GW00468400

CLONLIFFE HARRIERS

ATHLETIC CLUB

1886-2013

Dominic Branigan

ORIGINAL WRITING

ISBNs

PARENT : 978-1-78237-369-8

EPUB: 978-1-78237-370-4

MOBI: 978-1-78237-371-1

PDF: 978-1-78237-372-8

A cip catalogue for this book is available from the National Library.

Published by ORIGINAL WRITING LTD., Dublin, 2013

Printed & Bound in Ireland by LETTERTEC

ACKNOWLEDGEMENTS

Sincere thanks are due to the following for their assistance in making this work possible :

National Library of Ireland
Irish National Archives
Royal College Of Physicians Of Ireland
Ordinance Survey Ireland.
Irish Newspaper Archieve.
Irish Times Archieve.
Tony O'Donoghue for his outstanding record of Irish athletics 1873-1914.
Colm Murphy for his books on the Irish Athletics Championships 1884 to 1967.
Lindie Naughton and Johnny Watterson for Faster, Higher, Stronger, a history of Ireland's Olympians.
Ronnie Delany for his autobiography Staying The Distance
Padraig Griffin for his wonderfull book on the History of Irish Athletics.
Larry O'Reilly and Joseph Harden (RIP) for their recollections of conversations with the early giants of Clonliffe.
Killian Lonergan for his enormous work in compiling the largest amount of statistical information on any athletics club in Ireland and his contribution on the careers of many of the current Wasps. .
Ballymun Community Centre for their history of the Santry area.
Pat Baker for photos of club trophies.
Brendan Farren for loan of Mc Evoy Cup
Alan Mc Eachern for medals and memorabilia won by his father Norman.
Irish Runner Magazine.
Margaret O'Hogartaigh.
Dublin Diocesan College.
The families of Joe Peelo, Frank Ryder, Harry Cooney and Billy Morton.
Extracts from Ballymun a history by Dr Robert Somerville Woodward courtesy of Ballymun Regeneration Project.
Yves Pierre Boulange – "De Coubertin and Women's Sport"
The "members" of my editorial staff, Aidan Lucid, Mary Staunton, Monica O'Kelly, Killian Lonergan and Tony Mc Cashin.
To Mary, Ann, William and Miriam for "no job too small" and their continuing forbearance throughout the long gestation.
Garrett and Steven in Original Writing for their eternal patience.
To all those friends and family members of those no longer with us but who very generously contributed their own memories of being part of the Clonliffe family.
Finally, to the members of Clonliffe Harriers Athletic Club far too numerous to mention individually but particularly to Francis Mansfield, Kathryn Walley, John O'Leary, Noel Guiden and Paddy Marley.
Back cover photo courtesy of Sportsfile

*To my father William who introduced me to athletics,
and to all the past, present and future members of
Clonliffe Harriers Athletic Club*

EDITOR'S FOREWORD

As far as the sporting public is concerned Clonliffe Harriers needs no introduction. Since its foundation in 1886 the club's history has unfolded in the fields and athletic arenas not only of Ireland but in countries throughout the world and the club has always lived up to its motto "NIL DESPERANDUM"

The history of Irish athletics and that of Clonliffe Harriers are closely intertwined. From its very birth it has been involved in all aspects of our sport and as the years rolled by the club became more involved not only in competition, but in the promotion of local and international meetings which have witnessed many national and world record performances.

In addition, Clonliffe has been at the forefront in the administration of all aspects of our sport in Ireland. In many cases this has involved numerous attempts to bring about unity during the many "splits" which thwarted the aspirations of many promising athletic careers. Despite all these distractions we have produced an unequalled number of both male and female athletes who have not only brought national glory to Clonliffe but have competed with distinction at International level right up to and including the Olympic Games. Indeed the club holds the record for the number of members who have represented Ireland at the Olympics.

Then club President Sam Gray, in the 75th anniversary publication, very acutely describes the reasons for our survival and continued success.... "One may well ask how this famous club survived when one considers the many pitfalls which face amateur sports clubs such as Clonliffe Harriers. In my opinion, one of the greatest assets has been club and team spirit and the will to overcome all difficulties. During my time I have noticed all along the line, the great co-operation between the older and younger members. Throughout the years there has been this close link between past and present and I realise that we could not continue to exist without the injection of new blood into the club".

Billy Morton stated in that same publication that "We have come a long way" and the past 50 years has seen the success of the club more than surpass the great achievements of the first 75. Clonliffe Harriers have indeed come a long way since their foundation. From our humble beginnings in the back room of a house in Richmond Road in 1886 the club has, through the decades, experienced the highlights and heartbreaks that are the bread and butter of all sporting organisations.

The great Sam Gray put it very accurately when he spoke of team spirit and the will to overcome all difficulties. It is these attributes together with the unrivalled comradeship among members young and old, past and present, that has established Clonliffe Harriers at the very pinnacle of Irish Athletics.

Dominic Branigan
Morton Stadium
2013

PRESIDENT'S ADDRESS

It is with great pride and pleasure that I reflect on the history of this famous club and how it survived the test of time whilst maintaining its position at the forefront of Irish Athletics since its foundation in 1886.

We can now applaud the work done and time spent by the author Dominic Branigan in presenting us with a comprehensive history of our club.

My own memories of Clonliffe began in 1967 when myself and Hugo Duggan, along with the 2 McDaid brothers arrived in Santry. Our first meeting was with the famous Billy Morton along with Harry Cooney and Sam Grey. Very soon the stories began to evolve of the great teams of the past under club giants like Tommy Burton and Harry Cooney. The long term success of the club has been, in no small way due to the close attention paid to club structures over the decades, and the continuous injection of new members.

The club was founded on Richmond Road and moved to other locations including Kavanaghs of Glasnevin and finally to Santry where Billy Morton built a new stadium and cinder track. The next 40 years was an incredibly successful period as our cross country teams began to dominate the senior championships. In more recent times the track and field teams have achieved similar success.

Ever since our arrival in Santry in the 1950s Clonliffe has continually striven to improve facilities, not only for our members, but also for our extended family of friends and supporters. In the early days there was the nissen hut but this was soon surpassed in the 1970s with the building of the first club bar and new modern changing rooms, the brain child of Hon Sec Larry O'Reilly, Hon Tres Colm Brennan and Club Captain Christy Brady. Further upgrades took place in 1995. Under then president Maurice Ahern a new track and club house were completed to bring the facilities up to date.

This period also saw the arrival of legendary Clonliffe coach Lar O Byrne who, in is own words was "working with athletes and keeping the club focussed on what we are all about "Athletics ".

Throughout its history Clonliffe athletes have regularly gained selection on Irish Teams at European and World Championships as well as the Olympic Games.

The achievements of Jerry Kiernan in the LA Olympic Marathon , Danny Mc Daid in the World Cross Country in Limerick, coupled with Niall Bruton's victory in the World University games and Frank Murphy's second in European Championships, to name but a few, are forever etched in Clonliffe and Irish athletic history.

On the domestic front our own club promotions are in a very healthy state. The Clonliffe 2 Mile Invitation, the schools cross country and the Morton Games under meet director Noel Guiden are among the most successful events on the Irish athletic calendar .

We look forward to even bigger and better achievements in the years ahead.

Nil Desperandum

Paddy Marley
President

HONORARY SECRETARY'S ADDRESS

Nil desperandum .... (Never despair)

The motto of this great club, Clonliffe Harriers A.C. That 'Nil Desperandum' spirit has been evident throughout the course of the history of this club but particularly over the last 20 years, where despite a changing world Clonliffe Harriers has met the challenge head on to maintain its position as the best athletics club in Ireland.

The club's recent history has witnessed extraordinary developments. Traditionally regarded as a cross country club, the 1990s and 2000s have seen Clonliffe reinvent itself as a track and field club par excellence. Highly talented sprinters and field eventers, including unsung heroes like David Donegan who is rapidly closing in on his 20th national pole vault title, have augmented the middle and long distance athletes in propelling Clonliffe into the top men's track and field club in the country. Having won the national league title in 2008 they successfully defended it up to and including 2012. The club's women's section has also excelled in track and field winning Division 1 of the National League in 2011. As a result they gained promotion to the premier league and have retained that status ever since.

The club's dominance on the country, as one would expect, continues. The men's team this millennium has won the national on ten occasions with both Mark Kenneally and Sergiu Ciobanu taking the individual title in the famed black and amber singlet.

The juvenile section of the club in particular has blossomed in recent years. Driven by its captain Gladys Cooper it has exploded with huge numbers of young athletes training in Santry under a dedicated team of juvenile coaches. The fruits of this policy have resulted in a continuous conveyer belt of talented young athletes coming into the junior and senior ranks.

Clonliffe more than any other club is one which gives back to our sport. On an annual basis we are involved in the promotion and hosting of numerous events including the Brother Clonliffe Schools Invitational, a cross country event for schools athletes which has blossomed since its first race in 2009 to the most recent event in October of 2013 when 1400 young athletes competed in Santry Demesne. The club has also, on an ongoing basis, hosted the Aviva Leinster Schools Cross Country, as well as the Dublin and National Interclub Cross Country Championships. These events are run with military precision by a hardworking dedicated group of club members who give voluntarily and freely of their time. These volunteers played a pivotal role in the hosting of the European Cross Country Championships in Santry Demesne in 2009 and the European League Team Championships in 2013.

Billy Morton would no doubt be delighted to see Clonliffe once again host an international athletics Meet. The Morton Games is an event which, in a few short years, has grown from humble beginnings into a meeting which now attracts world class athletes, including Olympians, back to the scene of the original dream mile of the 6th of August 1958 with the Morton Mile as the centrepiece.

Clonliffe Harriers is a club which honours its past, embraces the present and is confident about its future.

Nil Desperandum

Noel Guiden
Honorary Secretary

CONTENTS

1895 National Junior CC Champions
Back Row: W Allen, J Stephen (President), PJ Byrne (Captain), H Temple, R Trench,
P Ewing
Middle Row : J Murtagh, GF Walker, GF Matthews, RD Gwynne,
Front Row : PJ Lonergan and SJ Warry.

THE EARLY DAYS

History Of Cross Country Running
 Though it is generally accepted that modern athletics was initiated in the second part of the 19th century, the first athletes were probably the Greeks who created the original Olympic Games in 776 BC. The 16th century annals of the four masters record that the last Tailteann games took place in 1169. In 1924, these games were revived and Clonliffe Harriers were very prominently represented. Following another staging in 1928 these games were abolished.

 Cross country running developed from several traditions. Professional runners in 18th century England kept race fit by following the hunting hounds on foot. In the 1820s, there had been foot steeplechases between local landmarks in the midlands and north of England. In 1834, the sport had come into the public schools as a paper chase known as the hares and hounds. In the paper chase, two runners, referred to as the "hares", would set out carrying bags, to lay a paper trail over suitable terrain. They were allowed to lay a false trail into a cul-de-sac in places, but they also had to lay a true trail leading to the finish line. If they were sighted by the pursuing runners, known as the "hounds", they were allowed to drop their bags and head for home. The object of the competition was for the hounds to catch the hares, similar to the sport of beagling. During the 1850s, the sport of athletics spread through the universities and in 1864, Oxford and Cambridge competed for the first time in what was to become one of the most fashionable meetings of the athletics calendar. In 1865, the Amateur Athletic Club was formed but was really only reflecting the class divisions of Victorian England. Its definition of an amateur excluded, "tradesmen, labourers, artisans and working mechanics".

1929 paper chase in progress. Note the two paper carriers on right.

The sport as we know it today was initiated in 1867 with an organised run at the Thames Harriers and Hounds Club. Clubs subsequently sprung up and the hares and hounds name preserved their connection with hunting. It did not take long for this trend to catch on in Ireland. The Irish Cross Country Association was founded in 1881 and their first championship was held that year in Dunboyne. It was won by City and Suburban Harriers who had their headquarters at Butterlys Field, which is now Croke Park. These athletes must have been known to the teenagers who founded Clonliffe Harriers five years later.

Amateurism

All the clubs competing in these events referred to themselves as "Harriers". Each club captain had to sign a declaration that all his men were amateurs. The thinking behind this rule of the cross country association may be explained by an editorial which appeared in the *Irish Sportsman* in 1886 under the heading "Amateurism In Sport". It read as follows, "We have always been in favour of young men enjoying their leisure time as much as possible in healthy muscular outdoor games. But when we take into account the hard hours of toil of many of our artisans, we question if ordinary working men save in exceptional circumstances, can afford to devote sufficient time for practice, so as to become bona fide athletes without incurring such pecuniary loss as would render money prizes a necessity. Thus, we must regard the general participation of such persons in our athletic contests as constituting a serious danger to the maintenance of amateurism in sport."

Pedestrianism

These strictly enforced rules of amateurism were in contrast to the proliferation of "professional" athletic events which were commonplace in the 19th century. "Pedestrianism" as it was known, saw both men and women competing for the equivalent of up to one year's pay for a single event and as a result many individuals of very limited means saw an opportunity to free themselves and their family from the poverty trap. These contests sometimes took the form of what we now term "Ultra Distances" and regularly ended with one or more of the competitors suffering from extreme exhaustion or severe injury.

In an early example of gender equality, women ("Pedestriennes") were recorded as competing in many such events. In 1857, a Mrs Jackson is reported as having walked 1,000 consecutive hours on the stage of the Franklin Hall in Philadelphia while in 1867 the *New York Herald* reported on a 100 mile race in Mexico between eight women.

Betting was rife in "amateur" athletics in 19th century England but under the rules of the Amateur Athletics Association (founded in 1880) athletes were forbidden to compete for money or even to run against professional runners. There were very stiff penalties for transgressing these laws and more than a few professional athletes were imprisoned for up to six months for masquerading as amateurs. By 1898, the top athletes at all distances from 100 yards to 20 miles had been disqualified and banned from ever again competing as amateurs. These strict rules actually boosted membership of the AAA and from 45 member clubs at its foundation, there were 296 clubs attached by 1898.

Significant Dates

1880	Founding of Amateur Athletic Association.
1881	Founding of Irish Cross Country Association.
1884	Founding of Gaelic Athletic Association.
1885	Founding of Irish Amateur Athletic Association.
1887	First ever international track and field contest takes place in Dublin. England defeats Ireland. This year also sees the staging of the first American Track and Field Championships.

The first officially ratified world records for track and field were issued on 16 April 1887 by the AAA, which had been inaugurated in 1880. Of the 15 events given ratification, four were held by Irishmen and all four were set in Ireland.

High Jump	1.98 metres	Pat Davin	Carrick-On-Suir	5-7-1880.
Long Jump	7.06 metres	Pat Davin	Portarlington	27-9-1883
Shot Putt	13.33 metres	James O'Brien	Dublin	3-7-1886
Hammer	36.40 metres	James Mitchell	Limerick	16-6-1886

The late 19th and early 20th centuries were a golden era for Irish athletics mainly in field events. Between 1881 and 1912, not a year passed when Ireland did not bring home at least one gold from the AAA championships. Eighty five were won altogether. Among the collection were 13 in the high jump including 2 each by Patrick Leahy and Peter O'Connor and 4 consecutively by Con Leahy. William Barry (5), James Mitchell (3) and Thomas Kiely (5) were among the 16 hammer champions. In the long jump no fewer than 20 titles were won (including six in a row by Peter O'Connor from 1901-1906). The shot putt saw the biggest haul with 22 wins (including 13 by Denis Horgan). In 1886, the year Clonliffe was founded, Irish athletes won AAA titles in the long jump (John Purcell), shot putt (James Mitchell), and the hammer throw (James Mitchell),

1886

To tell the full story of the club, one needs to go back to the founding fathers and the type of surroundings into which Clonliffe Harriers was born. Late 19th century Ireland was a country which was still recovering from the ravages of the famine during the 1840s. The population of 8 million in 1841 was reduced to six and a half million by 1851 and by the mid-1880s, it had reduced further to around five million. The latter decrease was mainly through emigration.

In 1886 Charles Stewart Parnell loomed large on the political pages of our newspapers. He was at the height of his popularity as his Irish Party held the balance of power in Parliament. That same year he had managed to convince Prime Minister Gladstone to introduce a Home Rule bill for Ireland. Unfortunately, this bill failed and it would be another 36 odd years before the country would achieve full political independence. Grover Cleveland was halfway through his first term in the White House. Having lost the 1888 election, he became the only president to regain the office when he was re-elected in 1892.

The following major events would have appeared on the business pages of the newspapers in 1886:

- Karl Benz launches the first petrol driven motor car.
- April – Fecundi Bacardi dies.
- May - John Pemberton produces first bottle of Coca Cola.
- Founding of Easons bookshop in Dublin.
- Ireland's first chip shop opened in Dublin.
- The Bern Convention issued laws for the protection of literary and artistic work.

Among the events recorded on the sports pages of 1886 were:

- First game of field hockey.
- Wilhelm Steinitz became the first world chess champion.
- Arthur Wharton from Ghana, goalkeeper of Preston North End, became the first coloured professional in the football league. He also won the AAA 100 yards in world record time of 10 seconds flat.
- The Grand National was won by Old Joe and Fred Archer won his fifth Derby on Ormonde, a horse which also won the Triple Crown in 1886.
- Baron Pierre De Coubertin visited Ireland to gather support for the rebirth of the Olympic Games.
- A horse named Arsenal won the Melborne Cup and Arsenal FC were founded.
- Oscar Traynor was born on 21st March. He was, in later life, instrumental in getting government funds for building of Clonliffe Stadium. He died in 1963.
- On 23rd August, Englishman Walter George set a new world mile record when he ran 4 minutes 12 seconds in Birmingham.
- The newly formed Irish Amateur Athletics Association, the first of many subsequent reincarnations, was enjoying its first full year of existence.
- On 24th April Marie Bremont was born in the French town of Noellet.
- The first overseas tour occurred when Kerry played Galway in Boston.
- In December, Dublin University Harriers was founded.

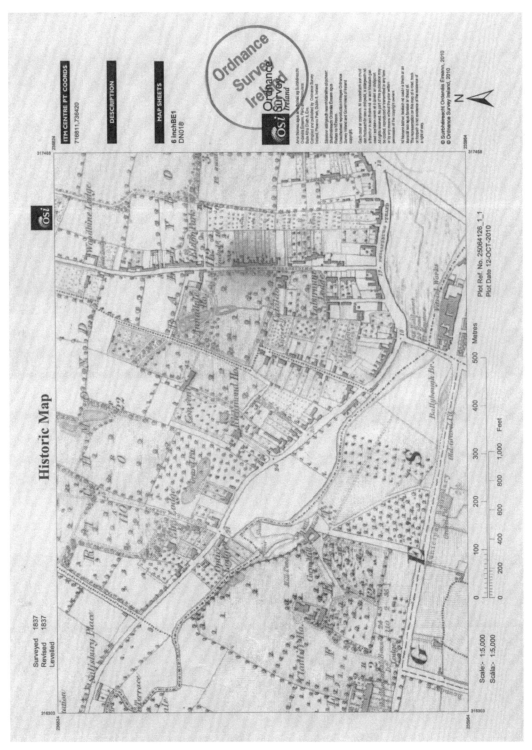

Map showing location of Knotts Cottage. Ordnance Survey Ireland/Government of Ireland. Copyright Permit No. MP 007613.

The Founders

In September 1886, a group of teenagers who subsequently became known as "The Lads" met at Knotts Cottage on the Richmond Road in Fairview on the north side of Dublin and founded the Clonliffe Harriers. While this event would not have made the front pages at the time, it was the beginning of the story of a sporting phenomenon which today sees the famous "Wasps" at the pinnacle of Irish Athletics. The enthusiasts who gathered on that day included the following men:

Joe Harden and Larry O'Reilly at original site of Knotts Cottage

Joe Harden and Larry O'Reilly at grave of Sam and Harry Warry.

Sam Warry

Born in 1871, Sam was a young 15 year old when he met at Knotts Cottage with his brother Henry (nicknamed Harry) and six others, to begin the legend. The son of Walter and Jemima, he had another brother Stanley and two sisters Jemima and Florence. Like his father, Sam was employed as a compositor in a printing company. They lived at 19 Oak Terrace off the North Circular Road. Sam first "featured" when he finished fifth in the National Junior CC Championships in 1891. He was subsequently a member of club teams which finished fifth in 1892 and sixth in 1893 before finally winning the title in 1895. Along with Joe Ingram, Sam was one of the first elected officers of the club serving as President and Captain from 1886 to 1890. Having never married, he died in 1913 at the age of 42.

Harry Warry

A brother of Sam, Harry was just 16 years old when he met the other Lads at Knotts Cottage. Like Sam, he also featured on winning Clonliffe teams. Harry married and moved to 97 Connaught St. Phibsborough and had a daughter Gladys who died in 1914 at the age of four years. Harry worked as a clerk for a pharmaceutical suppliers in Mountjoy Square in Dublin. Among his fellow employees was the wife of another "Wasp", Mrs Jack Cowell. Harry died at the age of 70 on 21 January 1930. His wife Sarah died at the age of 63 in 1936. Harry, Sarah and Gladys, along with Sam, are all buried in the Church Of Ireland Cemetery attached to St John The Baptist Church in Drumcondra Dublin.

Joseph Ingram

Born in 1870, Joe, like the Warry brothers, was also a teenager when he joined the other Lads at Knotts Cottage. He lived at 61 Clonliffe Road and was the person who suggested the club name. No record exists of any athletic achievements by Ingram. Joe was, however, deeply involved in administration at a national level and was elected as vice president of the Irish Cross Country Association in 1909. Along with Tommy Burton he was also a member of the International Committee of the ICCA.

He joined the Irish Railways Clearing House as a clerk in 1889 and soon rose to become secretary of the department. For his work in the First World War, he was awarded the OBE. Joe was an expert on Irish railways and later became head of the transport section of the Department of Industry and Commerce from where he retired in 1932. Having married in 1898, he initially lived in the family home before moving with his wife Jane to Crawford Road in Glasnevin where he reared four daughters: Eva, Ada, Florence and Edith. He also resided at 80 Iona Road in Glasnevin.

Joe continued his association with the Wasps throughout his life. His death at the age of 83 on Christmas Day 1951 marked the passing of the last of our founding members. Among those who attended his funeral was Sean T. O'Kelly, the then President of Ireland.

Joseph Ingram

Fred Mc Kittrick (AKA Fred Arthur)

Fred was 35 years old when he met with the Lads at Knotts Cottage in 1886. He worked as a legal accountant and insurance clerk. He was well known in Dublin theatrical circles where he used the stage name "Fred Arthur". Some of his most renowned performances were in pantomimes in the Theatre Royal. He was at different times, manager of the Tivoli and the Pavilion Theatre in Kingstown (now Dun Laoghaire). He passed away in Sydney, Australia in 1919.

Fred Mc Kittrick "Business Card"

The other four men who attended were: Thomas Fitzpatrick, Ben Pearson, John Thomas and Charles Webb. Unfortunately, at time of writing, there is no information available on these fellow founders.

It was initially decided to name the club Richmond Harriers but having discovered there was already a club of that name in existence nearby, they settled on the name Clonliffe Harriers after the road where Joe Ingram lived. Interestingly, the location of Knotts Cottage on the corner of Convent Avenue and Richmond Road was directly opposite a house occupied by the family of the famous Irish writer James Joyce in the late 1880s. This was the beginning of an association which Clonliffe would have with Joyce and his works right into the mid twentieth century.

The First "Social"

By this time a number of Harrier clubs had been in existence and as well as organising sporting events, they were also holding social nights such as smoking concerts and annual dinners. In November 1886, Haddington Harriers held their annual Dinner, Smoking Concert and Presentation of Prizes in the Wicklow Hotel where they presented a gold watch to one of their members, Hugh Brae, who was emigrating to Australia

In 1889, the Clonliffes took up new headquarters at 18 Richmond Road and it was on Saturday 21 September that year at this address that they held their very first Annual General Meeting. The only item on the agenda was the election of officers. Sam Warry was elected President and Captain while Joe Ingram was elected Club Secretary and Treasurer. This was followed by the first ever annual club supper. This "Dinner" consisted of the Lads bringing along their own food and beverages. It was not on the scale of the famous smoking concerts which dominated the later decades but it did have its benefits in that one of the local nuns from the nearby hospital grounds "noted the generous demeanour of the well behaved Protestant lads" and gave them permission to train in the grounds of their estate.

These social events were sometimes recalled by T.W. Murphy, a sports journalist of Shavian appearance who always wore knickerbockers and a beard. He had been a racing cyclist in the early days and throughout his life he dressed like a Victorian gentleman. He understood and appreciated the ritual of the traditional "smoking concerts" and prize-giving of the "Harrier" clubs and was a witty and entertaining after dinner speaker at Clonliffe Dinners right into the 1940s. Many of these dinners were held in Morans Hotel, which still trades in Talbot St. This annual event continued in the club until the latter part of the 20th century when it was subsequently replaced by an annual club dinner dance.

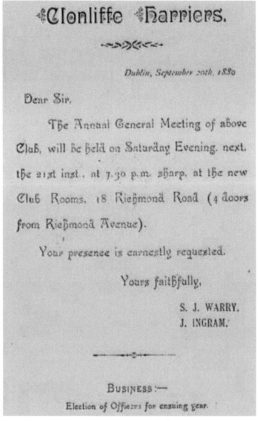

Notice Re 1889 Club AGM

Club Notices:

During the first few years of their existence and the age profile of many of "The Lads" Clonliffe did not feature prominently in any of the major championship races. They were, however, constantly recruiting new members and as can be seen from some of the Athletic Club notices below, were regularly staging "runs" from various locations around the city.

Saturday Sport 11 October 1890

Clonliffe Harriers

"This being the fourth year of their existence promises to be the most successful they have had yet. A full 40 members are already on the rolls under the captaincy of Mr C. Webb assisted by Mssrs Rafter and Warry as vice captains. It is hoped nothing will be found wanting to make these sturdy men gain a name for themselves worthy of their steel. At their runs so far this season no complaints could be made as to speed or attendance. The following may be noted as showing great promise as developing into long distance runners: W. Nugent, H. Cox and C. Webb. Any person desirous of becoming a member will kindly communicate with Mr J. Ingram, Hon. Sec. and Treasurer, Mountainview House, Richmond Road.

Next run will be today Saturday at five o'clock. Visitors invited."

Saturday Sport 25 October 1890
"Clonliffe will be proposed for membership of the Irish Cross Country Association as they wish to 'have a go' at Junior and senior championships."

Saturday Sport 30 October 1890
"Clonliffe ran up the Howth Road into field on left at St Lawrences Road. Did laps of four to six miles stretching out to Clontarf Yacht Club and ran home via the sea wall."

The opening run of the 1890/'91 cross country season took place on Saturday 1 November and was reported thus, 'From the club house on Richmond Road they ran through Goose Green and into the fields at Sion Hill. Among those in attendance were Tannan, Kirwan, Murphy, Warry, Cox, Nugent, Moore, Trench and Ingram. They next ran across into Norwood Demense where Kirwan nearly ended his career as a harrier at the river. Then it was back through the fields and into Kilmorry. Mrs Griffin provided shelter from the rain and offered hospitality and entertainment."

6 November 1890
"Clonliffe ran from Hanlon's Pub on North Circular Road."

8 November 1890
"Trench, S. Warry, H. Cox, W. Nugent and J. Ingram (Hon. Sec.) met at Dollymount Hotel at 3.30pm. Trench set pace through St Annes and out to Raheny."

Irish Times January 1902
"Clonliffe Harriers run to-night from Brian Boru at 8.30, wet or dry!"

During those early years it was common practice for harrier clubs to run from public houses as these were the only premises which could readily provide running water for washing down after a training session. In fact, the club used several of these establishments right up to the time they set up permanent home in Santry in the 1950s.

The First Big Breakthrough
The first ever National Junior Cross Country Championships were held in Clonskeagh on 21 February 1891. This event, not unlike today's novice championship, was to facilitate athletes who had never won a senior title or featured on a winning team. Appropriately enough, one of the club founders Sam Warry, competed in this race and became the first Clonliffe athlete to finish in the top 10 at a major championship event. In September of 1892 at the first ever track and field championships to be held in Butterly's Field (now Croke Park), George Blennerhassett Tincler became the first Clonliffe Irish National Champion when he won the mile in a time of 4 minutes 39.20 seconds. Tincler retained his title the following year with a time of 4 minutes 33.20 seconds.

Following Warry's fifth place in 1891, Clonliffe fielded their first full team in the 1892 National Juniors where they finished as fifth team. In 1893 they were sixth. The 1895 staging marked the historic breakthrough when the club took team gold for the first time. The race, run at Clonskeagh on 23rd February, was won with a total of 92 points, one ahead of Belfast Harriers with City and Suburban third on 108 points. PJ Lonergan, who subsequently served as club president, became the first Clonliffe man to win an individual cross country medal when he finished second in this race. The rest of the scoring six on that historic day were: GF Walker (7th), W. Allen (13th), club captain PJ Byrne (20th), R. Trench (22nd), P. Ewing (28th). The other team members were J. Murtagh, GF Matthews, RD Gwynne and Sam Warry. Many of these trailblazers went on to further triumphs in sporting and non-sporting fields and indeed a direct descendent of the Walker family can still be counted among our members.

This race also witnessed the beginning of the famous Wasps "sting in the tail". The fourth Belfast man finished in front of the fourth Clonliffe man but the fifth and sixth Wasps provided the sting to win the day. The team adjourned to a location, which even then was beginning to establish itself as a famous literary watering hole. Davy Byrnes in Duke Street was in its sixth year under the legendary owner and was subsequently frequented by, among others, James Joyce, who mentions it in *Ulysses*. It was also the starting location for the very first Bloomsday celebrations in 1954.

Clonliffe took bronze at the National Juniors in 1896 and followed with silver in 1897 and 1898 while there were top three finishes by GF Walker (third in 1896) and PJ Lonergan (second in 1898). On the track club captain PJ Byrne won the Leinster half mile and mile titles in 1895 before taking the Munster 440 yards and national half mile title in 1896. He was also second in the one mile championship in the same year.

These historical events and early championship victories were the first chapter in the story of Ireland's most remarkable and most successful athletic club and the beginning of a famous sporting odyssey which continues to this day.

THE BURTON YEARS

T Burton leads Clonliffe at 1924 Tailteann games in Croke park

Having spent the first 13 years of its existence on the Richmond Road, the club moved to a new home in 1898 when they took up residence at The Hut, a public house in the suburb of Phibsborough. This move was the beginning of an association with three interlinking parishes which would last for the next 54 years. While the 1895 National Junior victory was the first big event in the club's history, two other major milestones occurred in 1898 which are interlinked and are still commemorated to this day. The arrival of Tommy Burton marked the beginning of a career in Clonliffe that is without parallel in Irish athletics. He stayed with Clonliffe until his death 56 years later. This year, 1898, also saw the very first running of the Clonliffe two mile invitation, which is now the oldest continuously run club road race in Ireland and one of the oldest in the world. Since Tommy's passing, the winner of this race has been presented with the Tommy Burton trophy.

In 1901 the club had new sporting neighbours when Bohemians Soccer Club moved into Dalymount Park which was literally a short sprint from The Hut. The two clubs became very good neighbours and the Clonliffe Sports, created by Tommy Burton in 1912, were staged in Dalymount in 1915, 1916 and 1917. Indeed, some 50 years later when the club was busy raising much needed funds, a number of soccer games involving Clonliffe selections and English league teams were staged at the Phibsborough venue.

The year 1901 also saw the arrival of Clonliffe's first Olympian when Joe Deakin finished third in the National Junior Cross Country Championship. The course, at the present location of St Vincent's Hospital, contained three iron gates (each three feet high) and two water jumps (each 10ft wide). The team prizes went to Galway City (33 pts), Limerick Harriers (94 pts) and Donore Harriers (178 pts). The fifth Donore man home that day was a certain RJ "Bob" Payne who, in later years joined

Clonliffe and served as club president in 1950/51. In 1958 Bob was the official time-keeper for the three world records set at Santry by Herb Elliott and Albert Thomas.

Later in 1901 Clonliffe moved a few hundred yards along the Phibsborough Road to a new headquarters based at Brian Boru House. This pub is named after the 11th century Irish warrior who was the last high king of Ireland. It was on this site in 1014 AD that King Brian prepared his army for the famous battle of Clontarf against the invading Vikings, during which he lost his life. While based at this location, the Clonliffes continued their "association" with James Joyce, his family, and his literary masterpiece, *Ulysses*. Knotts Cottage - the club's first home - was directly across the road from one of the many houses occupied by the family in the late 19th and early 20th century. In the Hades chapter of *Ulysses*, the mourners at Paddy Dignam's funeral, "in silence drove along Phibsborough, 'cross Guns Bridge, Royal Canal, and Brian Boroimhe House." This sentence also implies that the cortege must similarly have passed The Hut. The novel is set on a day in June 1904, the same year that the Hedigans - the current owners - purchased the pub.

In 1903, the club again relocated when it moved further along the same road and based their winter training at Kavanaghs Pub next to the Old Gate of Glasnevin cemetery. This was the location at which they remained for the next 29 years. It was also the longest stay at any single location in the club's history until the move to its current home in Santry. When Clonliffe moved to this location they replicated the final stages of Paddy Dignam's funeral in *Ulysses*. The Joyce connection was further strengthened half a century later when James Joyce's nephew Fred served his apprenticeship as an optician under Billy Morton. Following Billy's passing, Fred Joyce purchased the Berkeley St. shop from the Morton Family.

The 1903 National Junior Cross Country was staged at Elm Park on Feb 7th. On a wild stormy day, P.J. McCaffrey from Claremorris but based in Scotland won the individual title in Clonliffe colours but was disqualified on residency grounds. An attempt to disqualify the club team failed and Clonliffe took the team gold. This year also sees the first record of the club competing in the National Seniors but with an incomplete team and no finishers in the top 10. McCafferty later became the first Clonliffe man to run for Ireland at the International Championships where he finished in 20th place. England won the team event on 25 points from Ireland on 78 and Scotland on 107.

The following year, 1904, saw yet another breakthrough when Oscar Cunningham (8th) and Joe Peelo (9th) became the first Wasps to finish in the top 10 at the national seniors. Clonliffe again did not have a complete team in a race won by John Daly of Galway who also led his club to the team gold. Peelo (35th) and Cunningham (42nd) were on the Irish team which finished fourth at the International CC.

Two years after the move to Glasnevin, Tommy Burton was elected club captain. He was to remain unopposed in this role for the next 41 years, the longest ever held by any club official and probably one of the longest held by any administrator in any sport in Ireland. Tommy joined Clonliffe in 1898 and had an association with the club in particular and Irish athletics in general which would last for the next 50 years. The sheer length of his term as captain together with the many individual and team victories under his stewardship make him one of the most influential figures in the history of the club. In addition he initiated the Clonliffe International sports and discovered and coached many athletes who brought great glory to their club and country.

Tommy was born in Tipperary in 1879, the son of Henry and Teresa Burton. The family moved to Dublin in the early 1880s. He was the eldest in a family of five which included his brother, John and three sisters: Mary, Margaret and Christina. He was employed as a rent collector for Dublin Corporation and during his early years in Clonliffe, the family lived on the North Circular Road, not far from where the club was headquartered at the time. Tommy was a regular competitor in cross country races and was a member of club teams which featured in the early years of the 20th century.

This is a notice which featured in *Freemans Journal* on Feb 28th 1909, "The team to represent Clonliffe Harriers will dress at Thomas Ashtons Clonskeagh today at 2.45pm for the National Juniors, fixed to commence at 3.30pm. All members are requested to meet as early as possible. Trams for Clonskeagh leave Nelson's Pillar via Nassau Street."

In 1909, Charlie Rothwell – another well known Clonliffe member joined and his contribution is outlined elsewhere in this publication. Around this time the following would be typical of the type of club notices in the press, "Run from (venue named) Tuesday. First pack starts at 8pm. New members and visitors welcome."

The Tuesday night runs were from Finglas Road, turn left at Finglas Bridge to Broom Bridge, Cabra Road, Doyles Corner and finish at starting point. There were usually three packs - slow, medium, and fast, who took off at about three to five minute intervals.

The Saturday runs, up to the end of December, were usually run on the same system of "packs" throughout the country. These runs included the use of the famous "hares and hounds" system of 19th century cross country running. A couple of members would get a 15 to 20 minute start with paper shavings in bags to lay a trail. The slow, medium and fast packs would start at intervals and follow the paper trail, with each pack trying to catch up with the one in front and the slow pack trying to catch the "hares". Larry O'Reilly, another Clonliffe lifer and who is still with us, is the last member still alive who took part in these races.

1908 opening run at The Old Gate

At the 1909 AGM of the Cross Country Association of Ireland in Belfast, J.T. Graham was elected vice president and Tommy Burton was elected as a club delegate in addition to being voted on to the international committee. Fellow club members C.F. Lonergan and Dan McAleese also served on this committee.

In the same year, the first marathon staged in Ireland over the standard 26 miles 385 yards was held in Croke Park. It was run over a 78 lap course and was attended by over 25,000 spectators. The race was won by Galwayman Tom Hynes in 2hr 51min from Pat Fagan and Frank Curtis. In 1910 the race, which was the subject of large scale betting, saw the first appearance of a Clonliffe athlete competing over the classic distance. The following report of the race appeared in *The Galway Observer*, "Eighteen athletes were in the field including the Olympic champion Johnny Hayes. Tom Hynes (Galway) never took up the running and was content to let the Spaniard Herander and Englishmen Goldsmith and Swan dictate the first 10 miles which was reached in 62 minutes. O'Flynn of Clonliffe then moved into the lead as the Spaniard dropped back. By the 18 mile mark, the Englishmen had also dropped out of contention and just after 19 miles, a disappointed O'Flynn retired with badly lacerated feet leaving Hynes in full control from whence he went on to win by a full lap from John Timmons of Oldcastle and Jack Lynch of Dublin. Olympic champion Hayes finished a dejected fourth."

1908 at the Old Gate

It was in 1909 that a Clonliffe team first featured in the Senior Inter Club Championship. Frank Ryder (18 years old at the time), took the individual bronze in a race which saw City and Suburban Harriers win with a total of 39 points from Willowfield on 86 and Clonliffe on 103.

Tommy Burton was on the panel for the championship in Clonskeagh in 1910 and led Clonliffe to the national senior title for the first time in its history. The eight mile race was run before a large attendance and the course, "was in capital order and plainly marked out beforehand". The rest of the team members were: Tom J. Downing (2nd), F.J. Ryder (4th), B. Parker (5th), P. Kelly (6th), as well as J. Malone, C.F. Rothwell, C.V. Gross, J.J. Higgins, M. Wilson, J. Quigley, G. Johnston and S. Pearson.

The first three teams were:

1.	Clonliffe Harriers	(2, 4, 5, 6, 22, 28)	67 pts
2.	City and Suburban	(1, 3, 12, 14, 15, 25)	70 pts
3.	Donore Harriers	(7, 9, 18, 20, 21, 26)	101 pts

Downing (14th), Ryder (22nd) and Parker (33rd) were on the Irish team later that year, which finished second to England at the International Cross Country.

The first man home, in second place overall, in 1910 was Tom Downing who had a stellar record in this event at that time. He finished second in 1904, seventh in 1906, first in 1907 and second in 1908 as a member of Haddington Harriers. In 1909 he switched to City and Suburban when he again won the individual gold before transferring to Clonliffe in 1910. Being an astute watcher of form Downing took a team silver in 1904 but he was on the winning teams every year, with three different clubs from 1906 to 1910. One month before the 1910 seniors and at the same venue, Clonliffe were the fourth team home in the National Juniors with Charlie Rothwell the leading finisher in eighth place. The team prize went to Willowfield Harriers.

In 1911, the club celebrated its 25th anniversary. Frank Ryder became the first in an illustrious line of club greats to win the individual title at the Senior Cross Country Championships in a race which saw Clonliffe, on 96 points, finish second behind Connaught Rangers on 40 points with Willowfield third on 135 points. Paul Kelly was the second Clonliffe man home in sixth place.

Extract From FJ Ryder scrapebook recording his individual victory at 1911 Senior CC.

The following report on the 1911 National Senior Cross Country Championship appeared in the *Irish Times*. "The championships, which took place last Saturday over a new course at Trimblestown, Merrion, Co. Dublin, was a highly successful event. The weather conditions were perfect and the attendance of spectators would, by its large proportions, go to show that greater interest is being taken in cross country running rather than heretofore. This is most gratifying. The distance was eight miles, made up of 10 laps. The number of laps spoiled the event from a spectator's viewpoint, particularly when the tailed off runners were passed by the leaders. All the cracks competed and as a running contest the event was singularly successful. Johnson of Donore led in the beginning. O'Neill took up the running in the second lap, followed closely by Ryder and Guthrie with Daly and Johnson in close order. It was clearly evident that the winner would spring from the leading trio. O'Neill and Ryder cut out a hot pace and Guthrie was soon left far in the rear. In the run home, Ryder and O'Neill ran shoulder to shoulder, and a desperate race between them ensued, ending with Ryder winning by about a couple of feet. Ryder has a beautiful style, is a splendidly built young fellow, strong, and well knit. I shall never forget his winning of the R.I.C. marathon last year. It was, in my opinion, one of his best performances, and he at once struck me as a runner who possessed the possibilities of really great accomplishments."

FJ Ryder wins 1911 Nat Snr XC Championship

Following Ryder home were: P. Kelly (6th), B. Baker (12th), M. Pearson (24th), C. Rothwell (26th), J. Comerford (27th), H. Ryland (28th) and T. Burton (29th).

The close packing of the last three scorers for Clonliffe was another example of the famous "Sting in the tail".

The top six finishers were as follows:

1.	F.J. Ryder	Clonliffe Harriers	45 min	47.2 sec
2.	Sgt. O'Neill	Connaught Rangers	45 min	47.4 sec
3.	F. Guthrie	Vegetarian Harriers	46 min	11 sec
4.	Cpl. Clarke	Connaught Rangers	46 min	37 sec
5.	Pte. Daly	Connaught Rangers	46 min	39 sec
6.	Paul Kelly	Clonliffe Harriers	46 min	45 sec

Team Placings were as follows:

1.	Connaught Rangers	(2, 4, 5, 8, 10, 11)	40 points.
2.	Clonliffe Harriers	(1, 6, 12, 24, 26, 27)	96 points
3.	Willowfield	(14, 17, 18, 25, 30, 31)	135 points
4.	Donore Harriers	(7, 9, 21, 35, 37, 41)	150 points

That same year a team of T.J. Kelly, T. O'Neill, A. O'Sullivan, C.V. Cross, H. Rylands, F.J. Ryder, B. Parker, J. Comerford, P. Kelly, C.F. Rothwell, and S. Pearson were crowned Irish Southern Cross Country Champions.

In June, W Murphy took gold in the 100 and 220 yards at the IAAA Track and Field Championships in the RDS show grounds. Future club president, CH Caulfield was fourth in the 120 yards hurdles. At the same venue in July, Murphy and Ryder represented Ireland against Scotland. Murphy was fourth in the 100 while Ryder finished second in the four mile race. Ryder was again on the Irish team which finished second to England at the International Cross Country. He was the 23rd man home.

These historic victories were the beginning of an era which witnessed the transformation of Clonliffe into a major force in athletics in Ireland and Tommy Burton was at the very centre of this success. In 1912 he promoted the first staging of what would, in subsequent years and decades, become the premier athletic event in Ireland. The Clonliffe International Sports Meetings grew in stature as the years passed and it was due to the entrepreneurship of Tommy, ably assisted by his fellow club members, that the cream of Irish athletics was able to compete on home soil against some of the best in the world. 1912 was also the year in which the International Amateur Athletic Federation, the governing body for athletics worldwide, was founded. The initial membership consisted of 17 nations. It currently has 212 members.

The 1912 and 1913 Clonliffe Meetings were held at the Royal Dublin Society grounds in Ballsbridge. Among the events on the card was the Clonliffe Sprint, a race over 130 yards (this was based on the length of the straight used by the club's sprinters in Richmond Road). The inaugural winner of this race was C.J. Farrell of Linfield Swifts while the 1913 win was taken by T.J. Cooke of Donore Harriers. The running high jump was won by P. Kirwan of Kilmacthomas in 1912 and D.A. Quinlan of DUHAC in 1913. In 1912 the half mile was won by Clonliffe man, J. West while Irwin beat Ryder in the mile with W.E. Murray of Donore in third place. The two miles (limited to Clonliffe members) was won by Vincent Ryder from Jim Manning and Charlie Rothwell. Among the participants in the first Clonliffe sports were John Flanagan, one of the greatest hammer throwers of the late 19th and early 20th century and Denis Horgan who was an equally successful shot putter. The 1913 meeting saw the first in a long line of memorable races at Clonliffe promotions. The invitation two mile race saw Scottish international and 1912 Olympian at 10,000 metres, George Wallach along with double Olympic medallist and English one mile champion, Eddie Owen come over to take on Clonliffe "crack" and Irish champion Frank Ryder. In a never to be forgotten race, Ryder took the spoils in a new Irish record time of 9 minutes and 42 seconds. The 1913 meeting was also notable for being the first one to stage a ladies race. The 100 yards was won by Lillie O'Mahony. At the end of 1912, the club had the sum of £1 2s 6d in the bank but in a sign of things to come the success of athletes in the field of competition resulted in extra costs and at the end of 1913 there was a deficit of £20.

In 1914, Tommy Burton was celebrating his tenth year as captain and it turned out to be one of the most successful in the long and distinguished history of the club. On 24th January at Baldoyle racecourse, Clonliffe took the team prize in the Southern Cross Country Championship of Ireland in magnificent style. Frank Ryder covered the six miles in 34 mins. and 9 secs. to take the individual title. He was followed home by: McAleese (2nd), Irwin (3rd), Guthrie (4th), Pearson (7th), and Barden (8th). Other finishers were: Rothwell (11th), Gross (13th), Wisdom (14th), Cronin (18th), Burton (25th) and Monahan (28th). Clonliffe finished on 25 points with Donore second on 57.

At the National Junior Cross Country Championships in Newtownards on February 14th, Irwin defeated 114 rivals to take the individual gold, covering the six miles in 34 mins. 11 secs. (only two seconds slower than Ryder's time in Baldoyle). Clonliffe were the fourth team home.

The National Senior Championships were held at Meadowbrook, Dundrum on 14th March and Clonliffe had one of their finest days ever. Irwin again turned the tables on Ryder to take the individual title with his club mate finishing a close second. The following is a brief extract from the *Irish Times* race report, "Coming down the hill for the completion of the first of five laps of the eight mile course, Murray (individual) and Ryder were together, the latter being first to cross the brook. On the second lap, Irwin joined the two leaders and these three then began to pull away from the rest of the field. On the third lap they had built up a 50 yard lead and entering the last lap were 120 yards in front. Irwin and Ryder entered the home straight together but a grand race down the hill to the finish saw Irwin pull ahead to win by 15 yards." Pearson (6th), Guthrie (11th), McAleese (19th) and Cronin (25th) completed the scoring six. The other finishers were: Rothwell (28th), Wisdom (30th), Gross (32nd), Barden (36th), Burton (40th) and Monahan (43rd). This was the first time that Clonliffe had won both the team and individual titles at this event and the club were to go on and repeat this double another eight times up and including 2013. It was also the only time that the same athlete won the National Senior and Junior Cross Country titles in the same year. To add to his cross country crowns, Irwin went on to win the Irish four miles title at the IAAA track and field championships in June in a time of 20 min. 52 sec. In second place was his fellow Wasp, J.G. Houlihan, who was tragically killed ten months later in World War One. Ryder, Irwin and Guthrie subsequently ran on the Irish team at the International Cross Country Championship.

Following his outstanding successes at home, Tommy Burton wanted to send his new national champions to compete in the English championships but was disappointed when some of his runners were unable to afford to take time off work. Tommy believed that Clonliffe would have won all before them that year. In July, at an international triangular between England, Scotland and Ireland at Hampden Park in Glasgow, Irwin finished third in the four mile event. The other Irish representative in this race was J.G. Houlihan.

Pictured above, wearing the famous Amber and Black
are the 12 all conquering Wasps team of 1914.

Back Row.
D. Mc Aleese, CF Rothwell, F. Guthrie, HC Irwin, CV Gross, J. Monahan

Front Row.
F.J.Ryder (Vice Captain), S.Pearson, T.P.Burton (Captain), J. J. Cronin,
W. Barden, CG Wisdom.

WASPS WHO ARE WITH THE COLOURS.

CLONLIFFE MEN WHO SERVED IN WORLD WAR ONE.

During the years when the club was headquartered in Glasnevin there were many highs and lows, some of which occurred outside the field of athletic competition.

The advent of the First World War in 1914 had a severe impact on the organisation of and participation in athletics and other sports, not only in Ireland, but in Great Britain and throughout Europe. Included in the tens of thousands of Irish people who volunteered were several Clonliffe men.

In January 1916 *The Saturday Herald* wrote a feature entitled :
"Wasps Who Are With The Colours".

"The name of Clonliffe Harriers is not one to be conjured with in the athletic world, for no club has a finer record since their formation. Dublin sportsmen are unlikely to forget the years 1892 and 1893 when George Blennerhassett Tincler won the Irish Mile Championship. Having left the amateur ranks and joined the professionals, he became the champion of the world at 1, 2, and 3 miles. In his prime he had no equal and was the greatest mile runner the world had ever seen.

Every season has seen the Clonliffes take higher honours and 1913-14 was their most successful ever. At the club AGM held on Sept 30th 1914, Mr Daniel Mc Aleese, the popular energetic secretary attributed this success to the most invaluable coaching, advice and attention of club captain Tommy Burton. "Without Tommy" Mr Mc Aleese stated "the team would have been like a ship without a compass. Suffice it to say that Mr Burton has been captain for the past ten years and during this time there has been a significant increase in the numbers joining the club. They currently have a membership of over 150 and have already held three annual sports. This has been one of the most trying years for the club as they follow the fortunes of their fellow members on the front with keen interest. They have the best wishes of their clubmen who all pray for their safe and speedy return."

Among those on the front are :

J. Baird
J. Bell
G. Bevin
P. Bradley
John Byrne
S.W. Campbell
J. Connell
J.E. Deakin   Irish 1 mile champion and 1908 Olympian.
M. Dolan
C.J. Doran V.P.
E. Dowling
M. Doyle   Killed in action 21-3-18.
H. Ellis   Killed in action at Passchendaele July 1917.
J.F. Elliott
C.J. Flynn   Died November 1918
M. Flynn
C.V. Gross.   Member of 1914 team.
F. Guthrie.   Member of 1914 team.
J.M. Hill
L. Houchin
J.G. Houlihan   Member of London Territorials and 2nd to Irwin
                     in Irish 4 miles c / ship in 1914. Killed in action
                     at Ypres 2 March 1915.
W. Hull.   Canadian contingent. Killed in action at
                     Neuve Chapelle 18.3.1915

H.C Irwin	Irish Cross Country and 4 miles track champion in 1914. Competed in 1920 Olympics.
G. Johnson	
J.P. Kearns	
T.J. Kelly V.P.	Served in the United States Army.
W. Madden	
T. Maguire	Awarded military medal at Passchendaele. Later to serve as coach in Trinity College for 30 years.
R. Mather	
W. Mc Clelland	
J. Miller	
J. Nicholson	
M. O'Loughlin	
S. Pearson	Member of 1914 team.
A. Pressler	
H.K. Purdy	
J. Purdy V.P.	
J. Rainey	
H. Reid	
W.T. Richardson	Killed in action at Poizieres 1st July 1916.
V.J. Roddy	
C.F. Rothwell	Member of 1914 team. Club member for over 50 years.
R.J. Rowlette	Club V.P and medical officer to 1920/24/28 Olympics. President of IAAA.
W. Ryder.	One of three Ryder brothers who competed for Clonliffe.
H. Sadler.	
F.L. Sheridan	
W. Stadius	
J. Smith	
R. Smith	
W. Sumner	
T.W. Thacker	
W.J. Tipping	
A. Wainwright	
J. West	
W. Wheeler	
C.G. Wisdom	Member of 1914 team.

W Hull
Killed in action at Neuve
Chapelle 18.3.1915

JG Houlihan
Killed in action at
Ypres 2.3.1915

Copy of post card to Tommy Burton from H. Sadler during World War One.

Despite being in the field of battle, the Clonliffe's never lost touch with their roots, and the following message was printed in the *Saturday Illustrated Post* in November 1914.

"Mr T Burton, the popular captain of the Clonliffe Harriers, has received from one of the club members, Lance Corporal H Sadler, who is at the front, an illustrated postcard, which is a most interesting souvenir of the Great War. The card is made of wood. The history of the communication is certainly a unique incident in the chronicles of an athletic organisation.

The term "Wasps" mentioned in the postcard, is the designation of the Clonliffe Harriers, the colours of which are black and amber, while the "Magpies" also referred to, are the Donore Harriers, whose colours are black and white. The postcard is the work of Clonliffe man Sadler, who is also a skilled draughtsman, and is his reply to an invitation to run, from his club captain.

Dear Tom.
Just a line from one of the "Wasps". I am still alright.
Good luck to all the "C.H."
Yours
H. Sadler ASC.

The impact of World War One can also be seen from the reports written on the Clonliffe Invitation race. In 1914, *The Irish Independent* reported, "This event took place under very favourable conditions. Owing to causes that have militated against all types of sporting events, the muster was not up to the level of former years, but under the conditions a turnout of 56 runners was regarded as fair. The honours of the afternoon went to F.J. Ryder, who has now secured this distinction so often at Clonliffe events that he is becoming entitled to be ranked as a veteran!"

The 1915 report stated, "owing to the fact that many members of the competing clubs were serving in H.M. forces, the total field of 36 was the smallest on record for this race."

While cross country was the main focus of Clonliffe in its early years, the arrival of Tommy Burton as club captain saw track and field activity take on a higher profile. The earliest track cracks were: P.J. Byrne who won the 880 yards title in 1896, George Blennerhasset Tincler, the one mile champion in 1892/'93 and Joe Deakin who took gold in the one and four mile championships in 1901. Tommy's inbuilt coaching ability soon recognised the potential in some of the club's top cross country runners and he began to encourage them to 'have a go' at track events. This policy met with immediate success when in 1905, Burton's first year as club captain, J.C. Healy finished second in the Irish 100 Yards Championship. In fact, the following year Tommy himself took the bronze medal in the one mile steeplechase. C.H. Caulfield took two further bronze medals in 1908 and 1909 at the 220 yards. National titles by Ryder in the mile in 1913 and his one mile/four mile double in 1919 were followed by Irwin completing the same double in 1921. In addition, Timothy Carroll won the Irish High Jump title in 1919 and 1923. Carroll had set a national record for this event in 1910 which stood until it was broken by Brendan O'Reilly in 1954. These victories were the foundations on which the athletic careers of many future Clonliffe stars were built and Tommy Burton was the man who initiated a phenomenon which today sees Clonliffe holding the Irish record for the number of Olympians and National Inter Club Cross Country team titles.

Club Affiliation Fees 1914/15

Cycling

In addition to their prowess in the athletic arenas, Clonliffe athletes quite often featured on the cycling pages of the national papers. The Flynns, Galways, Ryders and Walkers were regular competitors and winners of several races and this connection was further enhanced when cycling events were included in the Clonliffe sports meetings.

The following are some extracts from the sports pages of the time.

1910

From *Sunday Independent* of July 24th 1910, "On Sunday 17 July, 1910, W.J. Flynn of Clonliffe Harriers succeeded in lowering the existing record from Dublin to Galway on a three speed bicycle by 61 minutes. He covered the distance in 8 hrs. and 54 mins. leaving the GPO at 6.21am, reaching Athlone at 11.14am and Galway at 3.15pm. He has also run the 19.5 miles from Monasterevin to Kildare and back in a time of 1hr. 44 min. Flynn and his two brothers were on Clonliffe teams which won the Southern and National Junior Cross Country titles".

1916

The Versatility of the Wasps.

This is a report from Irish Cyclist Association annual 25 mile race in July 1916.

Extract from FJ Ryder scrapbook detailing result of Irish 100 mile cycle championship race in 1917

"A feature of Saturday's race was the evidence it afforded that petrol is expensive and difficult to procure. The field included three men who have been indulging in a quiet little flirtation with petroleum. Jack Samson returned after a long period of motor cycling, and it does not appear to have improved his legs. Another was J.J. O'Shea, but quite the most distinguished was F.J. Ryder of the Clonliffe Harriers, the hero of many a classic contest across country and a top notcher at that game as well as long distance running on the flat. We often wondered how a man who could run as Ryder could – we might even write in the present tense as he is by no means a has been – could find any use for any kind of bicycle, but the fact remains that he is an enthusiastic devotee of the motor cycle. He was making his debut in a cycle race on Saturday and quite a promising start it was. With a nice allotment of 12 minutes for the 25 miles from M. Walker, he was almost presented with the event. He did 1hr 18 min 59 sec for the distance and beat the scratch man Walker by nine minutes. P.G. Dardis with a handicap of five minutes, finished second, three minutes behind Ryder."

From 1915 to 1917 the Clonliffe International Sports Meetings were held at Dalymount Park, the home of Bohemians Soccer Club. Following this tenure the event moved to Lansdowne Road, the headquarters of the Irish Rugby Football Union. In 1922, it again moved location to Ireland's premier sports stadium at the headquarters of the Gaelic Athletic Association in Croke Park. This was in effect returning close to its original home as it was only a stone's throw from Knotts Cottage. Indeed, many of the track and field events in which the club competed in the late 19th and early 20th century were held at Butterlys Field which was the name of the stadium before it was purchased by the GAA in 1913.

During these years Tommy Burton had been bringing club athletes and teams to Great Britain to gain further experience and compete against stronger opposition. The First World War era saw many athletes from all over Ireland serving on the Western Front and this resulted in weaker competition for those who remained at home. As a result of these trips across the water, Tommy had built up a strong rapport with his British counterparts and consequently many of their top athletes travelled over to Dublin in subsequent years to compete against the best of the Irish.

In addition to his undoubted coaching skills, Tommy had a great eye for spotting young talent. It was he who noticed Frank Ryder as a teenager and turned him from a prominent under-age walker into an international class runner. When Norman McEachern joined Clonliffe as an 11 year-old boy, Tommy was quick to recognise Norman's ability and five years later took him to Glentoran sports in Belfast where Norman won the novices' half mile in 2min 06sec. Tommy described him as the best half miler he ever trained and Norman's subsequent career (documented in the Olympians chapter), added further proof to Burton's legendary talent.

At the National Track and Field Championships in the early summer of 1932, he saw Bob Tisdall winning the national 440 yards hurdles title. Arthur Wisdom, a Clonliffe man of many years standing, takes up the story, "A week after the 1932 Irish Championship, I was speaking to Tommy and he forecast that Tisdall would win the Olympic race and he gave me the winning time. He then reduced the time by $\frac{1}{5}$ of a second and explained that the atmosphere in Los Angeles was 'lighter' and consequently more conducive to faster times. This prediction was made in May. Tisdall went on to win the Olympic gold medal in a world record time in August."

In May 1936, Tommy went to the RUC Sports at Balmoral in Belfast to watch New Zealand athlete, Jack Lovelock win the invitation mile. The following are Tommy's own words from an article in the Clonliffe Diamond Jubilee publication, "After the race I accompanied him to his dressing room and told him I would be travelling to Berlin to see him win the 1,500 metres. He seemed astonished at my prediction and asked me for my name and address and would I be so kind as to correspond with him weekly up to the opening of the Olympics."

CLONLIFFE HARRIERS'
ANNUAL SPORTS

(Under the Rules of the National Athletic and Cycling Association of Ireland)

CROKE PARK, JONES'S ROAD, DUBLIN
ON SATURDAY, 19th SEPTEMBER, 1925

Commencing at **2.30** o'clock, p.m.

PROGRAMME OF EVENTS:

1. **The Clonliffe Sprint**
   (130 Yards Flat Handicap Open)
2. **300 Yards Flat Handicap** (Open)
3. **1,000 Yards Flat Handicap** (Open)
4. **Half-Mile Scratch Bicycle Race** (Open)
5. **Three Miles Bicycle Handicap** (Open)
6. **Five Miles Bicycle Handicap** (Open)
7. **Throwing the Javelin Hadicap** (Open)
8. **Four Miles Flat Handicap** (Open)

YOUTHS' ATHLETIC CHAMPIONSHIPS OF IRELAND

Open to Irish Youths, Youths born of Irish Parents, or who have been residing in Ireland for a period of six months immediately previous to the Championships, and who were over 14 years of age and under 18 on 1st January, 1925.

9. **100 Yards Flat Championship**
10. **220 Yards Flat Championship**
11. **440 Yards Flat Championship**
12. **Half-Mile Flat Championship**
13. **One Mile Flat Championship**
14. **Running High Jump Championship**
15. **Running Long Jump Championship**

A Certificate of Birth will be required from each Youth, which will be returned after the Meeting.   (This rule will not apply to those who sent in their Birth Certificates last year and who are still eligible.)

ENTRANCE FEE—One Shilling each Event

🔫 NO ENTRY WILL BE RECEIVED WITHOUT FEE 🔫

ENTRIES close on Saturday morning (first post), 12th September, with T. P. BURTON, Hon. Secretary Clonliffe Sports Committee, 9 Shanganagh Road, Drumcondra, Dublin

HANDICAPPER AND STARTER—A. C. HARTY

NOTE—The Sports Committee reserve the right of postponing the Meeting, if necessary, also of making any change in the Programme.

REGULATIONS

1. All Entry Forms shall be carefully preserved by the Handicapper.
2. No Handicapper has power to recognise an Entry which is not made on the Standard Entry Form. Competitors must, therefore, fill up this Form, as no other entry will be recognised.
3. Handicappers shall not receive entries.
4. A Competitor shall not be allowed to compete in any event for which his name does not appear on the Programme.
5. A "General Entry" shall not be accepted, and Competitors shall enter only for the Events in which they intend to compete.
6. Every Competitor shall wear complete clothing from the shoulders to the knees (e g., jerseys, with short sleeves to cover the shoulder, and loose knickers with slips), and in any event in which a water jump is included, the knickers and slips must be dark in colour.
7. A Competitor may be debarred from taking part in the Sports unless properly attired.

Corrigan & Wilson, Printers, 13 Sackville Place, Dublin

Notice re 1925 Clonliffe Meeting

Lovelock's coach learnt that Tommy had a very wide experience as a coach and mentor. In Berlin the coach discovered that Tommy was staying in the same hotel and sought his advice. On the day of the final, Tommy wrote out the race plan. His instructions were that Lovelock should keep at the back of the field until 300 metres from the finish then make a dash at top speed, to take the other runners by surprise, and not give them enough time to respond. Jack Lovelock won gold in a new world record time of 3 min 47.80 sec. Similar tactics were used 20 years later in 1956 when Ron Delany took gold in the 1,500 metres in Melbourne.

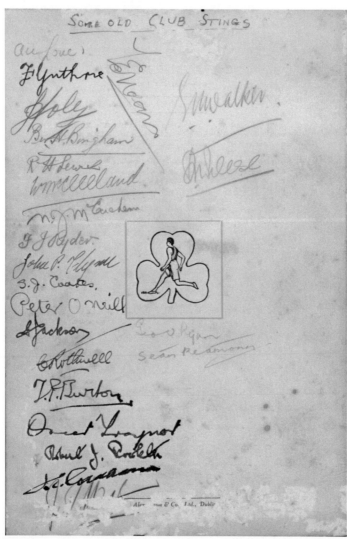

Dinner Card autographs include A Lowe, F Guthrie, BH Bingham, N Mc Eachern, FJ Ryder, C Rothwell, T Burton, O Traynor, S Reamonn, D Mc Aleese and G Walker.

International Cross Country Championship

The first International Cross Country Championships were held in Scotland in 1903. Clonliffe had a representative on the Irish team when P.J. McCafferty was the sixth Irishman home in 20th place. England won the team prize on 25 points with Ireland second on 78 points. Joe Peelo made the team in 1904, finishing 35th overall. F.J. Ryder made his first appearance on the team in 1909 when he finished in 23rd place. He subsequently finished 22nd in 1910, 23rd in 1911 and 31st in 1914. The advent of the First World War may have also deprived Ryder of greater glory in the International Cross Country as it was suspended from 1915 to 1919 when he was at or near his peak. Other Clonliffians to run for Ireland in this race included: T. Crowe (8th in 1920 and 6th in 1921), B.H. Bingham (3rd in 1921), and W. Kinsella (17th in 1922).

The 1920s - the third decade of Tommy Burton's captaincy - saw the arrival of a new bunch of cracks in the famous Black and Amber singlet. Tim Crowe (1920) and B.H. "Bev" Bingham (1921) were both to become national cross country champions while Norman McEachern established himself as the top 800 metre runner in Ireland and Clonliffe's first double Olympian. It also saw the arrival of yet another "lifer" in the form of Joe Peelo who was to remain a stalwart of the club for the next 50 years. The first government of the newly independent Ireland under the leadership of WT Cosgrave decided to revive the idea of the Tailteann Games, an ancient athletics event which predated even the original Olympics. The first renewal took place in Croke Park in August 1924. It was held just after the Olympics had finished and attracted many athletes on their way home from Paris. Clonliffe, led by their captain Tommy Burton, had a substantial representation at this event. A second renewal was held in 1928.

In 1925 Clonliffe again won the National Senior Cross Country title with Bingham taking the individual bronze. This win was most noteworthy for the fact that the team contained the three Walker brothers: Charlie (6th), George (8th) and Arthur (23rd). They were sons of G.F. Walker who was a member of the famous "breakthrough" team, which won the 1895 National Junior title and who later served as club president between 1902 and 1909. These three brothers featured in many club handicaps during their competitive days and their father had the pleasure of witnessing many of their exploits. The third generation of this remarkable family is represented by Frazer Walker who, like his ancestors, was on winning Clonliffe teams and who won Irish marathon titles in 1957 and 1958. Frazer's brother, Reggie was also an active member and served on the club committee with Billy Morton. The Walker Cup, a four mile track race, was donated by the family in 1966 and is still competed for today.

Throughout this decade the annual Clonliffe International Sports continued to attract athletes from near and far. At the 1921 event in Lansdowne Road where the track was 5 laps to the mile, a team from Salford Harriers ran an Irish all comers best time of 3 min 44.40 sec for the one mile relay. On July 2nd 1921, at an inter club meeting in College Park, a Clonliffe team of A. Wade, T.G. Wallis, J.R. Cowle and N. McEachern set an Irish record for the 4x440 yard relay when they ran 3 min 35.40 sec.

On 25th August 1922 the following notice appeared in The Irish Times, "The Clonliffe sports, which were due to have taken place at Lansdowne Road tomorrow, have been postponed due to the death of Michael Collins. A new date will be announced later." The sports were subsequently staged in Croke Park on 23rd September and included an appearance by Birchfield Harrier and multiple English champion CE Blewitt who won the invitation mile and three mile events. BH Bingham won the four miles in 1920, 1921 and 1926. One of the highlights of these sports was the 4x440 yards relay and Clonliffe teams won this event no fewer than eight times between 1915 and 1925, lowering their time from 3 min 47.80 sec to 3 min 39.40 sec.

1922/23 at Croke Park. Included are front row
(seated L to R) Dan McAleese (Hon Sec 1913/22 and future chairman of Rev Comms),
BH Bingham (Nat XC Champion 1921 and Irish International), CP Kenna, GN Walker
(Son of GF Walker and father of Frazer Walker), Joe Foley (who would later supervise
building of Santry Stadium), Tommy Burton (Renowned coach and club captain for over
40 years), GV Ryan (founder of Crusaders in 1942 and member of first AAU management
committee), Charlie Rothwell (Club Sec 1925/34 and member of committee which
purchased and developed Santry Stadium), Tom Maguire (LJ champion in 1910 and coach
to Trinity College Athletics for over 30 years), GF Walker (member of 1895 team and club
president 1902/07), JT Graham (Hon Sec 1902/04 and Club Pres 1910/11. Was also a
long serving official at Clonliffe meetings as well as being a member of IAAA and NACA
committees). Also included in 2nd row (7th from left) is Archie Cassidy a member of the
first Dail and many Clonliffe winning teams. On extreme right of this row is TE Nolan
(club Hon Tres 1914/30)

At the 1927 meeting in Croke Park, Dr Otto Peltzer of Germany who had set a world record of 1 min. 51.60 sec at the 1926 AAA Championships in Stamford Bridge, won the half mile in 1 min. 57 sec. AAA champion C. Ellis of Birchfield Harriers was second and Irish champion Norman McEachern finished in third place.

The high jump included Clonliffe man and Irish record holder, Timothy Carroll as well as the legendary Larry Stanley who won the AAA title in 1924. Among the competitors in the 1000 yard flat handicap in 1925 was one Frank Cahill of Donore Harriers who would later become a prominent official at race meetings right into the 1970s and was also a long time administrator both at club and national level. The club connection with cycling continued throughout this decade and bicycle races were regular events at Clonliffe meetings. Among those who competed was Bertie Donnelly, Irish champion over one, three, five and 10 miles and Olympian in 1928.

The success of these early sports meetings can be seen from the large number of advertisements in the programmes. Included in 1925 were ones for three hotels in Dublin. The Globe Hotel 95-97 Talbot Street had 200 bedrooms and did B&B for 4/11 (approx. 30 cents in today's money). The Tower Hotel at 33 Henry Street was "still going strong". Morans Hotel in Talbot Street was recently refurbished and had "electric lifts to all floors" and "hot and cold water in bedrooms".

In 1927, Norman McEachern broke the Irish 880 yards record when he ran 1 min. 53.50 sec at an international meeting in Fallowfield near Manchester. In 1928, Denis Cussen of Dublin University Harriers ran the 100 yards in 9.80 sec to become the first Irishman to break the 10 second barrier. He made the semi final of the 100 metres at the Amsterdam Olympics where he finished third. Only the first two qualified for the final.

At the 1928 Clonliffe Sports, a team from South London Harriers set an Irish All Comers record of 3 min 29.40 sec for the 4x440 yards relay. This time stood for well over 50 years. Olympic silver medallist, Jack London competed in 1928 and won the 100 yards in 10 seconds flat. As the decade drew to a close, Ireland was beginning to adapt to its newly established independence and participation in sport was on the rise. Nowhere was this more evident than in the sport of athletics. Greater numbers were appearing in cross country as well as track and field competitions. Throughout these years the Black and Amber singlet featured prominently at most major individual and team competitions.

1931 "Grand National" at Finglas. Front row shows 21 year old Billy Morton holding his bowler hat. Tommy Burton is on extreme right. Back row 6th from right is Joe Peelo.

In 1932, after many years running from "The Old Gate", the club yet again "decentralised" a few hundred yards along the Glasnevin Road to the Royal Oak public house on the outskirts of Finglas village. One day Mr John Craigie, the founder of Merville Dairies (which has since transformed into Premier Dairies and subsequently integrated into Glanbia), who was a renowned farmer and livestock dealer, was walking through his fields near Finglas when he came across Tommy Burton marking out a cross country course. Craigie asked Tommy what he was doing and when told, Craigie said, "I will show you a better course." The result was the famous half mile field, together with adjoining lands containing several jumps and ditches. These grounds at Barn Park became Clonliffe's new training ground and were enjoyed by club members until 1952. John Craigie soon became a member and later president and supported the club for many years.

As the club approached its 50th anniversary and Tommy Burton began his fourth decade as captain, a new generation of Wasps began to appear who would not only continue the high levels of success achieved by their predecessors but would lead the club through some of its most turbulent times. The arrival in 1928 of Sam Gray marked a lifelong connection which continued right up until his death 59 years later in 1987. Within a few short years, Sam was joined by Harry Cooney, Billy Morton and Fred "Mattie" Hewson among others. Along with already established stalwarts like Joe Peelo and Charlie Rothwell, these men brought Clonliffe from the fields of Finglas to the world renowned stadium in Santry which is now the permanent home long striven for by all Clonliffians since 1886. There were, however, several hurdles to be cleared and a few "temporary" headquarters to be enjoyed before this dream would be realised.

Dublin Jnr XC Champions 1935
Back Row L to R. P McCormack, P Higgins, F Burke, P O'Hara.
Front Row L to R S. Gray, H Cooney, T Burton (Capt), W Morton, J Foley.
(Note the stylish straps on the spikes !!)

When Sam and his fellow lifers joined, their main priority was to add to the growing list of Clonliffe successes in cross country, road, and track races. They first featured in club handicap races and Sam Gray established himself as the master when it came to getting his name on trophies like the Doran Shield and the Horan Cup. In the latter event he recorded the greatest number of fastest times when he "scored" eight times between 1933 and 1944. Indeed between 1932 and 1944, Sam was a top four finisher 11 times, winning the cup twice in 1936 and 1943. In 1936, J.J. O'Connor presented a trophy to be competed for over a four mile flat (sealed) handicap course. Sam Gray dominated this event during its first ten years when he had four top three finishes in addition to having the fastest time on five occasions. Harry and Billy, who were members of many winning teams alongside Sam, were to go on and win Irish marathon titles in future years.

Their first time to feature as members of a winning Clonliffe team was in 1935 when the club took the Dublin Junior Cross Country title. Sam Gray won the race and was followed home by: H. Cooney (2nd), W. Morton (4th), P. Higgins (6th), F. Burke (7th) and P. McCormack (14th), to give Clonliffe a winning total of 34 points. Donore, led home by Tommy Hopkins, were second on 96 points.

The 1935 Dublin senior cross country was won by Clonliffe's J.J. O'Connor with Higgins 7th and Gray 12th. J.J. O'Connor then went on to win the national senior in Thurles and become the fifth Wasp to take this title. Later in 1935, Billy Morton finished third in the national marathon in a time of 3 hrs. 2 min 52 sec. In 1936, he would win the event in a new Irish record time of 2 hrs. 48 min.

50th Anniversary opening run at Finglas.

The golden jubilee year was celebrated with a dinner in the Red Bank Restaurant on November 28th. Clonliffe had grown in its 50 years from a small gathering of eight "hopefuls" at Knotts Cottage in 1886 into one of the top athletic clubs in Ireland. Their aspirations had been realised as they annexed county and national titles in almost all disciplines of the sport. Many of their athletes had competed at the highest level representing their country at World and Olympic competitions. In the field of promoting the sport, Clonliffe had initiated their first International meeting in 1912 and, apart from the breaks during World War One, these contests had continued throughout the decades. In the area of administration the club was also to the fore in providing members to help with the management of the various athletic bodies which existed since 1886.

* * *

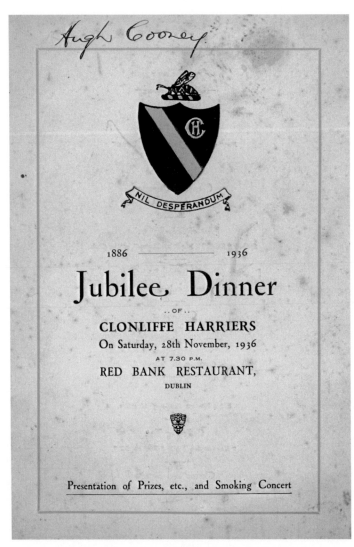

Programme for 50th Anniversary Dinner

When Clonliffe was founded in 1886, the sport of athletics in Ireland was administered by two separate bodies. The Irish Amateur Athletic Association (IAAA), which was founded in 1885, was mainly an urban based organisation. The Gaelic Athletic Association (GAA), which was founded in 1884, held their meetings mostly in rural locations. The year 1886 also saw the formation of the Cross Country Association of Ireland (CCAI) which catered for the winter activities of IAAA members. Clonliffe Harriers competed in IAAA and CCAI events during the first four decades of its existence with no small amount of success but the club was also well represented on the administrative side of the sport during its early years. Dr Robert Rowlette was a member of the management committee of the IAAA in 1904 and later served as its president from 1908 to 1920. He was one of the Irish delegates to attend the meeting which established the International Cross Country Union in 1903. This organisation promoted the International Cross Country Championships, which was the forerunner of the current World Cross Country Championship. When this event was held in Ireland for the first time in 1905, Dr Rowlette was elected President for the year. In 1909, J.T. Graham, V.P. McDonagh and T. Burton were elected to the management committee of the CCAI. Graham and Burton were also elected to the International Committee of the Association.

Following political differences in the early 20th century and the founding of the International Amateur Athletic Federation (IAAF) in 1913, a division developed in Irish athletics which resulted in the IAAA and GAA not permitting their members to compete in each other's events. After the signing of the Anglo Irish Treaty in 1921, the Irish Free State was established and this enabled the country to compete in international competitions, including the Olympics, as a stand-alone nation. Around this time the GAA was placing more emphasis on hurling and football and less importance on athletics and following negotiations among all the athletic bodies, the IAAA, CCAI and the athletic council of the GAA agreed to disband and form a single new body - the National Athletic and Cycling Association (NACA). This was the first time since the 1880s that athletics was administered by a single organisation.

On March 4th 1922, the Irish Southern Championship was the last Cross Country event run under the rules of the IAAA. The race was staged over the Phoenix Park racecourse with Clonliffe winning the individual and team gold medals. First man home was W Kinsella who was followed home by Walters, McEachern and Peelo. At the time of its dissolution, the IAAA president was JT Graham and TE Nolan was a member of its executive committee. Among the vice presidents were VP Mc Donagh, GF Walker, T Burton, D McAleese TW Murphy and Dr Rowlette. In addition to their administrative duties all of these Clonliffians were regularly to be found officiating at meetings ranging from the Dublin Tramway sports, the Post Office sports and the Civil Service sports right up to and including National Championships.

At the final IAAA track and field championships, Clonliffe's T.G. Wallis won the 120 yards hurdles while T.J. Carroll won the high jump. JT Graham, who had previously served as club president and honorary secretary, and Dr Rowlette were both on the inaugural committee of the NACA.

The new athletics association enjoyed its first full year of competition in 1923 and it proved to be a very successful one for Clonliffe. In January, B.H. Bingham finished second in the Dublin City Harriers Invitation Road Race and first in the Donore Harriers Invitation. Another Clonliffe man, A.J. Cassidy, who would later represent Donegal in Dáil Éireann, won the Harp Invitation race. At the Dublin Junior Cross Country in the Phoenix Park in February, Joe Peelo took the individual gold while Cassidy took the bronze. G.N. Walker (5th), N. McEachern (6th), C.P.

Kenna (10th), and C. Walters (11th) ensured Clonliffe took the team gold on 36 points from St James Gate on 84 and The Harps on 124. This was the first major race to be staged under the auspices of the new athletic association.

At the 1923 National Juniors in March, Kinsella in third place led home, Walters (6th), Walker (7th), Peelo (8th), Cassidy (9th) and McEachern (10th) for Clonliffe to take the team gold. Two weeks later at the same venue Bingham won the Dublin Seniors and Clonliffe again took the team gold with their scoring six in the first eight finishers. On the following weekend, Bingham finished just two seconds behind J.J. Ryan of Tipperary at the National Senior Cross Country Championships. Walters (6th), Kinsella (7th), Peelo (8th), Cassidy (11th), G. Walker (12th) C. Rothwell (13th) N. McEachern (16th) and C. Kenna (25th) followed him home to give Clonliffe the team gold for the third time in their history.

So, in the first year of the NACA, Clonliffe teams won the County Dublin Junior and Senior together with the National Junior and Senior team titles.

The first inter club track and field meeting of the new body was held in April at Morgans School in Castleknock where Harry Cooney won the 880 yards.

At the inaugural championships of the new association held in Croke Park in June 1923, Clonliffe's Norman McEachern finished second in the 880 yards, J.V. Peatt was third in the mile while there were gold medals for Tim Carroll (1.77m) in the high jump, P.J Bermingham (39.07) in the discus and M. O'Halloran (35.99) in the javelin. Bermingham added two further golds in the 56 lbs "slinging" and "over the bar" events. McEachern would go on to win the 880 yards titles in 1924/'26/'27 and 1928.

Club gold and silver medals won by Norman Mc Eachern

Tailteann games medals won by Norman Mc Eachern

***

Politics was the area of the sport which was to take up an inordinate amount of time and space in Irish athletics during the 1930s. Following a dispute over the participation of NACA athletes in a meeting in Belfast in 1924 which included "professional" non athletic events, thus compromising the amateur status of the association, a number of clubs in the north left the NACA and formed the NIAAA which was affiliated to the AAA of Great Britain. At a meeting of the IAAF in Stockholm in August 1934, a new rule governing membership of the federation stipulated that member countries were restricted by the political boundaries of the relevant nation and that each nation could only be represented by one athletic body. This effectively meant that athletes competing for clubs south of the border could only represent the republic of Ireland while competitors from north of the border would be part of teams representing Great Britain and Northern Ireland. Chief among the events affected by this ruling was the Olympic Games. There was much heated debate among the membership of the NACA as they considered themselves the representative body for both parts of Ireland. At a special congress held in Dublin later that year, a motion was passed rejecting the ruling of the IAAF in Stockholm. This led to Ireland being suspended from the Federation and their competitions including the Olympics. As a result, no athletes were eligible for the 1936 Games in Berlin. One of those affected by this ruling was Billy Morton who that year had won the Irish marathon title. It also prevented Pat O'Callaghan from attempting to win his third consecutive hammer gold.

It was always the priority of Clonliffe Harriers to promote and encourage the sport of athletics in Ireland and to allow all those who achieved the required standard to represent their country in international competition. Any obstacles placed in the path of such opportunities should not be welcomed. In order to gain access to international events, including the Olympics, a number of clubs including Clonliffe Harriers decided to secede from the NACA in 1937 and form the Amateur Athletic Union of Ireland. This new body subsequently applied for and was approved for membership of the International Amateur Athletic Federation and was thus eligible to participate in their competitions. This decision, or "split" as it became known, was to lead to a division in Irish athletics which would not be fully resolved for another 63 years.

In 1946 Clonliffe celebrated its diamond jubilee. Tommy Burton was in his fifth decade as captain and the club was firmly established at the top table of Irish athletics. WW Commiskey was club president, Harry Cooney was vice captain, Billy Morton was Hon Secretary, Arthur Wisdom was Hon Treasurer, Sam Gray was Assistant Treasurer while the committee members were Charlie Rothwell, ET Galway, JJ D'Arcy, George Wisdom, Joe Peelo and Mattie Hewson. All of the above had a long affiliation with the club with some of them going back to the very early years of the century. A celebratory dinner was held in December in the Four Courts Hotel. The end of the jubilee year also marked the end of the 41 year captaincy of Tommy Burton. His time in office had witnessed Clonliffe being transformed from a small local club on the north side of Dublin into one of the top clubs in Ireland and one of the most highly regarded in Europe. He had also overseen the achievement of a record number of team and individual national titles in all areas of the sport. He was the instigator of the Clonliffe International meetings which drew the cream of world athletics to Dublin and put Ireland firmly on the world athletics map. Tommy was also a tireless worker when it came to administration as can be seen from the many positions he held on various national and international committees over the years. However, more than anything else, Tommy will be forever remembered for his captaincy of Clonliffe Harriers and in particular, his unequalled capacity to unearth, nurture and guide young athletes of all ages and abilities to enjoy the sport to which he dedicated most of his life. Some of his protégés achieved the ultimate dream of competing at the Olympics and many were guided to county and national success but the vast majority of those who came into contact with him, whether as members of Clonliffe or other clubs, will remember him for his patience and generosity in giving the benefit of his knowledge to all those who sought it out.

During his later years he was a regular attendee at all club events, more often than not as an official. He passed away at the age of 75 in August 1954. Four years after his death, Clonliffe put up the Tommy Burton trophy for the winner of the two mile invitation race which is still competed for to this day.

Club photo taken at Ballymun Hockey Club Mobhi Road in 1946.
The last year of Tommy Burton's captaincy. Picture includes:
Front row L to R. F Walker, M Hewson, J Foley, J Lawton,
AN Other, J Mc Guigan.
2nd Row from left : H Cooney, C Walker, S Gray, W Morton,
R Galway, T Burton, WW Commiskey (club President).
(2nd from rt GV Ryan. Extreme rt A Wisdom)
3rd row (from left) C Rothwell, CC Walker, AN Other, Joe Foley.

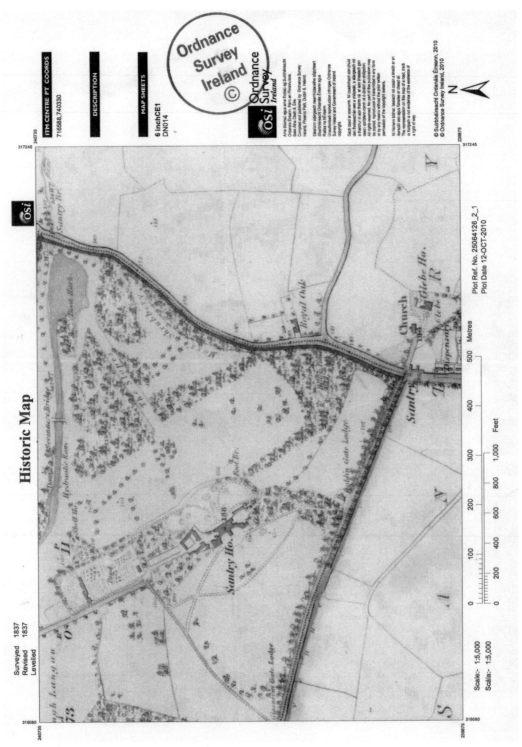

19th century map of Santry Court Estate. Ordnance Survey Ireland/Government of Ireland. Copyright Permit No. MP 007613.

A DREAM REALISED

Prehistory

In telling the story of Clonliffe Harriers, it is worth reflecting on the past history of the village that we now call our home. It is a history which is not without incident, both historical and otherwise.

The original name "Seantrabh" (Irish translation meaning "old tribe"), is first noted in the 9th century Annals Of The Four Masters, when it records the death of Cormac, son of Muirgheas, Abbott of Seantrabh. However, it is thought that the parish itself was founded in the 6th century by St Pappin, and a church bearing his name is located at the top end of Santry Avenue.

Henry II granted the lands to Hugo De Lacy following the Norman Invasion of 1169. These settlers were not warmongers but peace lovers who farmed the high quality agricultural ground and nurtured the extensive woodlands. Indeed the name "Clonliffe" has itself been translated as "The plain of the Liffey" and in the 16th century the townland became part of the extensive lands of the Cistercian Order, which was headquartered in St Marys Abbey less than four miles south in Dublin City centre. The last abbot of the abbey surrendered all these estates, including Santry, to Henry VIII in 1539.

In the 1620s, the lands were taken over by the Barry family who between themselves and their descendants the Domvilles, kept possession of the estate for over 300 years. The Barry family, a Protestant branch of a Cork family named Barrymore, acquired the estate after it had been confiscated from a Catholic, John Barnewell, who took part in the Kildare rebellion headed by Silken Thomas.

James (1603-1673) became the first Baron Barry of Santry in 1660. He was succeeded by Richard (1637-1694), Henry (1680-1735), and the fourth Baron, also Henry, who died without an heir at the age of 40 in 1750.

While all of the Barrys lived at Santry, and some are buried locally, it was not until 1702 that the third baron, who was then married to Brigit Domville, began the construction of what was to become Santry Court. This house was so grand that it soon achieved the name of "the miniature Palace of Versailles" due to the fine wall murals and large number of rooms. It was four storeys high in the Queen Anne style of architecture and resembled Blenheim Palace in England, the home of the Dukes of Marlborough and birthplace of Winston Churchill. By the mid 19th century, an east and west wing had been added making it by far the largest house in the area.

Original Santry Court mansion built in 1702. Courtesy of the National Library Of Ireland. Photo from the Edward King Tennison collection at Kilronan Castle Ballyfarnon County Roscommon.

The fourth baron inherited the estate in 1735 and became probably the most high profile member of the family. His only known portrait hangs in the national gallery of Ireland where he is depicted along with the other four founders of the infamous "Hellfire Club" located in the Dublin mountains. He is best remembered, however, for events which took place in August 1738. While out drinking at the Palmerstown Fair, he got into an altercation which resulted in his killing a local letter carrier. The subsequent trial found him guilty and he was sentenced to death. In fact, Barry signed his own death warrant which stated that he was to be executed the following year. He was given a Royal pardon later that year following the intervention of his uncle, Sir Compton Domville through whose Templeogue estate the water supply for Dublin City flowed. Having threatened to cut off this supply, Domville secured his nephew's release and subsequent return of all his lands at Santry.

When the last Baron Barry died, the Domvilles inherited Santry and moved there in 1751. The estate included almost 5,000 acres and ownership remained in the family until 1935. On moving in, it was found that there were some financial difficulties due to the building of Santry Court and the extravagant lifestyle of the last baron. When Thomas Domville died, the lands were taken over by his nephew Charles Pocklington, who changed his name to Domville to comply with the terms of his uncle's will. Charles was subsequently succeeded by his son Compton. In 1816, the title of Lord was granted to Compton and he became the first Lord Santry.

The rental income at the time allowed him to make extensive improvements to the house and gardens. In addition, a large number of trees were planted and a "pleasure garden" built on the estate. They also had the very unusual facility of gas lamps adorning the main avenue up to the house. These lamps were an expensive indulgence as only five percent of Dubliners had them in the mid 1800s.

This extravagance was not limited to the Lord of the estate. His wife Margaret, on a visit to Switzerland in 1839, became enchanted by the contours of the local houses and on her return, ordered a number of old cottages to be demolished and replaced with 18 new ones designed in the shape of Swiss chalets. These cottages, all bearing the names of plants and flowers, were still standing in 1963, but all bar one have now been replaced. The public house next to these cottages is today known as the Swiss Cottage, and was the local watering hole for many Clonliffe Wasps after they moved to Santry in the 1950s. Mr Eugene O'Reilly, who was the owner of "The Swiss" during these years, was a great friend to Clonliffe and a regular contributor to club fund raisers.

1798 Rising

The late eighteenth century saw another outbreak of lawlessness in the Santry area. From about the 11th century, the main highway from Dublin to the northern parts of the country passed through the village. The proximity of the extensive woodlands made it an ideal location to carry out highway robberies and these were frequent events over the centuries. In 1798, an uprising had begun in Ireland and on 23rd May, an attack was carried out on the northern mail coach below the walls of Santry estate. While the coach was stopped and burned, no possessions were taken and nobody was harmed. This act was to be the signal for the outbreak of the rising in Co. Dublin where more than 3,000 rebels had gathered at the time.

The Famine at Santry

Unlike most of rural Ireland at the time, Dublin City and its hinterland did not rely heavily on the potato. In fact, a survey in 1837 showed that only eight of Santry's

20 townlands grew potatoes.

The famine hit Dublin in 1845 but only about half the population depended on potatoes. The proximity of the city to trading ports meant it had access to foods such as bread and oatmeal. However, from 1847, food riots became common and in 1849 nearly 4,500 Dubliners died from cholera. The influx of rural inhabitants seeking food in Dublin also led to an increase in the number dying from general debility, consumption (TB) and dropsy.

During the famine the population of Santry dropped from 1,117 to 1,034, but some of this could have been due to emigration rather than starvation or other such diseases. The records of the North Dublin Union show that between 1848 and 1850, over 10,000 people passed through its doors but only 13 of these were from Santry.

End Of Domville Era

Charles Compton Domville (1822-1884) was the third son of Compton Pocklington and when he inherited in 1857, he began the largest upgrading of the house and gardens since the building began in 1702. In 1861 he married Margaret St Lawrence, daughter of the last Earl of Howth. He was the last of the Domvilles to reside permanently at Santry and died in 1884. During his life time, the estate became very profitable and in the 1870s, the rental income had increased to around £17,500 per annum. Charles and Margaret had no children and on his death the title passed to his brother William who only lived for two more months before passing away in September 1884. The lands were then inherited by his son Compton (1857-1935) who was never to marry and he only spent some of his time at Santry. Mary (died 1929), a sister of Compton subsequently married Sir William Poe (died 1934) and they lived on the estate until the 1920s.

After the Domvilles

On the death of the last surviving family member in 1935, the house and lands were purchased by the state thus ending over 300 years of continuous ownership of Santry Court. The family did, however, have one last moment in the public eye. At an auction in Battersby's in July 1946 an Irish record price of 4,000 Guineas was paid for a necklace containing 47 diamonds which was owned by Sir Compton Meade Domville. Also sold was the "Monteith Bowl", originally used as a punch bowl by the members of the Hellfire Club (550 Guineas).

Initially the house was under the control of the local regional Health Board and was used as a residential home for people with disabilities. The outbreak of World War Two changed this initiative and the estate was commandeered by the army for use as a practice firing range and general storage depot. It was also of strategic importance due to its proximity to the airport. Following the end of the war, there was little practical use for the grounds and a suspicious fire destroyed the house in 1947.

Arrival of Clonliffe

As early as the 1940s, the officers of Clonliffe Harriers expressed a desire to purchase land with a view to finding a permanent home for the club and a national stadium for athletics in Ireland. At the September 1949 meeting in College Park, Billy Morton announced to the crowd of over 7,000 spectators that Clonliffe were planning to build a cinder track and full details would be made known "in the near future".

In the early 1950s, urban regeneration saw many of the city centre residents relocated to newly built areas like Finglas where Clonliffe had been headquartered since

1936. Housing estates were being built on the fields used by the club for so many years and it was time for the committee to give more serious thought to fulfilling the dream of owning its own clubhouse and training grounds. For the next few years the club was located at "temporary" premises in St Francis Boxing Club in Phibsborough and Neptune Rowing Club at Islandbridge. They were allowed train in the Phoenix Park and to demonstrate their appreciation, they did a run at Christmas around all the occupied buildings delivering messages of goodwill to the inhabitants. Residences visited included many of the Gate Lodges as well as Aras An Uachtarain, occupied at the time by Sean T O'Kelly, The Papal Nunciature occupied by Msgr Albert Levame, and the American Embassy occupied by William Howard Taft III.

During this time, the club was fortunate to have well known businessman Michael McStay acting as its treasurer. Michael was also on the board of the eastern region health authority which had bought the Santry Hall estate after the war with a view to building a mental hospital on the lands. After some prolonged and sometimes difficult negotiations, Clonliffe finally took possession of 11 acres of the estate while Trinity College bought another section of land for their own sporting facilities and also to use as their book depository where there are currently over 3,000,000 books stored. The majority of the estate was sold to the Harris family. A 99 year lease was signed in November 1954 after which a celebratory party for 100 members and guests was held in their then headquarters at Neptune Rowing Club.

In October of 1957, Clonliffe held its first opening run over the lands of Santry.

First opening run at Santry 1957. Part of old mansion in background. Included in photo: John Tallon, Albert Muldoon, Frank Whyte, Don Appleby, Michael Kinsella, Larry Reid, Larry O'Reilly, Alex Ingle, Joe Dempsey, Mick Roe, Tommy Taylor, Sean O'Sullivan and John O'Leary.

Signing of lease on Santry Stadium in Nov 1954.
L to R - J Doran (Capt), D Johnston (Solr), A Wisdom (Hon Tres), W Morton (Hon Sec),
J Masterson (Grangegorman Hospital board member)

R Delany and W Morton turn first sod in 1957.

In June 1957, the first sod was turned by Lord Mayor Robert Briscoe. Along with members of the club, those in attendance included Olympic champion Ronnie Delaney. The shovel used to turn the first sod was supplied by Mr Bernard Mc Donough, an American businessman who was also the owner of the largest shovel factory in the world. The grandson of Irish emigrants he also donated one thousand dollars towards the building of the cinder track. Work began immediately on the construction of the new stadium and the following account is reproduced from the opening night programme in May 1958:

1957 opening run on steps of Santry Court. Included is renowned star of stage, screen and TV Jim Norton. Also included in back row extreme left is 1952 Olympian Paul Dolan.

The Stadium – A Dream Realised

The Clonliffe stadium is the only one of its kind in Ireland. Its running track is a replica of the Olympic track in Melbourne and was constructed by the En-Tous-Cas Company from Leicester who are sports ground specialists and the largest makers of hard lawn tennis courts in the world (The Irish agent for En-Tous-Cas was JJ Fitzgibbon who ran a sports shop in Duke Street and sold much of the clothing and equipment used by club members).

There are two grandstands, one a temporary tubular steel erection built by Mssrs Murphy Bros and the other a fine stand of reinforced concrete with a capacity for 9500 spectators and costing £9500 (€12000) built by Collen Bros under the splendid supervision of Mr Jack Flynn who can claim to know something about grandstands as he supervised the construction of the new stand at Leopardstown race course and the new terracing in Croke Park. Naturally the stadium had to be ring fenced and this was done very competently by Mssrs Kennan Ltd at a cost of £1000 (€1270). Apart from the surfacing material everything else used in the building of the stadium is of Irish manufacture and up to 100 men were kept in constant employment.

The track consists of seven 440 yard lanes each 4 feet wide. It takes twelve words to say it: it took four months to make it. Before anything can be done about the track itself, a road strong enough to carry heavy lorry traffic had to be laid down from the gate to the site consisting of 15 inches of hardcore filled in with small stones and cinders. Over 4000 tons of filling was used during construction. The building of the track was to say the least, very interesting. Trees had to be felled and roots taken out. Then an area of approx 200 x 100 yards was measured and nine inches of topsoil removed and heaped in mounds around the perimeter. The next step was the laying down and rolling in of a clinker ash foundation. This was covered with a lighter ash which was raked and rolled. Then came the layer of En-Tou-Cas surfacing which had to be shipped in from Leicester and was laid to a depth of 2 inches. The track was then thoroughly watered and rolled until it was flat and solid. Finally a top dressing of fine red ash was applied. The cost for the track alone was £8500 (€10800). Next came the stands and heavy equipment needed to stage an international athletic meeting. It is now hoped that the proceeds from the upcoming events will contribute substantially to the upkeep of the stadium. The public have always received good value at Clonliffe meetings and in the future we hope that they will regard a ticket to these events as a very sound investment.

Oct 1957. First opening run at Santry Court. L to R Billy Morton, Joe Peelo, Sam Gray, Charlie Rothwell, Jack Deegan, Charlie Walker.

The work was completed in time for the opening meeting on 19th and 20th May 1958 and the stage was now set to continue the sporting phenomena begun by Tommy Burton in 1912 and continued in the 1940s and early 1950s by Billy Morton. To launch the first season of Clonliffe International Sports Meetings in Santry, Billy held the by now obligatory press conference where he boldly proclaimed the now immortal words "Gentlemen, grass is on the way out". This caused a bit of a stir, as previous Clonliffe meetings in venues like College Park and Lansdowne Road had attracted huge crowds and produced many record performances. He then announced that the inaugural meeting at Clonliffe's new home would include the cream of British athletics including Olympic 5000 metres silver medallist Gordon Pirie, European 1,500 metres gold medallist Brian Hewson and then world mile record holder, Derek Ibbotson. (In September 1958 Ibbotson became the first true four minute miler when he clocked 4.00.00 at White City in London).

19 May 1958. Start of first ever mile race at Santry Stadium.
Included in photo are B Hewson, G Pirie, D Ibbotson and R Delany.

The highlight of the opening night was the 880 yards which saw Hewson beat Delaney. On the second night, what was to be the very first of innumerable unforgettable one mile races in Santry was staged. The field included the Olympic champion (Delany), the European champion (Hewson) and the world record holder (Ibbotson). Delaney gained his revenge to win in a time of 4.07.50 sec with Hewson 2nd in 4.08.10 and Ibbotson 3rd in 4.08.50.

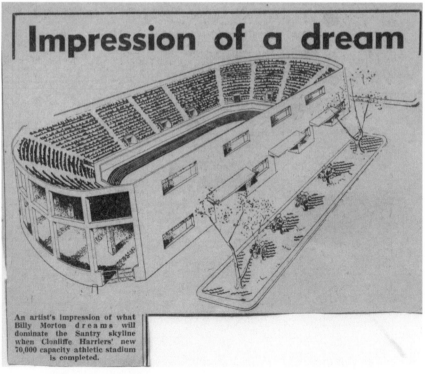

Impression of a dream

An artist's impression of what Billy Morton dreams will dominate the Santry skyline when Clonliffe Harriers' new 70,000 capacity athletic stadium is completed.

Billy's dream of National Athletics arena with 70000 capacity.

At the time the new stadium opened, no fewer than six Irish records were held by Clonliffe Athletes. Paul Dolan at 220 yards (21.60 sec), 300 yards (30.70 sec) and 440 yards (48.80 sec), while JJ Barry held the best times for 1,000 yards (2 min 16.20 sec), two miles (8 min 59 sec) and three miles (13 min 56.20 sec).

On 28th June the new stadium played host to the National track and field championships for the first time. Unfortunately it was not to be a memorable year for Clonliffe as the only National champion was Frazer Walker who successfully defended his marathon title in a new national record time of 2hr 32 min. He was followed home by fellow Wasps J Whelan (2hr 50min), L Reid (2hr 56min) and L Byrne (2hr 57min).

However, these minor setbacks were to be completely subsumed in the events of the next two months. 1958 saw the staging of the Empire (later the Commonwealth) Games in Cardiff, with track and field athletes from 37 countries taking part. With teams arriving well in advance, the redoubtable Billy Morton seized on the chance of getting some of them to come to Dublin beforehand. He travelled over to Wales and told those interested that Clonliffe now had one of the fastest tracks in the world and that they should come to Dublin and give it a go.

A week before the games began he held a meeting in Santry. On 9th July before a crowd of 7000 Australian Albert Thomas set a world record for the three miles when he blazed around the new cinder track in 13 min 10.8 sec.

This was enough to convince some of the other "cracks" to come to Dublin before heading home after the games. The Empire Games were staged at what is now the Millenium Stadium and Australia topped the medals table with England. Herb Elliott won two golds (880 yards and 1 mile) and Murray Halberg of New Zealand won the three miles. Two other Australians, Albert Thomas and Merv Lincoln were also among the medallists. Ten days after the games concluded, Clonliffe and Crusaders hosted a two day meeting in Santry which will go down in the annals as the greatest athletics event ever held in Ireland and one of the greatest sporting fiestas ever to hit our shores.

Having run on the track in July and seen the world three mile record being set, the Australian team returned along with the New Zealanders as well as Mike Agostini and George Kerr, two Canadian sprinters. The stadium capacity was now 17,500 and all tickets were sold by early in the day of August 6th. It was then decided that no money would be taken at the gates but when over 4,000 arrived without tickets, and acting on Garda advice, the organising committee had no choice but to take cash at the gates. While some people were a bit cramped, the evening that followed made it all worthwhile.

The 20,000 plus who attended the new Clonliffe Harriers stadium that night witnessed the greatest night of athletics ever seen in Ireland.

At 8.15pm on Wednesday 6 August 1958, the field lined up as follows in the meeting programme:

10.	M. Lincoln	Australia
11.	H. Elliott	Australia
24.	D. Power	Australia
25.	J. Russell	Australia
26.	A. Thomas	Australia
27	R. Delaney	Crusaders /Villanova
28	J. Mc Loughlin	Civil Service
29.	M. Hoey	Clonliffe Harriers
149.	M. Connolly	Donore Harriers
150.	D. Carbery	Crusaders
151.	T. O'Donoghue	Crusaders

The first lap was led out by Albie Thomas who took them around in 56 sec. The next lap was a little slower as they reached half way in 1 min 58 sec. On the third lap Lincoln took up the running and brought them to the bell in 2 min 59 sec at which point Elliott took to the front and gradually pulled away. In his autobiography, *The Golden Mile*, Elliott takes up the story, "I was on my own now. The track was uncluttered in front. I planned to keep it that way. I drove my feet into those kind resilient cinders and flew. I whizzed round the turn and could feel someone dogging me. It could have been Lincoln. It could have been Delaney. I didn't care. I felt that I could hold whoever it was. And then there was the tape, coming closer and closer, and I was through with the shouts of 20,000 Irishmen ringing in my ears. I looked over at the timekeepers and they were bouncing up and down, unable to restrain their excitement. One of them rushed over, his face flushed.

'Fantastic,' he said, 'it's just fantastic! Your time is 3.54.5!'"

The existing world record of 3 min 58 sec held by John Landy of New Zealand had been broken by the first four athletes and for the first time in history five men had run under four minutes in the same race.

The official result was as follows :

1	Herb Elliott	Australia	3 min 54.50 sec
2	Mervyn Lincoln	Australia	3 min 55.90 sec
3	Ron Delany	Ireland	3 min 57.50 sec
4	Murray Halberg	New Zealand	3 min 57.50 sec
5	Albert Thomas	Australia	3 min 58.60 sec

The sheer magnitude of the achievements in the mile ended up overshadowing some other first class performances that night. A new all comers record was set in the 100 yards when Mike Agostini of Canada ran 9.50 sec while Australian Ian Tomlinson set another all comers record of 50feet 4ins (46.02m) in the triple jump. Ken Gardner of Jamaica equalled the all comers record in the 120m hurdles when he was timed at 14.20sec while C Porter (Australia) equalled the Irish High Jump record when he cleared 6ft 7 in (2.00m).

On the second night Albert Thomas, who had started the summer of records in July returned for an attack on the two mile record. Returning the favour of the first night Herb Elliott was now the pace setter. After an opening lap of 63 sec the half mile was reached in 2min 10 sec and the mile in 4 min 22 sec. Thomas then went to the front with a 61 sec lap but Elliott led into lap 6 to get them to the 1.5 mile point in 6 min 30 sec. Thomas then took over for the final two laps to finish in a new world record time of 8 min 32 sec. Another member of the famous five who broke the 4 minute mile was also back on the track. Murray Halberg ran a world best time of 18 min 22 sec for the 4 miles thus completing an unforgettable two nights of athletics which has never since been equalled in Ireland.

The dream of Billy Morton and his fellow committee members first enunciated 10 years previously had finally come to fruition. The signing of the lease in 1954 had given Clonliffe Harriers a permanent home while the three world records set on the track in its first three months had forever put Santry Stadium on the world athletic map.

*Start of world mile
record race
6 Aug 1958*

*World record mile
6 August 1958*

*Herb Elliott wins
in 3 min 54.50 sec*

International Amateur Athletic Federation
FOUNDED IN 1912.
President ; THE LORD BURGHLEY, K.C.M.G.
Honorary Secretary-Treasurer ; D. T. P. PAIN.

APPLICATION FOR A *WORLD/OLYMPIC/EUROPEAN RECORD.
(*Cross out the words which are not applicable)

To : THE HONORARY SECRETARY OF THE I.A.A.F.

Application is hereby made for a * *WORLD* Record, in
support of which, the following information is submitted :—
*(State the nature of the application—World, Olympic or European)
Reference should be made to Rule 24 I.A.A.F. Competition Rules.

1. Event *ONE MILE FLAT* Men/Women
2. Record claimed (time, distance, height, points) *TIME*
3. Date and hour *6th AUGUST 1958 8.15 PM*
4. Where held (Ground, Place, Country) *CLONLIFFE HRS STADIUM SANTRY DUBLIN IRELAND*
5. Condition of track, runway or circle *GOOD*
6. Level or gradient of track, runway or circle *LEVEL*
7. Weight, measurement and material of implements
8. State of weather *GOOD*
9. Force and direction of wind
10. Name of Competitor, Club and Country *ELLIOTT HERBERT JAMES*
(Surname) (Christian names)
COBIVCY CLUB MELBOURNE. 69 STANLEY ST SCARBOROUGH WEST AUSTRALIA

(In relay events, the full names of the competitors should be stated)
(Signature of Referee) (Address)

TIMEKEEPERS' CERTIFICATES
I, the undersigned official timekeeper, of the event above-mentioned, do hereby certify that the time set opposite my signature was the exact time recorded by my watch, and that the watch used by me has been certified and approved by my National Association. (Refer to Rule 9.)

Time *3 min 54.5 sec* (Signature of Timekeeper) Address
Time *3 mins 54.5 sec* (Signature of Timekeeper) (Address)
Time *3 m 54.50* (Signature of Timekeeper) (Address)

I confirm that the above Timekeepers exhibited their watches to me and that the times as stated are correct.
(Signature of Referee or Chief Timekeeper)

STARTER'S CERTIFICATE
I hereby certify that I was the starter for the event above-mentioned, that it was a fair start and no advantage was given to or taken by the claimant. (Refer to Rules 10 and 27.)
(Signature of Starter) (Address)

Certification of world record

THE MORTON ERA

Billy Morton
© RTE Stills Library

When Tommy Burton joined in 1898, Clonliffe was still competing in the junior ranks but over the next 50 years he transformed it into one of the most well known and highly respected athletic clubs in the country. During the final years of his captaincy he was joined on the club committee by Billy Morton who would take over the reins and lead the club into a new era which would result in Clonliffe becoming one of the best known clubs in the world. Born in 1910, Billy was the son of harness maker Patrick Morton and his wife Mary. He spent his early years living in Sandwich Street just a few hundred yards from Trinity College where he would later promote many memorable Clonliffe International Meetings. He went to England to study opthomology and later returned to Dublin where he opened two shops in Berkeley Street and North Frederick Street in Dublin city just about half a mile from O'Connell Street, Dublin's main thoroughfare.

The Berkeley Street shop became famous among the athletic fraternity and the general public as it was frequently used to hold club committee meetings as well as being the venue for many "negotiations" between Billy and almost everybody connected with any aspect of the clubs activities. It was also a 'part time' opticians practice where half of Dublin bought their glasses. He was ably assisted by his wife Elizabeth and daughters Yvonne and Billie who frequently had to *"hold the fort"* while Billy dashed away, very often at short notice, to *"take care of Clonliffe business"*. Was it a coincidence that the lands bought at Santry were a mere 3 miles (10 minutes by car in those days) from the shop ?

Billy arrived in Clonliffe on 23 September 1926 and it was not very long before he established himself as a 'crack'. He was on the club team which took part in the 1928 Tailteann games and finished 2nd in the marathon at the 1932 renewal. In 1935 he was a member of the team which won the Dublin Junior Cross Country Title. He finished fourth behind Sam Gray and Harry Cooney who took first and second

53

respectively. The following year Billy won the National Marathon in a new Irish record time of 2 hours and 48 minutes. The difficulties within Irish athletics at that time resulted in no team being sent to the Berlin Olympics thus robbing him of an opportunity to compete on the highest stage. His Irish record would have placed him in the top fifteen finishers.

In 1942 he was elected Club Honorary Secretary and held that office for 38 years until his untimely death at the early age of fifty nine in 1969. He also served as Hon. Treasurer from 1964-69.

During his early years as club Secretary Billy began taking charge of the organisation of a new era in the history of the club. Along with stalwarts like Harry Cooney, Sam Gray, Charlie Rothwell, Arthur Wisdom, Mattie Hewson and Michael Mc Stay, Clonliffe continued the work begun back in the early years of the century by Tommy Burton, Dan Mc Aleese, T.E. Nolan and many others.

One of Billy's most famous characteristics was his showmanship and this manifested itself from the very beginning. He was Ireland's first, and finest, sports impresario and the first promoter to hold a press conference before his meetings where he would announce to the public that records would be broken and patrons would get great value for their money. Throughout his many years of promoting athletic events his photo, and the name of Clonliffe Harriers, appeared as frequently in the features and social columns as it did on the sports pages. Billy never failed to miss an opportunity to get publicity and apart from his numerous successes in staging sports meetings, in later years he was constantly in the news with his many and varied schemes to reduce the club debt.

Billy Morton's first Clonliffe Sports.

The Second World War years were lean times for athletics in Ireland but Clonliffe were determined to continue providing sporting outlets for both competitors and spectators and meetings were held throughout those troubled times. After the fifteenth Clonliffe International sports in 1928 the club, not unlike many other organisations around the world went through a lean time financially and no more big meetings were staged for 15 years.

Billy staged his first meeting on Saturday 14th August 1943 at Glenmalure Park in Milltown, the then home of Shamrock Rovers soccer Club. At the press launch he announced that an attempt would be made on the world hammer throw record. He could not have made a better start to his "career" when Bert Helion duly obliged by throwing a new world record of 192 feet and 11 inches (59.71 metres). Another of Billy's renowned tactics was to get well known personalities to attend the press conference or to present the prizes at the sports. For his first meeting he got no less a personality than the world famous boxer Jack Doyle (known as "The Gorgeous Gael") and his then wife the Mexican film star Movita Castaneda to present the prizes. Married in 1939 the famous couple divorced in 1944. Movita subsequently married Marlon Brando with whom she had two children. Doyle, who was also a famous singer in his prime, died in poverty in London in 1978 and was buried in his native Cobh. Among the competitors in the high jump were Irish champion Dick O'Rafferty and Ulick O'Connor, a well known Irish writer who would subsequently produce definitive biographies on Oliver St John Gogarty and Brendan Behan.

Group pictured in Barn Park Finglas in 1940s.

In addition to providing competition for athletes the profits raised from these sports meetings were donated to the *Evening Herald* Boot Fund, a charity set up to provide footwear for the less well off children of Dublin but especially for young newspaper sellers. This was another example of the generosity of Clonliffe and Billy to help out in raising funds for various charitable organisations. The annual Christmas run with presents to the young patients in Cappagh Orthopaedic hospital was by now well into its second decade.

Never one to let the grass grow under his feet Billy organised the first athletics meeting after World War Two in Lansdowne Road a mere three weeks after the cessation of hostilities. At the September 1945 meeting in College Park Douglas Wilson who would later represent Great Britain in the 1500 metres at the 1948 Olympics set a new Irish All Comers record when he won the mile in 4 min 15.80 sec. Seeing that the sporting public were now looking for more outlets to put the tragedy of the war years behind them Billy set about organising meetings in College Park and Lansdowne Road which drew crowds ranging from five to forty thousand spectators. Like Tommy Burton thirty years previously Billy's aim was to pitch the cream of Irish athletics against many of the top competitors from other countries and put Clonliffe back on the sporting map.

In 1946 Clonliffe celebrated their diamond jubilee by holding two major international meetings in College Park. The first one in July drew a crowd of over 8000 spectators and they were not disappointed. In the two mile event Sidney Wooderson of Blackheath Harriers, the then European 5000 metre champion, broke the Irish record of JJ O'Connor by no less than 29 seconds. His time of 9 min 05 sec was also announced as a world record for a grass track. In the high jump 18 year old Scot Alan Peterson became the first man to jump 6 feet 6 inches in Ireland and in the process broke the record held by Clonliffe's PJ Carroll set in 1910. Douglas Wilson equalled the Irish record for the 1000 yards. The *Irish Independent* concluded its report of the meeting by stating "to the Clonliffe Harriers and to Mr Morton in particular, who organised the meeting, the best thanks of the Dublin public are due for an athletic event which thrilled the crowd and will make athletics a topic of conversation for quite a while to come."

The second Jubilee meeting was again held in College Park in September but two days of incessant rain beforehand made the chances of record performances on the grass track virtually impossible. Despite the conditions a new Irish record was set in the Javelin when C Ryan of Hermes threw 169 ft 5.5 inches (51.66m) which was 9.5 inches further than the existing 12 year old record. The sprints turned out to be very competitive due to the handicap system with Clonliffe man, and Irish rugby international Louis Crowe beating E Mc Donald Bailey in the 100 yards. Bailey, who would later win bronze in the 100 metres at Helsinki in 1952 and subsequently break the world record, did gain revenge in the 220 yards when he finished in front of Paul Dolan (Clonliffe) and Crowe. His winning time was 22.60 sec. Arthur Wint won the 440 yards in 49.80 sec which was only 0.40 sec off the Irish record. Wint was the first Jamaican to win a gold medal at the Olympics when he took the 400 metres title at London in 1948. He also won silver in the 800 metres. The crowd of over 5000 were again given full value for money as Clonliffe managed to attract yet another generation of world class athletes to its famous sports meetings. After just three years in the job Billy Morton had established himself as a major sports promoter who could not only attract the worlds best athletes to Dublin but could provide the paying public with top class competition as well as National and World records.

In 1947 Dave Guiney became the first clubman to win an AAA title when he took gold in the Shot Putt with a throw of 47ft 6ins (14.47m). He retained the title in 1948 and represented Ireland at the Olympics in London. At the August 1947 Clonliffe meeting John Joe Barry set a new Irish 1 mile record when he ran 4 min 15.20 sec in College Park. Willem Slijkhuis (Nederlands) the bronze medallist over 1500 and 5000 metres at the 1948 Olympics ran the 4 miles in 19 min 44.40 sec to equal the Irish all comers record. Among those competing in the 100 yards event was Clonliffe's JC (Sean) Diffley who would in later years become a prominent athletics correspondent and life long friend and supporter of the club.

The London Olympics in 1948 provided Billy with a further opportunity to bring the worlds best to Dublin. Before doing so however he organised yet another publicity coup by raising funds to send up to 5000 eggs per week to the competitors in London. In true Morton fashion he announced to the press that "an export license had already been granted and that the eggs would be purchased for 3/6 per dozen". As post war rationing was still in existence in Great Britain and Ireland was then a major agricultural country any "sustenance" was warmly welcomed. It also proved to be the required carrot to attract athletes to Dublin after the Games.

Just 2 weeks before the opening ceremony a meeting was held in Lansdowne Road which saw E Mc Donald Bailey run an all comers record of 9.80 sec for the 100 yards while Bill Nankeville (GB) won the mile from JJ Barry and Douglas Wilson in a time of 4 min 17.40sec. After the Games a number of Dutch Olympians came to Dublin and competed at the Clonliffe International including Fanny Blankers Koen, winner of four gold medals in London. In the 100 yards event Blankers-Koen equalled the world record when she ran 10.80 sec. Prophetically, one of the adverts in the programme was for "houses built to last on beautifully situated sites at Santry" They were priced at £2000-00 (€2540-00) and required a deposit of £200-00. A grant for £275-00 was also available with "loans for balance available".

The success of these meetings prompted Billy to go to London in December 1948 and negotiate a deal to hold a major event the following year. It was to entail the largest expenditure on one event by any sports club in Ireland. Clonliffe would contribute £4000-00 being half the total cost. Teams were invited from USA, Sweden, Holland, Norway, France, Belgium and Great Britain to take on the best of the Irish.

The meeting took place on 8th and 9th June in Lansdowne Road and proved to be one of the greatest ever Clonliffe Internationals. On the first night no less than 4 Irish all comers records were set, each by an American athlete. D. Bolan won the 440 in 48.50 sec, D. Phillips cleared 6ft 6.25ins (1.98 metres) in the high jump while Olympic champion Harrison Dilliard ran 14.40 sec for the 120 yd hurdles. Dilliard was a four time Olympic gold medallist and one of only two men to win individual Olympic titles in hurdles and flat events. He was 100m champion in 1948 and 110h champion in 1952. The other is Kipchoge Keino who won the 1500 in 1968 and Steeplechase in 1972. The Mile was won by Fred Wilt (USA) in 4 mins 10 secs from JJ Barry (4.14) both inside the old record of 4mins 15secs. The 15 mile road race from Kilmacanogue to the Stadium was won by Jack Holden (GB) in 1hr 17min 43sec from Frank Cahill (Donore) and Harry Cooney (Clonliffe). This event was historic as it was the first time that a radio car had been used for a road race in Ireland relaying back details to the spectators in the Stadium. Multiple Olympic champion Fanny Blankers Koen won the 100 yards in 11.20 sec and the 80 yards hurdles in 11.60 sec.

The three mile event on the second night provided one of the greatest races in the history of the sport in Ireland. Clonliffe's and Ireland's great middle distance champion was back on the track to avenge his defeat to Wilt in the mile the previous night. In a never to be forgotten race fellow American Curtis Stone along with Wilt set a fast pace with Barry lying back in fourth until the half way point. The Irishman then moved into third but was still off the record pace which the Americans hoped would be too much for him. Barry gradually moved closer during the last lap and on the final bend he sprinted past his two opponents and breasted the tape with the cheers of over 30,000 fans ringing in his ears. When the times were announced the cheering became even louder. Barry had knocked no less than 34 seconds off the Irish and all comers record set by G Carstairs of Scotland in 1937. The winning time was 13 min 56.20 sec. Wilt, who was second and Stone were also inside the old record.

A sample of the list of prizes at this International meeting included :

3 miles flat :	1st	Solid Silver Candlesticks
	2nd	Sandwich Stand
	3rd	Cake basket
120 Yds Hurdles:	1st	Case of Silver Sauce Boats
	2nd	Fruit Dish and Spoon
	3rd	Bread Knife
Relay race :	1st	Parker Pen Set
	2nd	Silver Pencil Set
880 yds Invitation :	1st	Silver Salver
	2nd	Case of solid silver spoons
	3rd	Sugar and Cream on stand

Fanny Blankers Koen at Clonliffe Meeting Lansdowne Road 1949

A fantastic year for Irish athletics was concluded in front of 7000 spectators at the final Clonliffe International of 1949 in College Park in September. Among those competing were Olympic 800 metre champion Mal Whitfield and 19 year old double Olympic Decathlon gold medallist Bob Mathias. He won the high jump with 6ft1in (1.82m) but was beaten into second place in the Discus by rising new Irish star Cumin Clancy who threw 152ft 4ins (46.43m). Clancy, along with John Joe Barry and Jimmy Reardon were the first Irish athletes to go to the United States on athletic scholarships. American sprint champion Andy Stanfield set an all comers record for the 100 yards of 9.60 secs and in doing so broke the 20 year old record held by Denis Cussen. However, it was the running of Dutchman Willem Slijkhuis in the 4 mile event which really put the icing on the cake. His time of 19 mins 31 secs knocked 13 secs off the longest standing record in Irish athletics. The previous time had been set 62 years previously in 1887 (the year after Clonliffe was founded) by Tommy Conneff. As the decade drew to a close the reputation of Billy Morton was at an all time high and he was now regarded as the premier sports promoter in the country and as someone who always delivered on his promises.

1949 National Junior CC Champions.
Front Row : G Smyth, F Hewson (Vice Capt), L Reid,
Middle Row : N Mooney, F Sherwin, F Walker, D Appleby, G White, W McAuliffe,
Back Row : A Wisdom (Hon Tres), P Tunney, P O'Hara(Capt), C Rothwell
(President), J D'Arcy, W Corbett, W Morrissey, W Morton (Hon Sec).

While the main profile of the club during the 1940s centred around inter-national track and field meetings the club cross country handicap races continued to flourish. Large fields regularly turned up to compete for the Vice Presidents Cup for novices, the O'Connor Cup, The Irwin Cup, and the Horan Cup. Having won the Mc Evoy Cup outright in 1943 Sean Farren presented the Farren Cup as a replacement. When ET Galway won the Doran Shield outright in the same year he replaced in with the Galway Shield. During the summer various club handicaps were held including the 130 yards which had been competed for since the early days of the century. Clonliffe's reputation as a producer of fine international athletes reached yet another milestone in 1948 when Donegal man Paul Dolan (4x400 metres relay), Cork man Dave Guiney (shot putt) and Tipperary man John Joe Barry (1500 and 5000 metres) competed at the London Olympics. In addition, Dublin man Charlie Rothwell, a member of many cross country winning teams and former club president, acted as team manager.

The success of Billy's post war meetings also witnessed the arrival of yet another generation of Clonliffe "cracks". While the Senior Cross Country had been won only four times before the War, the club, in addition to victory in 1949 went on to take four consecutive championships in 1952/53/54 and 1955. The most consistent performer during this time was Don Appleby who followed his gold medal wins in 1949 and 1952 by finishing 4th in 1953 and 2nd in 1954 and 1955. The latter victory also saw Paddy Killeen take the individual title thus becoming the seventh clubman to achieve this honour. Other notable members of these teams were Frazer Walker, who would later become a multiple Irish Marathon champion, and Frank White who later ran in the 2 mile world record race at Santry in 1958 and subsequently became a life long administrator in the club. The team victory in 1955 was also notable for the performances of Paddy Killeen and Don Appleby who finished first and second thus replicating the feat achieved in 1914 when, in addition to winning the team gold, Irwin and Ryder finished first and second.

This era also saw a new breed of track and field stars who featured in many of the Clonliffe meetings as well as picking up National and International honours. Paul Dolan, a young civil servant from Ballyshannon arrived on the scene when he won the 100 in 1946 and the 440 in 1947 and 1949. He subsequently won the 100/220/440 in 1952 and competed in these three events at the Helsinki Olympics. John Joe Barry was the king of middle distance track events taking no fewer than three 880, three 1 mile and two 3 mile titles. Dave Guiney won the shot four times and was one of three Clonliffe men to compete at the London Olympics. Pole Vaulter PV Furlong was the first "Wasp" to win National titles in a discipline which, at the time of writing, is totally dominated by two Clonliffe men David Donegan and Anthony Mc Creary.

On 6th August 1953 a young Ronnie Delany made his first appearance at a Clonliffe sports when he won the 880 yards in College Park. After completing his first year at Villanova in May 1955, Billy sent him his ticket home to Ireland with a promise of some good races during his summer sojourn. Ronnie had not raced over 1 mile up to then but it was Billy who persuaded him that this might well be his best distance. At the Clonliffe August meeting Delany raced his first mile and duly proved Billy correct by setting a new Irish record of 4 min 05.8 sec in College Park. Within 16 months Ronnie was Olympic 1500 metres champion.

1950s in Santry. Included are C Rothwell (extreme left), Don Appleby (back row 3rd fom left), Sam Gray (extreme right back row) and Billy Morton (front row extreme right)

1953 National Senior CC Champions
Back L to R F Whelan, P Phelan, D Appleby, D Main, F White, F Walker, L Leach,
C O'Loughlin, J Johnson, R Payne (starter)
Front L to R J Whelan, L Reid, J Dempsey, W Mc Auliffe, D Roe, H Cooney

The commercial and financial success of the post war meetings meant that the club was now in a strong position to proceed to the next stage of its development. It was Billy's dream and that of his fellow clubmen that Clonliffe would one day buy their own ground and build a stadium which would be for the use of all the youth of Ireland. At the September 1949 meeting in College Park he first publicly announced that Clonliffe were planning on building an athletic ground with a cinder track and that *"Details would be made known in the near future"*.

The search went on for the next few years, and a 99 year lease was signed in November 1954 to purchase part of the Santry Court Estate. This agreement may have fulfilled Billy's dream but he was not a man to rest on his laurels and as soon as the track was ready he continued his campaign of attracting the cream of world athletics to Clonliffe's new home. His first year (1958) surpassed even his wildest dreams but this only drove him on to promote the sport and the stadium even further and he continued encouraging athletes of every club to come and use Ireland's National Athletics arena. This invitation was particularly significant as there had been a 'split' in Irish Athletics since 1937 and Billy hoped that building a facility which would be open to all who chose to use it might in some small way contribute to more talks taking place with a view to resolving the impasse.

There were a number of 'incidents' at various points in time which did not help in the resolution of this dispute but Billy was only interested in promoting athletics and providing young people with the facilities to enjoy the sport for as long as they wanted. His commitment to the solving of the problems which beleaguered Irish athletics for many decades was unrelenting. When he joined Clonliffe, the sport was run solely by the National Athletics and Cycling Association (NACA).

Following the initial division Billy made several attempts at resolving the impasse during the 1940s but to no avail. Another effort was made in 1952 when he met directly with the British Amateur Athletic Board but this again failed to yield a solution. Around this time he also sent a letter to the NACA asking for talks with a view to unifying Irish athletics. Included in this letter were the following words... "I feel that the time has come when all people in Irish athletics must get down to fixing up this whole question. I feel, as all people do, that it is only with one united body that our small country can put itself back on the athletic map" Unfortunately this effort also fell on hollow ground. The situation was further exasperated at the Helsinki Olympics. The AAU had selected a number of athletes for nomination to the Games but the Irish Olympic Council decided not to send any track and field team. Despite this rejection the AAU sought and received approval to compete from the IAAF. They then raised the necessary funds to send two athletes with Billy Morton acting as team manager. Clonliffe man Paul Dolan and marathon runner Joe West realised their dreams and competed on the highest stage. For the remainder of his life Billy constantly sought out ways and means to heal the division which had denied many Irish athletes a chance to compete at international competitions. When a solution was finally agreed in 1967 it involved the dissolution of the AAU and the NACA. Among those who attended the final meeting of the AAU were Billy Morton, Fred Hewson, Al Guy and Jack Deegan of Clonliffe Harriers. The resolutions dissolving the old body and approving the establishment of the BLE were put forward by Colm Brennan and Al Guy. All resolutions were passed unanimously and as a consequence Billy Morton had lived to see the end of the "split" and his many efforts of the previous 30 years finally realised.

Clonliffe International meeting Lansdowne Road 1950s

Gary Dempsey at Clonliffe International in Lansdowne Road

The 1960S

While the successes of the early meetings in Santry had drawn huge crowds, the years following saw a major change in the sporting and social priorities of the general public and unfortunately athletics was one of the sports which suffered quite significantly. Billy continued to try to bring International athletes to Dublin but the supporters failed to respond in sufficient numbers and this resulted in an increasing debt mountain building up in the club. Undaunted, he set about attracting in 'non-athletic' forms of entertainment in an effort to bring the crowds back in order to help reduce the financial burden.

These events were as wide and varied as could be imagined. For the 1965/66 year the money spinners which helped to keep the club afloat included :

Christmas Raffle	£ 65-00	
Annual Dance	£123-00	
Canadian Hell Drivers	£953-00	
Eintracht Film	£ 40-00	(1960 European Cup Final)
Flag Days	£335-00	
Tokyo Olympic Film	£127-00	
Dickie Rock Concert	£170-00	
Sept Mile Meeting	£368-00	(Featuring Kip Keino)

View of Santry Stadium in 1966.
Courtesy of Sportsfile

However, the biggest single amount generated that year was by the ladies when their house to house collection yielded £1180-00.

In 1967 a "Passion Play" was staged and yielded a profit of £1500-00. Rugby league tournaments were also staged as well as soccer games between a "Clonliffe Selection" and an English league team. In 1959 an International tennis tournament was held in Santry Stadium which featured some of the top players in the world including Wimbledon champions Tony Trabert, Lew Hoad, and Alex Olmedo.

Billy's cry for help !!
Courtesy of Sportsfile

While there were many profitable fundraisers there were also some losers, most notably the week long International Military Tattoo which was plagued with constant rain every day. However, the most constant sources of income were members subscriptions, donations, and of course the "Secret Bag". This innovation was introduced back in the 1940s to help garner some extra income mainly to pay for items like electricity and hot water. A bag was passed around the changing room after each training session and members were expected to make an anonymous donation. The total amount collected was published yearly as part of the annual accounts.

By the end of the 1960s the sport was changing on the international stage and the 'amateur' status of athletics was slowly being replaced by the arrival of professionalism in the form of the grand prix circuit. The wheel was turning full circle from the days of the late nineteenth century when pedestrianism and payment to competitors was outlawed. The promotion of athletic meetings was now becoming more of a business venture where it was necessary to engage major sponsors if big international names were to be attracted to Santry.

The Clonliffe association with the Joyce family continued throughout these years when Billy employed Fred Joyce, a nephew of the famous author, as an apprentice optician. Fred spent his career working in the shop and subsequently purchased the business from the family after Billy died. Fred's son Bob was a member of the club during the 1960s. While Clonliffe was famous for its "sting in the tail" which provided many famous victories, the Joyce family can also lay claim to leaving a final legacy to the club. Being was a classmate of Frank Murphy in O'Connells School where both began their athletic careers it was Bob who introduced the multiple Irish record holder and Olympian to Clonliffe.

The
Prime Minister
of Sport

"One man in his time plays many parts"
· AS YOU LIKE IT

Hibernian Insurance ad from Clonliffe Programme

Billy was a Clonliffe man through and through and this point is well illustrated in the concluding part of his address to the 1965 AGM :

"I have spent a lifetime in Clonliffe Harriers, seen very many changes and watched many faces come and go with all kinds of ideas but who never remained long enough to do anything. In bringing this to your notice I would ask you to give serious thought to to-nights election of officers. Do not be misled by the great talkers. What we in Clonliffe need are workers and badly at that.

As long as I am spared and you need me, I will be very happy to do whatever is necessary to keep the ideals of Clonliffe to the fore. At the same time I will not be afraid to speak my mind. I am not here to please any group or section. I call a spade a spade and under no circumstance will I change"

Apart from his family Billy's whole life revolved around Clonliffe, initially as a competitor and in later life as an administrator. Indeed he was often referred to as "Mr Athletics" or "The Prime Minister of Sport". While he passed away at a relatively young age he did live to see his dream of a national athletics arena created and it is a fitting testimony to his lifelong dedication to Clonliffe Harriers and the sport of athletics that the stadium now bears his name. The year after his passing the club committee inaugurated the Morton Mile and donated the Morton trophy to be presented to the winner of this yearly event. The mile had been the "Blue Riband" event of athletics for many years. The magical four minute barrier was an aspiration of most middle distance runners for almost a decade before Roger Bannister broke it in 1954. The famous race in Santry in August 1958 put the club on the world map and it was only fitting that this event was chosen to commemorate the contribution that Billy had made to Clonliffe and to Irish Athletics.

Joe Harden, Brendan Byrne, John O'Leary, Harry Cooney, Larry Reid and Paddy Byrne
at Duncairn Road Relays in Belfast 1960

Ashley Cooper prepares to deal with a smash from Mal Anderson (right foreground) in the final stages of the Men's Doubles match in the Professional Tennis Tournament at Santry yesterday. Anderson and Trabert beat Cooper and Hoad, 5-7, 8-6, 8-6.

PROFESSIONAL TENNIS

NOTHING LIKE IT EVER SEEN BEFORE

August 1959.
Professional Tennis at Santry.

1962 National Novices CC Champions.
Back Row : P Griffin, B Raftery, J O'Leary, C McArdle, A Sweeney, L Coogan, M Brady,
H Sydner.
Front Row : T Griffin, M McMorrow, R Heffernan, H Cooney Capt), Geo McIntyre,
M Ahern, L Murphy.

75th Anniversary 1961. 3rd from right in back row is
John Mc Donnell who later became the most successful coach in American college history.

THE FIRST LADIES

Significant Dates in Women's Athletics

1912   First Clonliffe International sports meeting included events for women.

1928   Women admitted to Olympic Games for first time.

1954   In the same month that Roger Bannister broke the four minute mile, fellow Britain Diane Leather broke the five minute mile when she ran 4 minutes 59.6 seconds in Birmingham.

1956   Thelma Hopkins of Northern Ireland breaks the world high jump record when she clears 5ft 8.50 inches (1.74 m) in Belfast. Having won gold at the 1954 Commonwealth Games she won silver at the Melbourne Olympics in 1956.

1963   Foundation of Clonliffe Harriers Ladies Section.

1964   Jackie Spence (Crusaders) 100, Mary Wood (Crusaders) 220, Hazel Tennison (Crusaders) 440 and Claire Walsh (Clonliffe) 440 are the first Irishwomen to compete at the AAA championships.

1965   Ann O'Brien sets world record when she runs 14,428 metres (9 miles 1133 yards) in one hour.

1966   Ann becomes first Irishwoman to break five minutes for mile when she runs 4 minutes 59 seconds in Santry. She also wins the first of 11 individual national track and field titles.
Clonliffe ladies win their first national inter club cross country title.

1967   Clonliffe ladies retain their cross country title.
Kathy Switzer becomes the first woman to register (as KV Switzer) and complete the Boston Marathon. During the race which was a male only event, Kathy was spotted by one of the officials who tried to forcibly remove her. He was himself "forcibly removed" and Kathy completed the course in 4 hours 20 minutes.

1968   Ann O'Brien wins first of four consecutive individual National Cross Country titles.
Claire Walsh wins first of 19 individual national track and field titles.
Wyomia Tyus of the USA becomes the first woman to retain the Olympic 100 metres title. Her winning time of 11.08 seconds is a world record.

1969   Ann O'Brien runs the second fastest 3,000 metres ever when she wins the WAAA championship in a time of 9 min 47.6 sec.

1970   Clonliffe Ladies win their third National Senior Inter Club CC.

1971   Clonliffe Ladies win AAA 4x400 and 4x800 metres titles.

1972   Claire Walsh becomes first Clonliffe lady to compete at the Olympics.
Mary Peters wins Pentathlon gold at Munich Olympics.
Boston marathon finally officially admits women.
Billie Jean King (winner of 39 grand slam tennis titles), becomes first
woman to win Sports Illustrated Sports Person of the Year.

1973   Bridget Cushen becomes the first Irish born woman to complete a
marathon when she runs 3 hr 27 min in England.

1976   Clonliffe Ladies win their fourth National Senior Inter Club CC.

1977   Michelle Walsh/Carroll wins the first of her 31 national sprint titles.
In the next 18 years she would win the 100 metres 15 times, the 200
metres 12 times and the 400 metres 4 times.

1978   Kathryn Davis becomes second Clonliffe lady to win National Cross
Country title.

1979   Greta Weitz wins the second of her five world CC titles in Limerick. In
November in New York, she becomes the first woman to run under 2
hours 30 minutes for the marathon.

1980   Jean Folan becomes the first Irishwoman to complete a marathon
in Ireland when she recorded a time of 3 hours 37 minutes at the
nationals in Tullamore.
At ladies marathon race in London in August, Mary Butler becomes
first Irishwoman to run under 3 hours 30 minutes when she ran
3:26.57.
Two weeks later at Nationals in Letterkenny, Carey May becomes first
Irishwoman under three hours when she clocks 2 hr 53 min.
In October, Carey again breaks Irish record when she runs 2 hr 42
min at the inaugural Radio Two Dublin City Marathon.

1986   In club centenary year Mary Donohue becomes third Clonliffe lady to
win National Cross Country title.

1988   Patrice Dockery and Ann Keenan represent Clonliffe and Ireland at
Seoul Olympiads.
Patrice and Ciara Peelo, granddaughter of Joe, are the flag carriers at
their respective opening ceremonies.

1989   Kathryn Walley wins Irish indoor 600 metre title in 1 min 41 sec.

1992   Catherina Mc Kiernan wins first of four consecutive silver medals at
world cross country championships.

1993   Cathy Shum wins Dublin City Marathon.

1994   Sonia O'Sullivan becomes first Irish female to win gold at European T&F when she takes the 3,000 metres title. Catherina Mc Kiernan is first Irishwoman to win European cross country title.

1995   Emer Haastrup wins Irish indoor 60 metre title in 7.95 sec. Sonia O'Sullivan wins world 5,000 metres in Gothenberg and becomes first Irishwoman to win a world track title.

1996   Marissa Smith wins Irish indoor 200 metre title in 25.02 sec.

1998   Sonia O'Sullivan becomes first Irishwoman to win world Cross Country title.

2000   Sonia O'Sullivan becomes first Irishwoman to win Olympic medal when she takes 5,000 metres silver in Sydney.

2003   Frances Ni Reamoin on Irish team at European Junior Cross Country Championship.

2004   Frances Ni Reamoin on Irish team at World Cross Country Championship.

2007   Frances Ni Reamoin on Irish team at European Under 23 Cross Country Championship.

2008   Clonliffe ladies celebrate their 45th anniversary.

2010   Becky Woods competes for Ireland at European under 23 Cross country championships in Portugal.

2011   Club 400 hurdler Sarah Woods helps DCU Mercy win National Womens Basketball final against Glanmire by 61 to 47.

2013   Clonliffe ladies celebrate their 50th anniversary.

Women's athletics, in common with other sports, struggled for some time to gain official recognition at both national and international level worldwide. It wasn't until the early 1920s that formal organisations and structures began to emerge. Baron Pierre De Courbetin, the founder of the modern Olympic Games, was not a supporter of women's athletics. At the first modern games in Athens, a woman, Melpomene, barred from the official race, ran the same marathon course as the men, finishing in 4 hours 30 minutes. De Coubertin said of the event "It is indecent that the spectators should be exposed to the risk of seeing the body of a woman being smashed before their very eyes. Besides, no matter how toughened a sportswoman may be, her organizm is not cut out to sustain certain shocks." The official report of the 1912 Games in Stockholm, written undoubtedly with De Coubertin's backing states: "An Olympiad with females would be impractical, uninteresting, unaesthetic and improper". It was not until after his retirement from the International Olympic Committee following the 1924 Games in Paris, that women's track and field events were first admitted starting with the Games in Amsterdam in 1928. Even then participation was restricted to the 100m, 800m, 4 x 100 relay, high jump and discus. The first two female track gold medallists were Betty Robinson (100m) and Lina Radke (800m) who represented the USA and Germany respectively. Some of the competitors in the 800 metres were so exhausted that distances longer than 200 metres were not included again until 1960. The 200m was not introduced until 1948, the 400m in 1964 and the 1,500m in 1972. The first Olympic Ladies Marathon was run in 1984 and the first 10,000m took place in 1988.

Despite these reservations by the IOC, organisers of domestic athletics were not found wanting when it came to promoting ladies events. When Clonliffe began staging their international sports meetings in 1912 the programme included a ladies sprint event. At the second meeting held at the RDS in 1913 the 100 yards was won by Lillie O'Mahony from Kathleen Kavanagh and Betty Magee. The 1916 renewal in Dalymount Park saw victory going to Peggy Mc Carthy who was followed home by Maud Gillen, Lillie Manning, Jane Barrett and May Manning. There were also ladies races at the Dublin tramway sports in Croke Park in 1923, the Post Office sports in Harolds Cross in 1928 and the inaugural Insurance Federation sports in Croke Park in 1930. Despite these events there was still some local opposition and a proposal put to the 1927 AGM of the National Athletics and Cycling Association by a Mr S. Bonner that some ladies events be included in their championship was roundly quashed with one delegate even going so far as to say that, at the 1914 event in the RDS, a ladies high jump had been included and "the sight of women's legs was not at all edifying".

An *Irish Times* editorial in May 1928 gave some support to the Pope (Pius XI) when he expressed concern at women's involvement in athletics. It stated *inter alia* "many girls are devoting themselves to public sports which demand violent exertion and sometimes it would seem, a notable scantiness of clothing. They compete for 'records' in 100 yards and quarter mile races. These performances are done before crowds of male spectators. His Holiness is surely in the right when he says that they are irreconcilable with women's reserve."

A similar proposal put to an NACA meeting in 1934 prompted a letter to the Dublin media from the then president of Blackrock College, Rev. John Charles McQuaid, stating *inter alia* that "mixed athletics and all cognate immodesties are abuses that right-minded people reprobate, wherever and whenever they exist". He further stated that women competing in the same sporting arena as men were "un-Irish and un-Catholic" and boys from his school would be prohibited from competing in any fixtures which featured ladies events. Due to the extent of the ensuing controversy, the NACA withdrew the proposal. This matter featured again following the establishment of a Ladies Section by Crusaders Athletic Club in 1947. Further protests from the now Archbishop McQuaid together with the small number of lady members prompted Crusaders to take a decision in March 1951 to discontinue its Ladies Section. It would be resurrected again in 1963.

At the August 1948 Clonliffe International Sports in Lansdowne Road, the Dutch athlete Fanny Blankers Koen, known as the "flying housewife" made her first appearance in Ireland. She was to return again the following year for the June Meeting. Fanny, the winner of four gold medals at the London Olympics, was the first female athletics superstar to compete in Ireland. During the next decade or so women's athletics in Ireland was never put on a properly organised footing. While there were ladies events as part of various meetings, most of the participants would have been members of other sporting clubs or organisations i.e. hockey.

1956 was an historic year for Irish athletics in general but for Irish womens athletics in particular. In May Thelma Hopkins broke the world high jump record when she cleared 5ft 81/2 in (1.74m) in Belfast. Later the same year she would win silver at the Melbourne Olympics. Thelma was joined at these games by Irelands very first female Olympian. Kilkenny born Maeve Kyle was part of this country's most successful Olympic team when she ran the 100 and 200 metre events. She was to subsequently compete at the Rome and Tokyo Olympics.

Following on from the economic gloom and mass emigration of the 1950s the early 1960s brought about a new era of economic development, not only in Ireland but in the UK, USA and Europe, where the EEC (now the EU) was well into its first decade of existence. For young people the 1960s saw what was probably the biggest revolution ever, not only in the way they expressed themselves individually but also as a section of society. Women in particular began to demonstrate their independence by supporting and forming many groups and societies which were exclusively or mainly catering for their gender. In 1960, Edna O'Brien published *Country Girls* and three years later, Valentina Tereshkowa was the first woman to travel into outer space and circle the planet 48 times in three days before returning safely to earth. In the United States the report on the status of women's issues, which had been commissioned in 1961 by JFK, was presented to the president.

Up and Running

During the 75th anniversary year in 1961, the possibility of opening the doors of Clonliffe Harriers to lady members was first mooted. Following two unsuccessful attempts, it was a case of third time lucky when the required quota to introduce a ladies section was finally achieved at the 1963 AGM. The motion, proposed by Billy Morton and seconded by Lar Byrne, only permitted ladies to become associate members, a restriction which prohibited the right to speak or vote at the annual general meeting. It was the best part of a decade before this situation was fully rectified thanks mainly to a new generation of more forward thinking male members.

On the 5 November 1963, the first formal meeting of the ladies section was held in Moran's Hotel Talbot Street to which Billy invited Maeve Kyle to address the attendees. As a further show of support, Maeve subsequently presented a trophy for a club pentathlon competition.

On Tuesday 17 December 1963, the club opened a new page in its illustrious history with the staging of its first ever ladies race. True to form, Billy had the media up in numbers to Santry the night before to give the race some publicity. One reporter described it thus, "Call them Morton's Marvels! They are the mustard keen lasses who just won't stay home knitting on these shivery nights but who three evenings a week and on Sunday mornings, bus it or pedal it out to Santry Stadium for group training sessions. Up to 30 girls are regularly in attendance and a full quota is expected tomorrow night for their first race."

Nov 1963-First meeting of ladies section. Pic includes Maeve Kyle, Billy Morton, Ann O'Brien and Claire Walsh

The run was over a 600 yard course on Santry Avenue and 32 athletes competed. The full result was as follows,

1st	Claire Dowling	1 min 37 secs
2nd	Ann Killeen	1 min 38 secs
3rd	Maeve O'Reilly	1 min 42 secs
4th	Deirdre Killeen	1 min 48 secs
5th	Muriel Malone	1 min 50 secs
6th	Rosemary Murphy	1 min 50 secs
7th	Anne O'Brien	1 min 50 secs
8th	Rita Keogh	1 min 50 secs
9th	Rita Murphy	1 min 55 secs
10th	Geraldine Ennis	
11th	Nora Hall	
12th	Maura Carey	
13th	Marie Doran	
14th	Leota Mc Alister	
15th	Olive Heaney	
16th	Kay O'Hehir	
17th	Margaret Lenihan	
18th	Margaret Eager	
19th	Georgina Mc Creevy	

Other finishers were: Theresa Keane, Margaret Armitage, Jean Neery, Ursula Sweetman, Elizabeth Beauchamp, Breda Fowler, Eileen Eager, Mary Corway, Anne Clarke, Una Eager, Hilary Morrison and Patricia Stafford.

Note   Deirdre Killeen was, in 1959, a member of the first group of women recruited into the Garda Siochana.

Line up for first ladies race Dec 1963

Claire Dowling wins first ladies race Dec 1963

The inaugural race had a first prize of a pair of silver candlesticks while the runner up received an electric table lamp! While this race was historic for being the first one staged involving Clonliffe girls only the club was merely resurrecting a practice begun 50 years previously by Tommy Burton.

In an interview with the press before the race, Billy Morton said, "One of the girls looks a world class quarter miler in the making. I would say there is an even money chance she will be a Tokyo Olympic candidate." While it proved to be a little over optimistic for an athlete in her first year of competition, Billy's prophecy did indeed come true. Claire Dowling (later Walsh) became the first Clonliffe lady to compete in the Olympic Games when she ran in Munich in 1972.

Club stalwart Frances Mansfield takes up the story of the early days. "Training took place four days a week under the guidance of Club Captain Harry Cooney who was ably assisted by Noel O'Rourke. The training of women for athletics in Ireland was uncharted territory. Not much was known about it and as a result the training was not very intense. The longest distance that we were allowed run was four laps of the track. Each session began with a warm up in the Nissen Hut followed by circuit training. The stabilizers for the hurdles were used for weight training. We were also introduced to high jumping. The landing area consisted of old tyres and sacks of foam. Billy got Irish high jump record holder Brendan O' Reilly to give us a demonstration and teach us some techniques. I remember the first night we got a break from training was when Billy came in and sent us home early as a mark of respect for President Kennedy who had been assassinated earlier that evening.

The Nissen Hut was the hub of the club. The changing area was a wooden shed under the stand near the main entrance to the stadium. Conditions were very primitive. No showers were available to the ladies. Whoever was first up to the club filled a kettle and put it on a pot belly stove adjacent to the training area. This was the only hot water that was available for washing. Despite not having full membership rights, the ladies still organised themselves by nominating a captain and a treasurer. Sums of money were contributed on a voluntary basis and when enough was collected we had showers installed."

On 29 February 1964, the ladies held their first club cross country race. It was a handicap run over a one mile course and was won by Rita Keogh from Olive Heaney and Ann O'Brien.

The details of the race were:

		Time	H.Cap	Time	Place	
1st	Claire Dowling	6.57	Scr.	6.57	8th	
2nd	Ann O'Brien	7.00	0.40	6.20	3rd	
3rd	Rosemary Murphy	7.10	0.15	6.55	7th	
4th	Rita Keogh	7.13	1.10	6.03	1st	
5th	Noreen Eager	7.32	0.40	6.52	6th	
6th	Olive Heaney	7.59	1.50	6.09	2nd	
7th	Jane Neery	8.14	1.50	6.24	4th	
8th	Ursula Sweetman	8.39	1.50	6.49	5th	

Other finishers were: Muriel Malone, Patricia Stafford, Patricia Burke, Gertrude Ryder and Eileen Murphy.

Before long it was realised that women were capable of running long distances without any problems. Some of them were even doing one hour time trials on the track. Crusaders, who had been re-formed earlier in 1963 was the only other club that catered for women in the south of Ireland. Competition was scarce and so to keep the ladies interested, a club track and field league was held twice a week during the summer and cross country handicap races were held on Sunday mornings in the winter. Everyone competed in these events and they were a great incentive for the girls to remain in the sport. Everyone was encouraged to compete in all the events and it was not long before athletes displayed their talent and preference for certain disciplines. Inspired by world class competitors like Thelma Hopkins, Maeve Kyle and Mary Peters, ladies athletics was thriving in Northern Ireland and to gain extra experience and competition, the Clonliffe girls regularly travelled north to test themselves against the local athletes.

Height of Fashion

On the fashion front, the ladies in the 1960s wore whatever they could find was suitable for running. Singlets tended to be of the high necked variety. Running shorts were not available in the shops, so skirts were the only option. The ladies subsequently decided to make their own shorts from a pattern. There was, however, an ongoing problem with splitting zips!

It is recalled that when Billy first saw the shorts he was heard to utter, "Jaysus, you're not going out in them. If the Archbishop sees ye, ye will all be excommunicated!" Tracksuits were almost impossible to find so on one trip to Holland the team bought some in the local Marks & Spencer. Adidas subsequently brought tracksuits into Ireland. At that stage, one pair of road shoes and one pair of spikes cost £5.00 and that was regarded as expensive!

Feb 1965. First ladies club team at Westland Row prior to departure to England. Back Row L to R – F Hewson, M Norton, E Diskin, C Dowling, H Cooney, S Kinsella, J Coffey, P Burke, M Stewart, W Morton,
Front Row L to R – K Keogh, F Quinn, R Keogh, O Heaney, U Sweetman, A O'Brien.

In February 1965, the Clonliffe ladies set yet another milestone in the history of Irish athletics when a group 13 athletes became the first female club team to compete outside Ireland. Under the captaincy of Harry Cooney they competed in a two mile cross country race in Bury in England. Ann O'Brien finished second behind Mary Hodson, a semi-finalist in the Tokyo Olympics and in front of the Lancashire Cross Country Champion, Joyce Ashcroft. Fifth place was taken by Dorothy Shirley, a silver medallist in the high jump at the Rome Olympics. The team event was won by the host club Bury and Radcliffe with Clonliffe finishing in third place. The following morning Ann finished third in a 660 yards race while Emer Diskin was second in the 60 yards at a track and field meeting in Warrington. The girls travelled over and back by train and boat completely at their own expense.

1966 saw yet another first for the still fledgling Clonliffe ladies section when they won their first ever national senior inter clubs cross country championship. The team consisting of Rita Keogh, Ann O'Brien, Nuala O'Brien and Claire Walsh were the groundbreakers and the feat was repeated in 1967 when the same 4 girls added a second national team title. Their third championship came in 1970 when Ann, Claire, Mary Byrne and Rita triumphed in Thurles. This year also saw Ann winning the third of 4 consecutive individual titles in these championships and later in 1970 she finished 9th in the world cross country in Maryland USA while leading Ireland to the team bronze.

In addition to these cross country victories the late 1960s saw the emergence of Claire Walsh and Ann O'Brien as the two leading track and field athletes in Ireland. Their tallies of individual titles are documented elsewhere in this publication but suffice it to say that, along with Maeve Kyle, the two Clonliffe girls set the standard for women's athletics in Ireland which was, in later years, followed by people like Mary Purcell, Michelle Walsh, Catherina Mc Kiernan and Sonia O'Sullivan.

The talents of the ladies, however, were not confined to competitive athletics. They also spearheaded the many forms of fundraising for Santry Stadium which had a huge debt, amounting to £14,000 in 1966. The girls were regular visitors to both private and public houses with their collection boxes helping to keep the club finances above water. Innovative schemes were constantly being used to raise funds and one such was an 84 mile run by long distance specialist Noel Henry from Dublin to Lanesborough in County Longford. Noel covered the distance in 12 hr 8 min and was accompanied on part of the run by Ann O'Brien who ran four separate 6 mile stretches along the way. Being the site of Ireland's first turf powered electricity generating station the runners were met at the town entrance and escorted to their destination by the locals carrying torches of lit sods of turf.

Like their male colleagues the Clonliffe ladies were also to the fore in the development of athletics in Ireland and were members of various county and national committees. With the creation of a new national athletics body, BLE, in 1967, a ladies committee was formed which included members of Clonliffe. Unfortunately, this committee was only a short time in existence as it was felt that for women's athletics to progress, it should be amalgamated with the men. In 1979, Kay Guy (nee O'Hehir) one of the founding ladies, became the first female to be elected to the management committee of the BLE.

Juvenile girls, who were mostly younger sisters of the senior athletes, now began to join the club. They had no separate section and had to train and compete with the seniors. With the foundation of BLOE this situation was redressed. The former NACA had a thriving juvenile boys section and they were approached to put on events for juvenile girls. They agreed on condition that a female member would be on the committee to give advice on what would be appropriate events for these young athletes. Frances Mansfield was co-opted on to this committee. At first the only two events were the 100m and long jump. As more clubs enrolled, this programme was expanded. The BLOE proved to be a very successful initiative and laid the foundations for more than a few senior careers.

In 1967 Billy Morton instigated the women's home countries cross country international. In 1969 he donated the Billy Morton trophy to be presented to the winning team and was also made patron of the International women's cross country association. This event, sadly only lasted a short number of years.

The high success rate of the pioneering Clonliffe ladies in domestic competition prompted them to contemplate spreading their wings and taking on the best of the foreign competition in the women's AAA championships. Their times at home led them to believe that they could more than hold their own and this proved to be correct as they met with almost instant success. The story is related here by one of those who participated in these victories.

The Story Behind The Photographs - Reminiscences Of Jean O'Neill

1971 WAAA 4x400 relay champions. J O'Neill, A O'Brien,
P O'Dwyer, C Walsh.

In 1969, Ann O'Brien became the first Clonliffe lady to compete at the WAAA Championships where she took gold in the 3,000 metres.

We noted the times the women were running in the WAAAs, especially in the 400, looked at our own "stable" of women and thought "why not, let's enter their club relays." This commenced a very successful few years for the Clonliffe ladies. In June 1970, Ann retained her 3,000 metres title and Claire was second in the 800 in 2.04.90. The race was won by Sheila Carey and in third place was

Lillian Board. We then eagerly awaited our turn competing in the 4 x 400 relay. We were sponsored by Collection General Investigation Ltd.

The following weekend sisters Claire Walsh and Jean O'Neill, along with Ann O'Brien and Padraigin O'Dwyer arrived in Crystal Palace. It was the first time for Padraigin and myself to run on tartan. The new modern complex had fabulous dressing rooms and clean modern showers, which was a far cry from our usual "away" track of a wet field surrounded by hedges!

The running sequence was Padraigin, myself, Ann and finally Claire. Having led for the first two laps with Claire running the anchor leg in 53.7 to give us second place, we were absolutely thrilled with our performance as it exceeded all our expectations and justified our entering and travelling to London. Edinburgh Southern Harriers won in 3.44.10 (they retained their title from 1969 when they won in 3.46.60 – we made them run faster to retain it!). Our time was 3.45.80 (splits 56.40, 57.10, 58.50 and 53.70). Our silver medal performance was a national record and a club record which lasted for 18 years.

There was no going back now. In 1971, we entered the 4 x 400 and 4 x 800 held on different weekends. For the 4 x 800, 16 year old Jean Appleby replaced Padraigin. She ran 2.16, I ran 2.14 handing over the lead to Ann who ran 2.12 handing a slight lead to race favourites Barnet AC. On the last leg Claire tracked the Barnet girl before passing her with 10 metres to go and taking the title in 8.48.80 to their 8.49.80. Claire ran a brilliant 2.04.90 equalling her PB and breaking the Irish record. The team time was the third fastest time in the world.

Three weeks later the 4 x 400 team of Padraigin, Jean, Ann and Claire, took the gold medal in a time of 3.49.10 from Bury and Radcliffe (3.50.20). Being overseas winners, we were not allowed take the trophy home so the proof of the victory is in the photo. In 1972 we entered the 4 x 400 and the medley (2 x 200, 1 x 400 and 1 x 800) relay. Claire, Padraigin and the two Jeans had to settle for silver in the 4 x 400 (3.48.50) behind Wolverhampton and Bilston and bronze in the medley (4.09.60) behind Airdale/Spen Valley and Bury and Radcliffe.

So ended a golden era for the Clonliffe ladies.

1970 and 1971 also saw victories for the Clonliffe ladies in the Omega/Tissot league. This event was the predominant club team competition at the time and was a precursor of the current national league.

1972 saw what was probably the last barrier preventing women participating in sport when "Title IX" legislation was introduced in the United States. This prevented gender discrimination in schools which receive government funding and over the following 35 years resulted in a 1000% increase in women's participation in schools athletics and a 500% increase in University athletics. Despite this it was not until the 2012 Olympics in London that women were permitted to compete in every sport at the games.

As the ladies section entered its second decade a new generation of girls were carrying the Black and Amber to further glory. While 1976 proved to be a landmark year for the men when they finally won the inter club cross country it was the ladies who led the way when they themselves took the corresponding title 3 weeks beforehand. The team consisting of Padraigin O'Dwyer (3rd), Jean Appleby (7th), Kathryn Davis (9th) and Patricia Appleby (10th) won the women's senior title in Ennis. Jean and Patricia are daughters of Don Appleby who was Clonliffe's leading cross coun-try runner in the late 1940s and early 1950s. Following her second place finish in 1971 and fifth in 1976 while running for Raheny Shamrocks Kathryn Davis (now with Clonliffe) finally took gold in the national cross country at Ballyfin in 1978 when she beat Dervla Mellerick (UCG) and Siobhan Lonergan (DCH) . She thus became, after Ann O'Brien, the second Clonliffe woman to win this title. The ladies were beaten by 1 point for team gold (30 to 31) by Dublin City Harriers. Kathryn and Jean were selected on the Irish team for the world championships the following month in Glasgow.

One of Clonliffe's best ever relay teams.
K Davis (1987 Senior CC Champion), K Walley (600 metres champion 1989)
AK Buckley (3 time Senior CC Champion and 1988 Olympian) and T Casserley.

It has not always been plain sailing for the ladies section and it went through a bad patch at the beginning of the 1980s with dwindling numbers. However, with the help of people like Claire Walsh, Kathryn Davis, Frances Mansfield and Kathryn Walley the numbers began to increase again.

J Wyse, N Walsh and A Archbald
pictured in Lifford in 1980s

Following the creation of the running boom in the early 1980s, spearheaded by the success of the Dublin City Marathon, a proposal to run an all female 10km race through the streets of Dublin was mooted. Having gained sponsorship from the now sadly defunct *Evening Press* newspaper, this race, within a very short number of years, became the largest all female road race in the world, and currently attracts fields of over 40,000 participants raising several millions of Euros for charity. When this race was first announced, one of Clonliffes founding female athletes Frances Mansfield, remembered the challenges faced in the early days of the ladies section. She decided to place an ad in the paper asking local women to turn up at Williams Supermarket in Walkinstown to "meet and train" together for the race. Having expected about eight to 10 to show up, Frances was "flabbergasted" when over 100 showed up. These girls who wanted to run for fun while simultaneously raising money for charity subsequently inspired other groups to spring up in Dublin and all over Ireland. The introduction of these groups by Frances played no small part in leading to the massive success of this event.

Mary Donohue
1986 National Senior CC Champion

One of the ladies who ran in the first women's mini marathon in 1983 was Mary Donohue. Finishing 66th in a time of 43.23 minutes it would have been a brave person to predict that she would soon be wearing the Clonliffe singlet and representing Ireland on the International stage. By the end of that year she had joined the club and following some top class performances on road, cross country and track Mary was very quickly ranked among the dominant female athletes in the country. These achievements culminated in her victory at the National Cross Country on home ground in 1986 followed that summer with a gold medal over 3000 metres at the national track and field championships.

While Mary was the find of the 1984 season she was soon joined in Clonliffe by Ann Keenan-Buckley and very soon these two stars were going head to head in Dublin, Eastern Region, National and open races while simultaneously offering a great one two punch for the Black and Amber. With Ann Archibold finishing second in the 1984 Dublin City marathon the mid to late 80s saw these team mates propel Clonliffe back to the forefront of womens athletics in Ireland for the first time since the heady days of the late 60s and early 70s. These performances culminated in Anne qualifying for the 1988 Olympic Games in Seoul.

Edith, Ann and Caroline Kearney

The early 1980s also saw the arrival into Clonliffe of the club's first world champion. Having grounded herself in cross country running Anne Kearney took up the triathlon and began a sequence of victories which saw her win 8 Irish and 2 world titles alongside a European silver and a bronze in the Ironman. She was one of the leading influences in the early growth of the sport in Ireland who was greatly loved and respected by everyone who knew her. Ann tragically suffered from cancer and sadly, passed away in 2004. Ann's daughter Caroline was a former swimming champion when she joined Clonliffe and, like her mother, took up the triathlon. She won the Irish championship in 2001, 2002 and 2003 and was regarded as a genuine medal hope for the Beijing Olympics when, at the age of 24 she was killed in a road crash while training in France in 2006. The annual Caroline Kearney memorial triathlon is held every year in Westmeath in her honour.

Ladies 21st Anniversary Re-Union 1984

Over the next ten years Clonliffe women had many successes, particularly in the sprints, while training under the tutelage of Tommy Coyle. Athletes like Geraldine Keogh, Marisa Smith, Emer Hasstrup and Adrienne O'Hara earned the honour of representing their country while Joanne Heffernan and Paula Carty added some quality to the hurdles. In 1993 Cathy Shum won the National marathon and 2 years later added the ladies mini marathon. Mary Donohue also won the mini marathon in 1994.The summer of 1995 ended on a high for the ladies when they won the Tissot track and field league final. Managed by Jean Carr and Tommy Coyle, the team consisted of Emer Haastrup (100/200), Patricia O'Clerigh and Marissa Smith (400), Siobhan Brown (800), Debbie Kenny (100 hurdles), Fiona Scully (400 hurdles), Donna Dowler, Emma Cooper (1500), Kathryn Freeman, Mary Donoghue (3000), Pamela Cooper (Javelin/shot putt), Louise Moriarity (HJ), Audrey Farrelly (LJ/Triple), Frances Mansfield (hammer/discus) and Teresa O'Leary (walk). In 1989, 1993 and 1994 Geraldine Keogh represented Clonliffe and Ireland on the 4x400 team at the European Cup. The 1993 team also saw Emer Haastrup compete in the 100m and 4x100 relay while Mary Donohue ran the 10000 metres.

The Ladies Section also continued to prosper throughout the noughties with different groupings dedicated to beginners, cross country, track and field, and mountain running. Under the stewardship of Pamela Cooper they competed with distinction in the National Track and Field league over the latter part of the decade making the division one final in 2008 and finishing third in 2009. Like the men in 2008 the ladies finally tasted success when they had their first victory in this competition in 2011 when winning the division 1 title and gaining promotion to the premier division.

P Walsh, M Ni Dhuchon, E Haastrup, F Scully, M Smith.

In November of 2008 the club celebrated the 45th anniversary of the founding of the Ladies Section with a special 600 metre race held in Santry replicating the very first race held in 1963. In addition there was a 2 Mile race held in the park which attracted a substantial ladies field. The events were organized under the leadership of former indoor 600 metres champion Kathryn Walley and concluded with a memorable evening of meeting old friends and reminiscing in the club bar.

On the masters scene the Clonliffe ladies have not been found wanting with Mags Greenan becoming the club's latest world champion by winning 3 consecutive world mountain running titles in 2008/9/10. She has also won several titles at county and national level at home in Ireland. Former indoor national track champion Kathryn Walley has been a regular medallist both indoors and outdoors including a treble (60m/100/400m) gold winning performance at the 2009 Irish championships.

A new century saw yet another generation of ladies join the club and carry on the proud tradition begun nearly half a century earlier. Under the captaincies of Mags Greenan, Brona Ni Bhriain and Pamela Cooper the number of female members has literally exploded and age categories from under 10 right up to senior level has put even more pressure on already hard pressed coaches. The policy however has paid dividends with Frances Ni Reamonn, Becky Woods and Sara Mc Cormack all gaining their international singlets. Most recently Sara was a member of the Irish team which won gold at the European Cross Country championships in Budapest in 2012 in a race won by her team mate and Ireland's latest athletic superstar Fionnuala Britton. As the ladies celebrate their 50th anniversary they can look back on a proud record of achievements which places them at the very top of their sport in Ireland and they can also look forward with more than a little confidence that the future can be just as bright.

Junior women at Dublin cross country 2011

Ladies National league division 1 champions 2011

National senior women cross country 3rd 2013

Sara McCormack

Clonliffe ladies at 2010 National CC in Phoenix Park

Belevedere House Feb 2011

Clonliffe ladies at 2011 Invitation race at Old Gate

SILVERWARE AND CLUB RACES

Like any sporting organisation, the club is the grassroots which provides the seed that can eventually grow into local, regional, national or international success. The provision of competition at club level has always been an important part of Clonliffe history. Handicap races have been staged from as early as the 1890s and, as can be seen from some of the brief profiles below, all the greats of Clonliffe were regular participants in these events. It gave the "crocks" a chance to "have a go" at the "cracks" and on many a day, to overcome them. Indeed it was considered your duty to try and put one over on the handicapper in order to get your name on one of the trophies. Members were almost obliged to "hold back" or "fake it" in an effort to get a good handicap. It was the duty of the handicapper, usually the club captain, to "know his man" so that a race was run to form.

Clonliffe today has many club races covering all distances and providing members with an opportunity for some "local" success. Below are profiles and brief histories of some of the earliest and longest standing of the club handicaps which are still being contested today. Most of these races have continued to survive through the generosity of various members who have sponsored them and continue to do so. Many other races have been added to the club calendar over the years and some of them have also been included as part of the club Grand Prix series which is contested throughout the whole year.

One of longest running is the Christmas cake race which is held every December. The tradition was started by Harry Cooney back in the 1950s with the intention of rounding off the year and giving members an opportunity to socialise and reminisce before the festive break. It has also given many members who are away on scholarships and travel back for Christmas a chance to test their fitness against the "home" team. The tradition was that the wife of the club captain would bake the cake which was to be presented to the winner and this practice begun by Mrs Cooney continues to this day.

The Doran Shield

This is the oldest recorded race in the club. It was a five mile flat cross country handicap, which was first run in 1896. The shield was presented by Vice President CJ Doran and the first winner was T. Clarke who was followed home by JM Heneghan, SJ Coates and S. Warry. The fastest time was by scratch man J. McArdle who covered the distance in 27 minutes 15 seconds. This trophy was competed for by many of the early club "cracks" including: GF Walker, WJ Flynn, J. Deakin, CF Rothwell, JJ Gorry, FJ Ryder and Arthur Wisdom. Among the winners were: E. Comerford (1911), J. Foley (1915), TP Burton (1917), PJ Howlin (1918), BH Bingham (1920), D. McAleese (1921), S. Gray (1933 and 1937) and JJ O'Connor in 1934.

Following his wins in 1926, 1927 and 1931, ET Galway had his fourth overall victory in 1943 and became the outright winner of the trophy. He subsequently donated a new trophy known as the "Galway Shield" to be competed for under the same conditions. During the 40 years of its running, the fastest time for the Doran Shield was run in 1914 when HC Irwin completed the five miles in 26 minutes 10 seconds. In the nine years from 1936 to 1944, Sam Gray had the fastest time on eight occasions.

Doran Shield

The Horan Cup

Presented by Vice President Michael Horan, this flat handicap cross country event takes place over a six mile course and was first competed for in 1908 when it was won by T. Hassell who was followed home by IE Ronan, JT Graham and J. Bracken. The fastest time was H. Mullally who covered the distance in 38 minutes 07 seconds. Among the early winners were: D. McAleese (1921), AP Walker (1924), CC Walker (1928), H. Cooney (1932), F. Hewson (1935), S. Reamonn (1939), and S. Gray (1943). This is the longest surviving club race in Clonliffe and is still competed for today.

Horan Cup

The O'Connor Cup

Presented by former Irish Cross Country Champion JJ O'Connor, this four mile flat sealed handicap was first run in 1936 when it was won by M. Murphy (off handicap of 1min 25 secs) in a time of 21 minutes 12 seconds. Second man home was M. Finglas (21-25) and third was Sam Gray (21-27). Finglas was the scratch man and also had the fastest time. Like the Horan Cup, this race is also still contested today. W. Fitzpatrick (1937), J. Williams (1940), S. Reamonn (1942) and A. Moore (1945) were among the early winners.

O'Connor Cup

The Grand National / Irwin Cup

A six mile handicap obstacle race first run in 1910 when it was won by CG Wisdom from TJ Downing, A. Morton and J. Malone. Downing, running off scratch, had the best time with 33 minutes 05 seconds.

From 1932 onwards, the Irwin Cup, purchased by members to perpetuate the memory of the late HC Irwin, was awarded for this event with the club gold medal going to the member doing the fastest time. Over the years this trophy has been won by many prominent "Wasps" like Joe Foley, FJ Ryder, Charlie Rothwell, Sean Reamonn, Joe Peelo, Billy Morton, Vincent Walker and George Smyth. In 1911 this race took place at Finglas Wood when the course was described as being "for the greater part uphill and included three fences and a water jump on each of the seven laps. Events took place under the close scrutiny of a designated starter and timekeeper together with three judges, four lap counters and six stewards. A total of 29 runners competed - 21 runners completed the course, led by G. Ryan who beat the previous year's winner CG Wisdom into second place." Still in competition, the Irwin Cup is part of the Club Grand Prix series.

Irwin Cup

The Walker Cup

This was first presented in 1966 by the family who have the longest continuous association with Clonliffe dating back to the 1890s. This four mile track race is competed for every September and is a very popular "end of season" event, which is now integrated into the Club Grand Prix series. In 1970 it was won by 15 year old Gerry Brady who with a handicap of 9 mins, had a winning time of 25 min 30 sec.

The Walker Cup

The Harry McEvoy Cup

This trophy holds the distinction for the shortest number of runnings in club handicap history. Donated by Harry McEvoy in 1938, the race was a seven mile point to point paper chase cross country event.

In its first year it was won by P. O'Hara. In 1939 the winner was J. Maher who was followed by J. Foley in 1940. Sean Farren then completed a hat trick in 1941/'42/'43 to win the trophy outright. The 1941 renewal had to be postponed due to high winds blowing away the paper trail. The Farren family, well known sportswear retailers in Dublin, subsequently presented a trophy bearing the family name for a similar event.

Harry McEvoy was the instigator in 1929 of the annual Clonliffe Christmas Run to Cappagh Hospital. Club athletes collected new and used toys each year and presented them to the children who were patients there. This event was continued until the early 1970s when the continuing urban sprawl and consequent traffic volumes meant it was no longer feasible.

Mc Evoy Cup

POST MORTON ERA

While the early decades of the clubs existence saw consistent success and international representation the post war decades were relatively calm as regards team victories. During the early 1970s the "baby boomer" generation began to appear in the club. Many of the older generation who had single-handedly carried Clonliffe through many difficult and sometimes life threatening situations had lowered their profile. Indeed many of them had gone to their eternal reward.

The untimely passing of Billy Morton in 1969 marked something of a watershed in the annals of Clonliffe. It witnessed a changing of the guard and a changing of the ethos within the club. Long serving "lifers" like Harry Cooney, Mattie Hewson and Sam Gray were now being succeeded by people like Laro Byrne, Christy Brady, Paddy Marley and Peter Mc Dermott. Beginning under their tutelage Clonliffe embarked on an era of unprecedented success at club and national level.

On the administration front a new approach was taken to tackling the long standing and persistent financial difficulties which had created an almost unbearable burden on the club during the previous decade. The days of raffles, fashion shows, collecting in local hostelries or passing buckets around at sports meetings were abandoned and the administration of the club was conducted in a more businesslike manner. A new committee in the early 1970s was able to negotiate a bank loan which was subsidised by the sale of a tranche of life memberships. The funds were used to build modern changing facilities under the terracing to replace those in the Nissen hut. It was also decided to build a club bar in order to generate an ongoing source of revenue.

In November of 1973, in true Clonliffe tradition, a press conference was called at which Honorary Secretary Larry O'Reilly and Honorary Treasurer Colm Brennan announced that the new facilities and a new club bar would be opened the following summer. In addition the stadium was to be re-named the Morton Stadium after the man who had done so much to bring it into being. When the club initially built the facility it was known as the Clonliffe Harriers Stadium but in 1962, in an effort to attract some badly needed funds, Billy re-named it the John F Kennedy stadium. The American President did actually pass it on his way from Dublin Airport in June 1963 but unfortunately the hoped for cash never materialised. The new club bar under the terrace did however generate income which began making big inroads into the club debt.

While these initiatives greatly helped the financial situation, they were not the only source of funds. In the late 1960s a new sporting phenomenon, the Community Games, was initiated by Joe Connolly a local councillor in the Walkinstown area of Dublin. It was set up to deal with the lack of leisure facilities for young people in the greater Dublin area. The first staging attracted over 3000 entrants and the second games had over 5000 participants. By 1970 over 10,000 young people representing 67 residents associations in Dublin alone were participating. In addition to athletic events there were a number of other sports including basketball, table tennis, volleyball, football, hurling and soccer. The games were re-named the Mini Olympics and the opening was marked by a parade of all participants in the city centre followed by a relay of the torch from O'Connell Street to Santry. The only venue capable of catering for this number of competitors was Santry Stadium. The success of this initiative was immediate and resulted in local and regional games being staged throughout the country with the national finals being held in Santry. With such large numbers the various events had to be staged over two weekends and this, at the time, provided the club with a lucrative source of income. Holding the catering rights to the stadium meant that members were press ganged into selling everything from ice creams, sweets, and crisps to tea, coffee and hot food. While Joe Harden was ensconced under the stand dispensing hot food and drinks to all and sundry, Ted Collins was "highly visible" under the terracing. He is fondly remembered for his stark warnings that "nobody will get any sweets until you form an orderly queue". The opening of the new bar subsequently provided a refuge for some distraught "coaches" as well as providing further relief to the long suffering club treasurer. The huge success of the Community Games resulted in a wider range of events being added to the programme and in a short number of years they were transferred to a bigger campus in Mosney and subsequently to their current home at the Athlone Institute of Technology.

These initiatives securing the future of the club and the stadium coincided with the re-birth of Clonliffe as the major force in Irish athletics.

Irish team at 1974 European T&F in Rome.
L to R D McDaid, C Walsh, M Purcell, J Hartnett, N Cusack,
E Leddy, E Coghlan.
At front team coaches P Griffin and R Long.

At the National Inter clubs Cross Country in Mallow in 1971 Danny Mc Daid, Padraig Keane, George Mc Intyre and Frank Murphy Junior took the silver medal. This feat was repeated the following year in Clonmel when Padraig was first club man home finishing in sixth place overall. His fellow medallists were again Danny and George with Brendan Mooney completing the scoring team. Clonliffe finished fourth in 1974 and took the bronze medals in 1975.

Club President Paddy Marley presents Christy Brady with lifetime achievement award.
Courtesy of Sportsfile

These performances gave club captain Christy Brady and coach Lar Byrne the belief that the big prize was now within reach and at Ballinasloe in 1976 history was made when Clonliffe broke the 18 year winning streak of Donore Harriers and took their first team victory since 1955 when, coincidentally Clonliffe man Paddy Killeen also won the individual gold. The scoring team on that memorable afternoon was led home by 19 year old Gerry Finnegan (9th) with Jerry Kiernan (12th), Frank Murphy Jnr (14th), and Padraig Keane (19th). Another club stalwart Tony Murphy was also a member of this historic panel. The race was won by the great Donie Walsh of Leevale who was claiming the third of his four individual titles. The closeness of the competition at the front of this race can be gauged from the fact that only 59 seconds separated Finnegan from the winner. This performance earned Gerry his first Irish singlet when he was picked for the World Cross Country at Chepstow in the following month. Kiernan was first reserve on the same team. Ironically, Danny Mc Daid, who had only recently returned to Donegal after a glittering career in the Black and Amber, finished second to Walsh in this race. In the Junior race Clonliffe finished second to Dundrum.

On the weekend following the Inter Club victory Clonliffe knocked over 2 minutes off the course record when they won the Liffey Valley 5x2 mile cross country relay in the Phoenix Park with a time of 47 min 27 sec. One month later a team of Martin Green, Denis Noonan, Padraig Keane, Frank Murphy, Jerry Kiernan and Gerry Finnegan won the National 21.5 mile road relay championship.

These three wins in almost as many weeks were the starting point in an unending run of team and individual victories which continues to this day. Since 1976 Clonliffe have won no fewer than 23 team and 8 individual gold medals at the National Inter Clubs. At Ennis in 1977 the team title was retained when Keane was first man home in 4th place, closely followed by Kiernan (5th), Finnegan (18th), and Murphy in 20th. This race was won by Gerry Deegan of Waterford who was taking the first of his five individual titles in a six year spree. It was also notable for the fact that Gerry Finnegan ran the race with his arm in plaster.

While the runners were beginning to make their mark the Clonliffe walkers (not to be confused with THE Clonliffe Walkers!) were also striking gold. In 1974 Johnny O'Leary won the Irish 10K (49 min 42 sec) and 20K (1 hr 34 min 06 sec) track walking titles. The following year Tommy Griffin took the 10K gold in 50 min 53 sec. 1976 saw Johnny regain the 20K title with a time of 1 hr 42 min 46 sec. a feat he repeated in 1978 with a time of 1 hr 36 min 21 sec. Both Johnny and Tom would go on in later years to serve as officers of the club and remain to this day two of the most well regarded men in Clonliffe.

The ladies were also establishing themselves among the top clubs in the country with the O'Brien and Dowling sisters leading the way. The work started by Harry Cooney in 1963 was producing Irish champions and record breakers and Clonliffe ladies relay teams won gold medals at the WAAA championships in Great Britain. Claire Walsh became the first Clonliffe lady, and only the second Irishwoman, to compete at the Olympic Games. Indeed, only three weeks before the men had their historic victory in Ballinasloe the senior ladies won their corresponding event in Ennis. More details on the achievements of the ladies can be found elsewhere in this publication.

By the late 1970s rising costs in other areas soon made it well nigh impossible to cope with the overall running of the stadium. The cinder track, which had seen so many Irish and world record performances was now becoming outdated and a more modern surface was required. The club was not in a position to administer the day to day upkeep of the stadium and subsequently entered into an agreement to form a new management committee involving Clonliffe Harriers, Dublin Corporation and Dublin County Council which would manage the running of the facility. The club would continue to have its own changing facilities and maintain its own exclusive training times on Tuesday, Thursday, Saturday and Sunday. It would also have ownership of the club bar which even by this early stage in its life was enjoying a famous reputation for post race festivities. However the main benefit arising from this new arrangement was the laying of a new world class tartan track together with floodlighting which enabled members to train all year round regardless of weather conditions.

This new agreement copperfastened the future of the Stadium as the national athletics arena, which was one of the primary aims of the Billy Morton led committee in the 1950s. The benefit for club members was the preservation of a permanent home within the stadium for club activities both sporting and social. The last race on the old cinder track was held in July 1979 and among those taking part was Harry Power who had also taken part in the first race on the surface in 1958. The last race was won by Eamon Tierney who also won the first race on the new tartan surface. The new track was opened with an international meeting in August 1980 which featured, among others, double Olympic Decathlon champion Daley Thompson, European 400 metre gold medallist David Jenkins in the sprints. The Morton Mile featured

John Walker, Ray Flynn, Steve Scott, former 1500 metre world record holder Filbert Bayi and American Craig Masback.

While the 1970s saw Clonliffe establish itself as one of the top clubs in Ireland the next decade would see that position improved beyond all recognition. 1981 saw the election of Paddy Marley into the role of club captain. Paddy had been an athlete of no mean repute and to this day is probably the most highly respected member of Clonliffe. In addition he has played innumerable roles on various committees of the governing body of Irish athletics over the past few decades and continues to do so to-day. His many years of service were justly rewarded in 1992 when he was appointed team manager to the track and field team at the Barcelona Olympics. Like two of his predecessors, Tommy Burton and Harry Cooney, Paddy is a Clonliffe "lifer" and is unswerving in his desire to make Clonliffe Harriers the best club in Ireland. Under his captaincy a new golden age unfolded as the club approached its centenary year. The trailblazers of the 1970s were now joined by another generation of Wasps, who were virtually unbeatable when it came to Inter Club team events. Eight National team titles and four individual wins were annexed during this decade. In the 1980 race at the Phoenix Park, the scoring four were Gerry Finnegan(9th), Jerry Kiernan (18th), Denis Noonan (23rd), and Eamon Tierney (24th). In 1989 at Killenaule, the first four home were Richard Mulligan (6th), Jerry Kiernan (9th), Gerry Brady (16th), and Gerry Finnegan (28th).

Kiernan (84), Harvey (86), and Taylor (87 and 88) took the 4 individual gold medals. During the course of the decade, a total of 14 Wasps were used on the "scoring four". Most appearances were by Kiernan (8), and Harvey (6), while Brady and Finnegan had 4 each.

Under 14 and Under 16 BLOE CC Champions 1970.
(front) GBrady, J Byrne, J Greene.
(back) M Greene, D Carroll, M Byrne, P Campbell.

1982 European Inter Clubs. L to R J O'Leary, N Harvey,
E Tierney, G Brady, J Kiernan. Kneeling P Marley and D Noonan.

Full details of these and other performances can be seen at Killian's Corner.

The victories in the National Inter Clubs Cross Country not only lifted morale within the club but it also significantly raised the bar in relation to the standard of training and competition for places on club teams. The 1980s saw the re-birth of road running in Ireland and large fields of several hundred runners were not uncommon as the frenzy spread to all corners of the nation. While many were inspired by the advent of the Dublin City Marathon and the Ladies Mini Marathon there was also a fierce and very competitive element at the sharp end of the sport. It was a decade described as "a golden age of road running" where the quality of athlete representing his or her club was never higher and no prize was won without "bursting your boiler". Runners trained hard and raced hard and there was a "no prisoners" ethos among the top echelons of individual and club competition.

Despite the onslaught of mass participation events more often than not it was the regular club runners who were to be found at the front of these fields. Athletes like John Woods, Gerry Curtis, Dick Hooper, Roy Dooney, John Griffin and John O'Toole were among those leading the charge. Clonliffe Harriers were not shy of the challenge and in providing athletes like Dave Taylor, Padraig Keane, Eamon Tierney, Noel Harvey, Jerry Kiernan, Gerry Finnegan, Gerry Brady, Frank Murphy Jnr, Denis Noonan and Richard Mulligan were annexing individual and team titles all over Ireland and were counted among the very best in the land. All races were fiercely contested and course records were being beaten everywhere from Hollymount to Ballycotton. Clonliffe athletes were regulars on Irish teams and the continuous wins in the National Cross Country meant that the club was more often than not representing Ireland at the European Inter Club championships.

These developments were in no small way the result of some major achievements by Irish athletes on the International stage. The double successes of John Treacy in the world cross country together with the fantastic silver medal performance of the Danny Mc Daid led Irish team in Limerick in 1979 lifted the profile of the sport in Ireland. Eamon Coghlan's 5000 metre gold at the inaugural world championships in Helsinki in 1983, Treacy and Kiernan's performances in Los Angeles, and the two golds won by Marcus O'Sullivan and Frank O'Meara at the world indoors in Indianapolis in 1987 gave the general sporting public a new sense of confidence that Ireland could indeed compete at the highest level.

On the world athletic podium the two dominant figures were Carl Lewis and Edwin Moses. Lewis arrived in style when he won gold in the 100m, 4x100 relay and long jump in Helsinki in 1983. The following year in Los Angeles he equalled the achievement of Jesse Owens in 1936 by winning four gold medals at one Olympiad. While Lewis was setting out on a glittering career Moses was bringing to a close a record of achievements which will stand very near the top of any athletic achievement in the history of the sport. His dominance of the 400 hurdles is as near to perfection as one can get. Olympic gold in 76 and 84 (boycott prevented him going to Moscow 1980) together with bronze in 88 alongside world championship gold in 83 and 87. He had 27 of the first 32 sub 48 sec runs. Probably his most remarkable achievement is his 122 consecutive wins over a period of 9 years 9 months and 9 days between 1977 and 1987.

1984 National Cross Country Champions.
Back L to R G Shiel, G Brady, E Tierney, M Byrne, N Harvey, J Kiernan.
Front L to R P Keane, F White (Hon Sec), C Brennan (President), P Marley (captain), D Noonan

Marathon Mania

After attending the New York City Marathon in November 1979, Louis Hogan, then head of the newly launched RTE Radio Two, proposed a Dublin version to BLE. Having been informed there would be no market for such an event in Ireland Louis then approached the Business Houses Athletic Association, who immediately embraced the concept and kick started the running boom in Ireland which continues to this day. The Dublin City Marathon has attracted tens of thousands of runners of all ages and nationalities since 1980. Indeed, some of its founding fathers were also responsible for initiating the women's mini-marathon, which is now the largest women only road race in the world. In addition to bringing out the masses this latest initiative also played a role in raising the standard at the more competitive end of the sport. Some of the top ranking club athletes began to tackle the ultimate distance event and it was soon not uncommon to see sub 2 hr 20 min finishing times. Winner of the first Dublin City Marathon Dick Hooper, along with 1974 Boston Marathon winner Neil Cusack and Clonliffe's double Olympian Danny Mc Daid were among the trendsetters and were joined in the 1980s by athletes like Jerry Kiernan, Roy Dooney, John Woods, Louis Kenny and Kingston Mills.

Marathon mania reached its high point at the Los Angeles Olympics in 1984. This race also witnessed one of the greatest ever individual performances by a Clonliffe athlete. Jerry Kiernan ran his first marathon in Dublin in 1982 and for over 20 miles (reached in 1 hr 38 min) he was on world record pace. Severe cramp overtook him in the last couple of miles but he did recover to win the race in 2 hrs 13 min 45 sec, a course record which stood for 23 years.

Having spent the previous two months living and training in San Diego Jerry had become accustomed to the oppressive heat and being able to concentrate exclusively on his preparation felt he was in peak condition going into the race. On the start line with him in Los Angeles were five time National champion Dick Hooper and double world cross country champion John Treacy. The weather on race day was very hot and humid but this did not deter the Irish. While Dick did suffer a little, he did manage to finish 51st in 2 hrs 24 min 51 sec. Up front, Treacy was staying with the leaders while Jerry was following closely in the chasing group. Past the 18 mile mark BBC commentators Brendan Foster and David Coleman suddenly became animated when they saw an Irish singlet joining the leading group. It was our Jerry ! With still some way to go, those of us back home were out of our armchairs cheering on the two Irishmen. For a few brief miles we thought we might be looking at a possible 2 medals and one of them for Clonliffe Harriers. However, as the race reached its climax, Jerry again suffered an attack of cramp which caused him to lose contact with the leaders as they approached the final few miles towards the stadium.

By the time the race finished at 3am Irish time, we had witnessed one of our greatest ever days at the Olympics. John Treacy had fought a magnificent battle over the closing miles to take the silver medal in 2 hrs 9 min 56 sec, and Jerry had finished an incredible 9th in 2 hrs 12 min 20 sec, less than 3 minutes behind gold medallist Carlos Lopes of Portugal. The Clonliffe man finished just behind then world champion Rob De Castella (Australia) and in front of marathon greats Rod Dixon (NZ), Hugh Jones (GB), Toshihiko Seko (Japan), and 3 time NYC winner and pre race favourite Alberto Salazar (USA). The race was run in 90 degree heat and only 87 of the 107 starters completed the course.

Jerry had achieved this feat with only 6 weeks of full time training as he was a full time teacher back in Dublin. In a poll of club members this performance is consistently regarded as the best ever by a Clonliffe athlete. It must surely also be regarded as among the best ever by any Irish athlete.

The three athletes who represented Ireland in that never to be forgotten race are still major figures in our sport. John is currently chief executive of the Irish Sports Council, Dick is a passionate coach for his club, and great Clonliffe north side rivals Raheny Shamrocks, as well as heading up the marathon mission team. Jerry has his own stable of runners in addition to coaching teams at a national level.

Ballyhaise 1988. Clonliffe athletes L to R N Harvey, Keane, Brady, Mulligan.

G Finnegan leads G Brady, J Kiernan, R Mulligan. Ballyhaise 1988

J Kiernan. Ballyhaise 1988

David Taylor wins National Senior CC at Ballyhaise 1988

Apart from burning up the roads Clonliffe athletes were also winning National titles on the track.

1981	Jerry Kiernan	10000 metres	28.55.90
1986	Dave Taylor	5000 metres	13.50.91
1986	Mary Donohue	3000 metres	9.16.06
1987	Dave Taylor	1500 metres	3.47.94
1987	Ann Buckley	3000 metres	9.29.45
1989	Richard Mulligan	10000 metres	30.14.09
1990	Richard Mulligan	10000 metres	30.06.52

Early on the morning of 11th December 1985 yet another club stalwart Frank White passed away. Frank joined Clonliffe back in the 1950s and was a member of the teams who won four National cross country titles in succession between 1952 and 1955. He also ran in the world 2 mile record race won by Albert Thomas in August 1958. In later years Frank was a prominent administrator in Clonliffe and was club secretary from 1983 to 1985. He also served as national BLE competitions secretary and was a regular visitor to the annual International Cross Country championships. Frank was deeply involved in the centenary year preparations but the illness which he bore with such fortitude for many months finally overtook him just 3 weeks before the celebrations commenced.

Centenary Celebrations

As the club reached its centenary year, Ireland and the world had changed more in the time since "The lads" first met at Knotts Cottage than in all of the preceding centuries put together. However, as in many aspects of life, the more things changed the more they remained the same.

The 1980s, like the 1880s saw mass emigration from Ireland, but for different reasons. The economic recession resulted in many thousands of young people leaving to seek their future on foreign shores.

Among the items on the political pages were :
• Recession in Ireland.
• Margaret Thatcher in her seventh year as Prime Minister.
• Ronald Regan halfway through his second term as American President.
• Mikhail Gorbachev in early stages of dismantling Communism.
• Opening of Knock Airport.

Among the items on the sports pages were :
• Maradona leading Argentina to World Cup Victory.
• Alan Hansen leading Liverpool to the League / FA Cup double.
• Kerry winning their 8th All Ireland in 12 years.
• Ireland losing all 4 of their 5 nations games.

While Parnell was the uncrowned King of Ireland in 1886, Mick O'Dwyer was the uncrowned King of Irish sport in 1986. However as his reign came to an end Clonliffe's centenary year saw the arrival of another uncrowned king in the person of Jack Charlton who was to subsequently lead the whole country on the greatest sporting frenzy in its history.

"John, Tom and Laro solving the problems of the world"

In the midst of these sporting activities Clonliffe celebrated its centenary in 1986. The festivities commenced with the running of the club cross country championship on new years day. At a wet and muddy Santry, club athletes past and present assembled for a great day's sport which culminated with the first of many celebratory evenings in the famous Clonliffe Bar. As a tribute to its long and dedicated service to Irish athletics, the club was granted permission to stage the national Cross Country Championships on its own home ground. On Sunday 24th February all members not participating were commandeered by the committee to "help out on the day". Course director Johnny O'Leary ensured that a tough but fair course was laid out and that, in true Clonliffe tradition, spectators would get full value for their money.

Just like their predecessors in 1976 the senior ladies race provided a kick start to a memorable day when Mary Donoghue became the first Clonliffe woman since Kathryn Davis in 1978, to win the individual title. The form book for the senior mens race suggested that Clonliffe had a real opportunity of picking up a few medals on home ground. In the weeks beforehand Jerry Kiernan who had been setting the roads of Ireland on fire was expected to challenge for his second individual title but would face some stiff opposition from pre race favourite John Woods (Liverpool), as well as Roy Dooney (DCH) and previous winner Dave Taylor (Clonliffe). Unfortunately Jerry suffered an injury just before the race and was forced to withdraw. Noel Harvey was out injured for 7 weeks in November and December and did not feel he had a gold medal performance in him. Following his marriage to Sandra in December he began to settle back into training.

As the race unfolded Noel stayed in the leading pack with all the pre race favourites. Around the 3 mile mark John Woods fell and brought down Mulligan and Taylor. Being just before the half way point this disruption did not have a major effect as all three quickly regained their places in the leading group.

As the race neared its climax on the final lap Mulligan, Woods and Dooney were in command but Harvey was only slightly adrift. The race report in the *Irish Independent* described the finish thus "when they re-emerged from behind the tall pines Harvey was still there and when Dooney and Mulligan made their final efforts it was the man in the Black and Amber who had the answer to score a fine win in 36 min 20 sec, fast running for the 7.5 mile course". Noel was followed home by Mulligan, Dooney and Woods. To put the icing on the centenary cake, the Wasps also won the senior men's team title. Behind Harvey were Dave Taylor (5th), Eugene Curran (15th), Derek Redmond (20th), Gerry Finnegan (28th), Eamon Tierney (31st), and Padraig Keane (42nd).

It proved to be yet another unforgettable occasion in Clonliffe's long and distinguished history. For the first time ever the same club provided the ladies and men's individual champions in the same year. It was also a record for Clonliffe which saw the largest ever number of club athletes racing in the National Senior event. The 19 who ran that day were Noel Harvey, Dave Taylor, Eugene Curran, Derek Redmond, Gerry Finnegan, Eamonn Tierney, Padraig Keane, Gerry Wyse, Denis Noonan, Liam Marley, David Dunne, Martin Treacy, Jim Cleary, Jim Mc Glynn, John Murphy, Loughlin Campion, Noel Guiden, Dermot Higgins and Jim Hyland. To demonstrate these performances were not a flash in the pan both the ladies and men went on to take the National Road Relay titles later that year.

Centenary year also saw the return of the 2 mile invitation to its traditional course from Finglas village to the Old Gate at Glasnevin. The event was now being sponsored by Eugene Kavanagh, owner of the "Gravediggers" pub, a venue which served as club headquarters for many years in the earlier part of the century. Indeed, many of the photographs featuring club members at opening runs were taken either outside this pub or next to it at the Old Gate into Glasnevin Cemetery.

During the summer, an international meeting was held in the Morton Stadium and the celebrations culminated in a gala dinner held at the Grand Hotel Malahide. Male and female members from the past and the present were in attendance as well as numerous honorary guests from all walks of Irish life. The address was given by 1948 Clonliffe Olympian Dave Guiney who regaled his audience with tales and anecdotes covering many eras of the clubs history. This event was also the last major gathering where "lifers" like Arthur Wisdom, Sam Gray and Harry Cooney celebrated with all their fellow Wasps.

This decade saw the continuation of the clubs commitment to the administration of the sport in Ireland and competition was just as keen as it was among the Clonliffe medal winners. At the 1987 AGM of the BLE Laro Byrne and Paddy Marley locked horns for the final place on the management committee. When the ballots were counted there was a dead heat with each candidate receiving 91 votes. Paddy edged it on the second count and Laro was subsequently elected on to the senior activities committee.

John O'Leary
Holder of 5 Irish Walking titles and Clonliffe chief course designer

In June of 1987 one of the true greats of Clonliffe Harriers passed to his eternal reward. Sam Gray first donned the black and amber singlet in 1928 beginning an association with the club which lasted right up to the time of his death. During those 59 years Sam was to the forefront, not only as an athlete, but in his later years, as a staunch and loyal administrator. He won practically all of the club trophies as well as featuring on many a Clonliffe team at national championships. He served as president from 1952 to 1963 but was also a constant confidant of successive committee members and a genial companion at any club gathering he attended. Along with Harry Cooney and Billy Morton, Sam was one of the main people responsible for keeping the club going during the decades before and after Clonliffe arrived in Santry.

The following tribute was penned by his good friend and fellow Clonliffe club mate Larry O'Reilly in the *Irish Press* "Sam Gray has gone from Clonliffe Harriers. He won't be there on Saturday afternoons to watch us run or to time a race, and to come down to the pub afterwards and talk of sport, as Clonliffe have done for a hundred years. Fifty years ago he was the best runner in the club. Old members at his funeral said that he ran like a stag, with great courage and a stride that would break your heart. He won almost every trophy in Clonliffe and was on the International Cross Country team in 1939.

He was one of a group of friends which included Billy Morton and Harry Cooney, who ran over the fields of Finglas in the 1930s and 40s.

In 1943 they decided to revive the old Clonliffe meetings (started by Tommy Burton in 1912). There were no international athletes but they got Bert Helion to attempt a world record in the hammer and they invited Jack Doyle to present the prizes. They were already beginning to show their flair !!

When the Second World War was over they began to promote a series of international athletic meetings that were to enthral the Dublin public for the next 25 years. There were summer evenings in Lansdowne Road and College Park, with sporting moments that are forever etched into our memories. They would not have been possible without the likes of Sam Gray.

He was club president, at Billy's side during the glory years and during the unrelenting years of the stadium debt. He was completely loyal to Billy and supportive in all his endeavours. They built the stadium in the days before government grants and Sam was one of the leading fundraisers, collecting in pubs and knocking on doors. The fact that the stadium is still in existence is due in no small part to the role played by Sam in keeping Billy's dream alive.

What this small band of ex cross country runners achieved was unique. They were dedicated amateurs and it cost them dear to be interested in the sport. They operated in an era before grand prix meetings and highly paid athletes..

When Herb Elliott broke the world mile record in 1958, it was a great night at the gate. When Sam counted the takings, he went to the modest hotel where the Australians were staying and offered to pay for any extra expenses they might have incurred. The Australians would not hear of it, so Sam presented Elliott with one of his Clonliffe gold medals. He had won more of them than anyone else during his running days.

He gave many of them away to special friends of Clonliffe or to true amateur sportsmen of the kind that is bred in the mud of cross country running. Sam had a dapper athletic appearance, who seemed 20 years younger than his age and 2 weeks before he died he came up to the club to be with his fellow Clonliffes. It was indeed a very sad day as we knew it was to be his last Saturday with us.

Sam Gray was still courageous and still breaking our hearts."

1991-2001

The unparalleled successes of the 1980s looked an almost impossible act to follow as the next decade dawned in Santry. But, as the saying goes "When one door closes another one opens" and so it proved to be. A new era brought some new faces to the fore in Clonliffe. The outstanding success of Paddy Marley during the 1980s now provided a challenge to his replacement Peter Mc Dermott. A member of four National Inter Clubs winning panels under Paddy Marley he was also a teacher at St Aidans school in Whitehall which was a prolific "feeder" of athletic talent to Clonliffe and continues to be so to this day. As such Peter was in the unique position of being able to recognise potential future Wasps from the very first day they donned a pair of spikes. True to form he was soon into his stride and in 1991 the Inter Club trophy was once more returned to the Clonliffe Bar when Richard Mulligan (2nd), Noel Cullen (7th), Derek Redmond (14th), and Gerry Brady (24th), were the scoring four in Limerick. One year later at Santry Mulligan (4th), Cullen (8th), Kiernan (9th), and Redmond (25th) gave Clonliffe their sixth title in 7 years. For the rest of the decade the club took three team silver and four team bronze medals, together with one fourth place finish, at these championships. Amazingly, just like the 1980s, only 14 athletes were used in the "scoring four". Most appearances were by Noel Cullen (10), Richard Mulligan (6), while Jerry Kiernan, Gerry Brady, and Cian Mc Loughlin had 4 each.

The outstanding athlete of this decade was Noel Cullen who, in addition to winning the Dublin senior, took individual gold at the 1993 inter clubs in the Phoenix Park. His form over the country earned him international recognition when he was selected for European cross country championships. In addition Noel was also a prolific road racer and was a twice winner of the club 2 mile invitation with a best time of 8 min 32 sec in 1992. Like his cross country form Noel's exploits on the road earned him a place on the Irish team at the European cup competition which was staged in Santry in 1994.

Off the field of competition this decade began with a major coup by club Olympian Frank Murphy. He was a member of the famous Scruffy Murphys lotto syndicate which managed to enter the majority of possible combinations into the system before the organisers realised their plan and shut down the machines. The syndicate won the jackpot but their triumph resulted in the numbers being increased from 36 to 48. In May of 1993 one of the Clonliffes reached heights never achieved in the clubs history. John Bourke was a member of the first Irish expedition to climb to the top of Mount Everest. He acted as advance base camp manager and while he was not amongst those designated to "summit", he did climb to 6600 metres (21650 ft).

Another first was achieved in 1994 when local Santry athlete Niall Bruton became the first Wasp to win the famous Wannamaker Mile at the Millrose Games in New York. He was also the first ever college student to win this race and the latest in a long line of Irish winners including Ronnie Delany (4), Eamon Coghlan (7), Marcus O'Sullivan (6) and Ronnie Carroll (1) who, between them have won 19 of the 88 renewals. This year also saw Mary Donoghue win the ladies mini marathon and Eamon Tierney take the national marathon title.

1995 saw the arrival of Fr Ted on our television screens and this show provided yet another link between the club and the world of show business. Former Wasp Jim Norton played the role of Bishop Brennan and he was also to be seen in Harry Potter films as well as winning many awards for his stage career. The capture and trial of OJ Simpson was led by police commissioner Willie Williams who competed as part of an American team at a Clonliffe meeting in College Park in 1954.

In parallel with its sporting successes the club was constantly seeking opportunities to improve the overall standard of facilities for its members.

When Clonliffe first arrived in Santry in the mid 1950s they built what was then a world class cinder track alongside spectator accommodation for several thousand people. A Nissen hut was also procured which was to provide changing facilities and limited room for indoor training. The nerve centre of this structure was the boiler room which generated the hot water for the showers. Because it was the warmest room in the building and despite its miniscule floor space it was also frequently used for committee meetings. Two decades later new changing facilities and a club bar were built under the terracing. In addition a new committee room was built alongside. Like their predecessors these facilities eventually outgrew their functionality and in 1995 the current changing rooms and club bar were opened. The original club bar which had provided many a memorable night of celebration and the nissen hut which had seen world record makers and breakers pass through its doors were shortly after consigned to history. Below are tributes penned by two of Clonliffes greatest servants.

"Farewell To The Nissen Hut"

Clonliffe Harriers moved to its present headquarters in 1957 and an exciting new phase in the club's history commenced. The ambition of the club, pushed forward by Billy Morton, was being realised. The club had a distinguished record of achievement in track, cross country, and distance running. The best athletes in the world were attracted to compete in the major meetings staged by Clonliffe. Now these meetings were being staged with pride at its new track and very soon the whole world would be aware that the track at Santry was a very special place to run. Three world records in the summer of 1958 would guarantee this.

But Clonliffe had not just acquired a new home and wonderful cinder track. Another facility played an important part in the activities of the club for the next 40 years: The Nissen Hut !! It had been serving the members well for about 5 years when the ladies section was formed in 1963. The first time we entered this hallowed establishment was on a cold and windy October night and we were being introduced to our future mentors Harry Cooney and Noel O'Rourke. It was here we trained, socialised, and in general it was the meeting place before the first club bar was built.

We received a warm welcome as we entered the changing rooms in the nissen hut but soon realised that "warming up" involved cramming into the boiler room across the corridor. Many a cold night we huddled around the belly stove as we chatted and laughed. The stove had to be lit each day at 4 o'clock to heat the water for the showers. One of our vivid memories was seeing Charlie Rothwell huffing and puffing to get the fire going. He would also religiously wind up the antique clock that was in the boiler room (what ever happened to that clock?) This boiler also caused a disturbance in the Morton household every Sunday morning when Billy set out early to light it for the members after their cross country runs. No Sunday lie in for Mrs Morton and family.

We learned all about athletics in that hut. Encouraged to have a go at everything, we hurdled, high jumped, long jumped, put the shot and even practiced starts. Technical terms like scissors, western roll, run up and take off board all became familiar to us. We were too self conscious to "have a go" outdoors but in the hut we were prepared to try everything. The net covered rubber cuttings served as landing areas for the jumps and the coke which was used for the boiler was used as the landing area for the shot, and Harry always knew where we should stand to ensure it reached the "landing area". When we got to know the male members we played indoor football with them as part of our warm up. It was also while training in the hut that we were first shown a javelin made from wood.

In December 1963 we had our first race. On arrival at the hut we were met by photographers and reporters there to record the event. Entries and pre-race photos were later followed by speeches and presentation of prizes and on this historic occasion, certificates of participation to all. We ladies were now beginning to appreciate just how versatile the nissen hut was and while new to us it was a routine occurrence at all events staged in the stadium.

In the early seventies, and in order to clear the club's heavy debt burden, a new committee set about building a bar and new changing facilities under the terrace. The hut still remained but was now being let out as a storage facility to help gather more cash for the club. Towards the end of this decade, plans were being discussed for a major development of the stadium but no time scale or commencement dates were being set. In the meantime the club set about re-organising the facilities in the hut to allow it to return to some of its former uses. Structural repairs, panelling to the side walls, major re-painting and improvements to the floor enabled us to once again use it as an indoor training area.

While training resumed, the hut now saw itself resounding to the energies of the younger members attending parties and discos. Life, and bright lights had once more returned to the hut! Club, and other social events as well as facilities relating to the organising of meetings in the stadium, some of them unheard of in 1958 such as dope testing, control and treatment rooms were now taking place there. While talk of grand plans were taking place "outside", the hut stayed alive, having adapted to meet the needs of the time.

Eventually the plans to turn the stadium into a venue with international standard facilities became a reality and while our hut remained for a few short years, time and the elements soon took their toll and it was subsequently demolished. The opening of the new clubhouse in 1995 finally signalled its end. It had been there in 1958 to accommodate the world record breakers alongside the new cinder track. It had outlasted many of the original features of the stadium and some of the subsequent "improvements".

It acquired the versatility of a decathlete and fulfilled all the requirements set for it in 1957.

It set no records and is not mentioned in the archives, but the Nissen hut will always hold fond memories for the couple of generations of Clonliffes it served in many different roles during our first 40 years in Santry.

Claire Walsh
1995.

Opening of Nissen hut 1957. Included are H Cooney, A Wisdom, C Rothwell, W Morton, F Hewson, R Walker and F Walker.

Damage to Nissen Hut following explosions at Santry in June 1959.

"Indoor training" in Nissen hut.

Epitaph To The Original Clonliffe Bar

It was a proud and happy gathering of members who assembled for the opening of our new clubhouse on Saturday 2nd September 1995. It felt good to be part of this august assembly of 3 generations of Clonliffians. Shortly before the opening, I stood in our new bar and gazed across the courtyard towards our original bar and the memories came flooding back as I thought of all the good people, many of them no longer with us, I had met there and of all the happy times we had.

It was back in the early seventies that the officers of the club Michael Hoey (president) Larry O'Reilly (Hon Sec) and Colm Brennan (Hon Tres) took on the monumental task of building and fitting out the club's first bar in order to help clear our huge debts. This job was undertaken on the proverbial "shoe string" budget as the club was in dire financial straits at the time.

So it behoves all of us to remember their deeds with gratitude.

Of course, building it was one thing, running it was another but the members were not found wanting as there was no shortage of volunteers to help out.

When I recall to mind all the greats I met and drank with there, Harry Cooney, Sam Gray and Mattie Hewson, men who had worked so hard over the years to ensure Clonliffe Harriers would have a permanent home in Santry. Over the years the old bar was a rendezvous for members and friends to gather and socialise and the highlight there each Christmas was the captain's cake race. Eamon Coghlan held his stag party there and many a lively 21st birthday was celebrated here.

Now, as I gaze out, I see Larry O'Reilly leading a group up the stairs, to sample the fare of the new bar just as he did at the opening of the first club bar all those years ago. As club captain Peter Mc Dermott and I clink glasses, I look at the trophy cabinet and yearn for the day I will see the National Inter Clubs cross country and national League trophies rest side by side on that hallowed shelf. It can and will be achieved, of that I am sure.

I am confident the new complex will serve the club well in the years to come, and when, if ever, the time comes for someone to write it's epitaph, may their memories be as nostalgic as mine are for the original bar.

Farewell, a thousand thanks. Goodbye to my old friend.

Nil Desperandum.   Lar Byrne.   1995.

Harry Power "volunteering" in original Clonliffe bar in 1985.

In 1994 the club lost yet another of its "lifers". After more than 60 years of unflinching service to the club, both as a competitor and administrator, Harry Cooney passed to his eternal reward.

Below is a short excerpt from an appreciation by Frances Mansfield.
(Printed in Clonliffe newsheet Dec 1994).

October 22 1994 was a sad day in the history of our club. Harry Cooney, a life member, died at the age of 83 years.

When the ladies section started up in 1963, it was Harry who "took charge" and organised all aspects of the training and racing regimes. He acted as coach and mentor and was always there to encourage and cajole and give much sought after advice. When Billy began his dream of building a permanent home for Clonliffe and a national stadium for athletics in Ireland, Harry was one of his main supporters. He became a trustee of the club when a loan was being arranged to build the stadium and when the club went into debt, the bailiffs even called to take possession of Harry's home. He was prepared to put a lot at risk in order to secure the future of athletics in his club and country. His family (wife Mary, sons Hugh and Gene) were frequently roped in to help raise funds to keep the club alive.

He travelled everywhere with club teams and was renowned for getting the sing songs going at the back of the bus. His own part piece was "The Sheik of Araby" usually followed by "The Jolly Sailor". Irish athletics in general and Clonliffe Harriers in particular owe Harry an indeterminate debt of gratitude.

The decade and the century drew to a close with yet another Inter Club title at the ALSSA complex beside Dublin Airport. Clonliffe's twenty first championship also marked the final appearances of two of the clubs greatest team runners when Gerry Brady and Jerry Kiernan completed their collections of team golds. As the new century dawned the legacies of those who led Clonliffe from The Old Gate at Glasnevin to Santry had been superseded by another generation of Wasps who had brought undreamt of success to the club and had set the bar even higher for the next generation.

Another good day's racing in Donegal in 1980s.
P Woods, D Mc Kinley, K Walley, A Baldwin, M Treacy, T Treacy.

New kids on the block 1970s style

Club 4x100m club records holders. B McHale,
P Woods, T Coyle (coach), M Penco, V Ragazolli.

THE NEXT GENERATION

One evening after training in the early years of the century club captain Peter Mc Dermott and Joe Cooper were walking across the infield in the Morton Stadium when Joe casually asked who he thought might be the next Clonliffe captain. Peter simply replied "Ah I'm sure they will get some poor eejit to take it on"!

Indeed, it could be said that under Joe Cooper's captaincy, Clonliffe have enjoyed their greatest unbroken run of success since the clubs foundation in 1886. Like his two predecessors, Joe kept Clonliffe in the medals at the Inter Club cross country championships. However, with Joe the exceptions were the silver medal positions in 2001-2-3 and the bronze in 2011. All the others were gold !!

Joe was soon joined at the helm by Noel Guiden who, on being elected Honorary Secretary, brought a whole new dimension to the organisation of the various activities within the club. While Joe was producing winners on the track, road and cross country Noel was at the forefront of renewing the grand prix series as well as signing up Hireco as the club's first ever official club sponsor. He was also involved in getting Brother sewing machines to sponsor the Brother At Your Side schools cross country event which attracts over 1000 athletes to Santry every October. To mark the 50th anniversary of the world record mile set in 1958, Noel set about attracting additional sponsorship in order to raise the profile of the long running Morton Memorial Mile and bring international athletics back to Dublin. This meeting has grown from strength to strength over the past number of years and several athletes from around the world used the Morton meeting as their final warm up before the London Olympics in 2012. The Morton Games, alongside the Cork City Sports is the only meeting staged in Ireland which manages to attract international competitors. While working tirelessly to keep Clonliffe at the top of Irish athletics Noel is also involved in under age coaching not to mention recruiting new members to ensure the legend of the Wasps continues to survive long into the future.

With Peter Mc Dermott continuing as senior coach to nearly all the Irish based athletes on these teams, training sessions in Santry Demense, Phoenix Park and Malahide Castle proved to be the breeding ground for many a National winning team. The integration into the senior squad of future scoring athletes such as Colm Rooney, Gary O'Hanlon, Chris Cariss, Brian Mac Mahon, David Flynn, John Heneghan and Sergiu Ciobanu throughout these years ensured the conveyor belt of excellence was evident for all to see.

Joe Cooper's first National Cross Country in charge would prove to be a pivotal one. Held on the Roscommon race course, the 2004 event was to be the start of the 7 in a row, and a 9 out of 10 year Championship winning streak. The senior men's team consisted of Rory Byrne, Paolo Doglio, Kevin English, Killian Lonergan, Cian McLoughlin, Gary O'Hanlon, Colm Rooney and William Stafford. The influence from the teams of the 70's and 80's was very obvious as Jerry Kiernan was coaching McLouglin and Byrne, while Peter McDermott coached Lonergan, O'Hanlon, Rooney and Stafford. Another stalwart of those earlier teams, Padraig Keane, had been involved in the local organising committee and Paddy Marley was of course the AAI Competition secretary at the time! With Keane and McDermott being Roscommon men, the travelling support hoped this would be the x-factor needed to overturn the 3 point deficit from 2003 and hence stop DSD from capturing their fourth title in a row.

While the journey from Dublin to Roscommon was an easy one, some team members had earned their share of air miles as well. Ever the team man, Paolo had travelled from his home in Italy for the race while Killian had just completed a month's training in South Africa. McLoughlin was back from Germany and Byrne had flown in from his home in London. Following an excellent junior career Rooney was running his first National as a senior. After swearing from the sidelines of the 2003 event never to miss another Nationals Gary had successfully kept his injuries at bay. William was running only his second Nationals and was eager to contribute in any way he could.

With perennial National and Dublin rivals Dundrum South Dublin and Raheny Shamrocks also bidding for the title it was always going to be a tight affair decided over the second half of the 12km course. Reigning champions DSD posed the biggest threat, and it wasn't until the last quarter of the race that the mathematicians on the side of the course were somewhat confident of a Clonliffe victory. Killian finished 5th, just behind Mark Kenneally running for Raheny, Cian 7th, Paolo 12th and Rory 17th. The scoring total of 41 points was seven better than DSD's 48. Gary came home in 19th, Colm 38th, Kevin 41st and William 64th. As on more than a few previous memorable performances by the men, the ladies also got among the medals. Thanks to top six finishes from Francis Nic Reamoinn and Nicola Fallon, club celebrations were further enhanced by the Junior Women's team taking home silver medals.

Joined at the post event meal by training partner and soon to be a Clonliffe club member Mark Kenneally, Joe put the question to those gathered as to how many titles they thought this team could win. With optimistic estimates of three to five being the standard reply, Joe confidently stood his ground in predicting ten! Though his optimism was ridiculed, history now shows that a return of nine wins from ten proved nobody was right, but nobody was closer than Joe!

The post script to this race was that Mark would finish second three times in this race for Clonliffe before picking up his 2010 win. Gary was as good as his 2003 promise and didn't fail to start in any of the next nine Championships. Colm Rooney would go on to win the coveted National Senior 1500m title in 2008. Killian would compete in the World Cross Country Championships the following month and Cian made a valiant attempt in qualifying for the Olympic marathon two months later in London. Sadly, Rory Byrne was never to race a National Cross Country again. The opportunity of leaving the National Cross Country Championships on a winning team was one of the main reasons he had joined Clonliffe Harriers from Blackrock AC a few years beforehand. However the following spring Rory was to collapse while out running in London and it was soon discovered he had a brain tumour. Battling through this illness for the next four and half years, Rory passed away at the age of 35 in late 2009

The two winning performances by Mark Kenneally and Sergiu Ciobanu means that thirteen Clonliffe men have now won the individual gold in this championship. With four of Joe's nine titles being won by ten points or less, the result has been far from a foregone conclusion until very near the end of the race and each team member has noted that the exceptional on course support of his fellow club mates has played a major role in achieving these titles.

Incredibly, only four more runners were used in the "scoring four" (18 compared to 14 in the 80s and 90s) in the nine victories under Joe's captaincy. Most appearances were by Killian Lonergan, Mark Kenneally and Sergiu Ciobanu with five each while Cian Mc Loughlin appeared four times. In addition Paulo Doglio, Chris Cariss, and Gary O'Hanlon have each taken home three team golds. As Clonliffe celebrated their 125th anniversary they enjoyed their longest unbroken spell as Ireland's leading cross country club having won seven successive titles.

During this period Clonliffe also achieved no fewer than 16 individual top ten finishes. The most consistent athlete over this time has been Mark Kenneally. His record in this event is truly remarkable and has contributed in no small way to the club's victories in recent years. Since coming on the scene his record is as follows : 2005 (2nd), 2006 (6th) 2007 (2nd), 2009 (2nd) and finally in the Phoenix Park in March 2010 Mark struck gold. Sergiu has an equally impressive record in this event finishing as follows : 2007 (19th), 2008 (9th), 2009 (10th), 2010 (9th), 2011 (6th), 2012 (2nd) and 2013 (1st). In addition Alistair Cragg won silver in 2008, while Killian Lonergan picked up an individual bronze in 2006. Sergiu became the seventh clubman under Joe's captaincy to win an individual medal at these championships when he took the gold in Tullamore in 2013.

2009 National Junior CC Champions.
J Cooper (Capt), C McGuinness, E Murray, L Brady, E McDonnell
M McDonald, B McDonald (Coach).
J Logue, D Fitzmaurice, J Rossiter, T Kavanagh, D Moran.

European Junior Clubs track & field Portugal 2012

Clonliffe At The Europeans

Following the breakthrough victory at the inter clubs in 1976 Clonliffe has been a regular contestant at the European clubs cross country and while no medals have been achieved to date the performances of individuals and teams are very impressive. At the 1981 event in Varese Jerry Kiernan (16th), Noel Harvey (25th), Denis Noonan (37th), Gerry Brady (49th) and Eamon Tierney (58th) saw Clonliffe finish 9th of 17 teams in a race which had 82 finishers. In Lyon in 1983 Kiernan(7th), Harvey (8th), Finnegan (19th), and Noonan (32nd) achieved 5th place just 2 points off the bronze medal. In more recent times the current trail blazers have striven with no small degree of success to match the performances of their colleagues from the 1980s. They have had no fewer than 8 top 10 placings in the past 12 years with a best result of fifth in Mantova in 2005. The team that day consisted of Killian Lonergan (10th), Mark Kenneally (24th), Cian Mc Loughlin (26th), Gary O'Hanlon (32nd), Colm Rooney (56th) and Aidan Bailey (62nd) and it is safe to say that the quest for further success continues!

Brian Gregan 4 x 400 National relays 2012

Jayme Rossiter
National Intermediate CC Champion 2012

Track And Field League Wins

Since its foundation in 1886 Clonliffe Harriers has produced many outstanding track and field athletes, as evidenced by the record number of Olympians, who have represented both their club and country with great distinction. The earliest track stars were George Blennerhassett Tincler who won the 1 mile championship of Ireland in 1892 and 1893, and Patrick J Byrne who took the half mile title in 1896. These pioneers were followed on a regular basis over the intervening decades by many Wasps who collected medals at national championships.

Being a Harrier club meant that the main emphasis was on cross country running while track and field was generally given a lower priority. The advent of the GV Ryan and Louis Vandendries, and the subsequent national league inter club events did add some incentives to produce more "summer" stars but the club was invariably down the field when it came to replicating the team successes enjoyed over the country. When Joe Cooper became captain one of his aims was to place additional emphasis on building a strong track and field team with the intention of taking on the best in the land. Aided and abetted by sprints coach John Shiels and field event coach Bart Rogers he slowly but surely set about his task. Not unlike the progress of the cross country teams of the early 1970s the early years of the decade saw the club progress into the top echelons until the big breakthrough finally came in 2008 when Clonliffe, for the first time in their history, won the National Track and Field League Championship final in Tullamore. This victory, alongside the win in the Inter Club Cross Country Championship earlier that year, meant that Clonliffe were the first club in Irish athletic history to hold both National titles simultaneously. To cap a memorable year the club also won their third consecutive road relay championship.

The historic track and field victory on 29th July 2008 was recorded thus on the club website by Killian Lonergan :

"David Duval and Davis Love fought for years to lose the tag, Colin Montgomerie, Sergio Garcia and Jim Furyk would love to lose it – that of `best player never to win a major`. On Sunday Clonliffe Harriers removed itself from the list of 'biggest club never to win the National League'. This team victory was not something achieved this past weekend, nor in the two qualification rounds in May and June. The nucleus of this team has been forming for the past number of years. With a runner-up placing in 2006 and 2007, we have been knocking on the door for some time. North Down, the champions these past 2 years, were steely competitors and were not easily going to give up the opportunity to become one of the few teams ever to win the title 3 years in a row.

Due in no small part to the Clonliffe reputation of being a cross country or long distance running club, capturing this title had become captain Joe Coopers Holy Grail for these past 7 years. The team that Joe built was not constructed overnight nor was it done without the assistance of the club's many coaches.

The naming of an O'Leary in our starting line up, in the walk, will have raised an eyebrow or two. The man in question was not our 1992 Olympian Bobby but his father Johnny.

Johnny was presented with an award last autumn to commemorate his 50 plus years of service, and his collection of a National Senior medal at this stage of his career is another wonderful acknowledgement of his enduring contribution to the Wasps. Having got the call 3 weeks ago, his daily regime took in walks in St Annes Park Raheny with the mantra of "I would never see Joe let down" ringing in his ears.

That self same mantra acted as a great motivating force yesterday in Tullamore.

Another display of Clonliffe commitment was in the showing of Jeremy Lyons, who, having blazed an early season trail in the 110 and 400 hurdles, and being sidelined by injury, nevertheless spent the day with clipboard in hand, constantly updating Joe on the scoring positions.

Jeremy's place was taken over by Chris Minn, who despite not being the No 1 hurdler, always had the desire to see the club do well Once again, he stepped up to the mark, and when asked to don the black and amber in both hurdle races, he earned the points that could easily have been lost through Jeremy's withdrawal.

Another early season club record breaker, Paul Marry, despite having picked up an injury, answered Joe's call, knowing he probably only had one or two throws in him. Fortunately his arm held out and he secured another win.

Out of view of the main arena, Eamon Byrne was busy squeezing out the extra centimetres in the hammer. A graduate of the Phil Conway school of hard knocks in Belvedere College Eamon knew how a teams momentum can be built up even from outside the arena. Another Conway graduate Luke Mangan was picking up maximum points in the shot putt, thus adding to this schoolboys growing status.

On the track Colm Rooney won the 1500 metres just a week after taking the national title at the same distance. Mark Kenneally took the 5000 metres while David Flynn, who departed on scholarship the following week to Fayettville, won the 3000 metres steeplechase.

Meanwhile back "in the field" recently crowned national champion Dave Donegan, comfortably took max points in the pole vault. Yet more max points were gained by John Laffey in the 400 metres, while Conor Healy finished 3rd in the 800 metres.

Mario Matuzzi was 3rd in the triple jump, while John Hartnett placed 2nd in the High Jump. In the 200 metres Cormac Doherty got a flyer from the blocks and took 1st spot.

The spirit and commitment of "The Lads" was shown when John Conroy took part in the high jump and 56lbs for weight. Neither event being down his alley, he answered Joe's last minute call to compete in these events.

Down to the last 2 events of the day and Jeremy "clipboard" Lyons still had us in the frame for overall victory.

Having lost out in the 4x100 metres, all our hopes were pinned on the 4x400. Having drawn lane 1, we put John Laffey on the first leg and he handed over in the lead. Colm Rooney took up the charge and having been cut off at the start he managed to hold on and hand over to Conor Healy in 3rd. Conor held his place and having passed "camp Clonliffe" at the 300 metre mark, he moved fluidly down the back straight and handed over to Eoin Mc Donnell in 2nd place. Still not 19 years old, Eoin held his nerve and ran an even paced lap to finish in 2nd place.

With the announcement taking over an hour, Joe had issued his own statement saying "If we do win, remember, I am too old to be thrown into the water jump". Cleverly enough, he passed his wallet, watch and phone for safe keeping to Johnny O'Leary. The sums proved to be correct and Clonliffe were declared the winners for the first time. That evening, yet another National trophy made the journey to the legendary Clonliffe Bar." The club now had the unique distinction of representing Ireland at two European Inter Club Competitions in the same year. The Cross Country was held in Turkey while the Track and Field was held in Slovakia.

While the first victory is always the sweetest, the real test comes when the title has to be defended. On 9th August 2009, and following some astute selections by

Captain Cooper, the wasps travelled back to Tullamore in search of back to back wins. With the best 15 results from the 21 events counting, Clonliffe had 6 firsts, (John Laffey-400, Mark Kenneally-5000, Jeremy Lyons-400H, David Donegan-pole vault, Tomas Rauktys-56lbs, and Fagan, Laffey,Healy, Lyons in the 4x400 relay.

Six in second, (Conor Healy-800, Aidan Bailey-1500, Jayme Rossiter-3000m st, Denis Delaney-javelin, Luke Mangan-shot, 4x100 relay.

The remaining scorers were

Jeremy Lyons- 110h
Danny Kavanagh-100
Patrick O'Connor-200
Martin Hunt-hammer
Tomas Rauktys-discus
Stephen Comiskey-long jump
Marco Matiuzzo-triple jump
Marcin Nowak-high jump
Tommy Griffin jnr-walk

Among those who contributed in the qualifying rounds in Antrim and Santry were Larry Brady, Kevin English and Anthony Mc Creery. The wasps were clear winners with 123 points from Crusaders on 102 and Raheny Shamrocks on 99.

With an entertaining and well choreographed march to the rostrum, the cup was collected for its second trip to the Morton Stadium.

Joe still denies he had the water jump drained before the presentation !!!

"The key to a great team in any sport is that it's a case of never resting on its laurels, and always building for the future" The successful defence of the league title again in 2010 displayed this mantra in no small manner. Athletes who had been on the periphery in the previous 2 years became star performers as Clonliffe secured a 3-in-row. The combination of fresh blood and experience particularly from the field eventers made it another day to remember. In the end, Joe was delighted with another days work well done while simultaneously shunning comparisons with the legendary Brian Cody when it comes to managerial greatness. The backroom staff was completed by another Clonliffe stalwart Killian Lonergan.

National And International Winners

While the team victories in Cross Country and Track and Field Championships continued unabated there were also many individual national titles annexed during these years. Under Joe's captaincy 13 different athletes have won no fewer than 16 indoor and 25 outdoor Irish Championships (details of these victories are listed in the appendix). The club also annexed the National Road Relay titles in 1998/1999/2002/2006/2007/2008. Throughout the decade Clonliffe was continuing to provide athletes for International, European, and World championship competitions. Mark Kenneally, Killian Lonergan and Colm Rooney all wore the green singlet while Alistair Cragg became the clubs first international track gold medallist when he won the European indoor 3000 metres in Madrid in 2005. He has competed at the Athens, Beijing and London Olympics as well as the European outdoors in 2006 and 2010.

Pole Vault

The noughties also saw yet another breakthrough for the "Harriers". The club was becoming a "centre of excellence" for the pole vault. David Donegan came on the scene when he won the Irish title in 2002, and duly followed that up with six more titles. His winning vault of 4.91 metres in 2009 is currently the championship record. He was justly awarded a place on the Irish team for the 2009 European Cup. David vaulted 5 metres at the Cork City sports in July 2010 to equal the National Record and become only the second Irish athlete to clear this height. His fellow clubman Anthony Mc Creary has a PB of 4.90 metres, achieved in winning the 2007 Nationals which ranks him joint 5th in the all time list. The bar has been set high by these 2 seniors but the club also has, in Ian Rogers, a national junior champion (2009), so the Wasps continue to reach great heights!

David Donegan after equalling Irish Pole Vault Record in Cork.
David has won 16 National titles indoors and outdoors.

Marathon

The advent of the running boom in the early 1980s very quickly led to the inauguration of the Dublin City Marathon which attracted the biggest fields at any road race in Ireland up to that time. Clonliffe have had a long and distinguished association the marathon distance which began in the early years of the twentieth century and in 1936 saw Billy Morton become the first Wasp to win this title. In doing so he also broke the Irish record. This victory was followed in the 50s by Frazer Walker and Harry Cooney, the 70s by Danny Mc Daid, and the 90s by Jerry Kiernan, Richard Mulligan and Eamon Tierney. The new century has seen the event now safely in the hands of the new kids on the block. Following Cian Mc Loughlins success in 2006, Sergiu Ciobanu stormed onto the scene with victories in 2009 and 2010.

Under Age

The ongoing success of any sporting club can only be guaranteed by a continuous flow of young talent being recruited, encouraged and coached to follow in the footsteps of their predecessors. To achieve this goal dedicated and committed coaches are a vital part of the process and Clonliffe has, in recent years, been extremely fortunate in having some of the finest under age coaches of any club in Ireland. The progress of the under age system in the club has been a major development over the past decade and juvenile coaches Gladys Cooper, Marian Halligan, Gerry Carr, Mick Fogarty and Noel Guiden are already seeing some of their prodigies winning national titles in their relevant age groups. Particular credit must be given to Gladys Cooper and her team of coaches whose trojan work has seen this section grow to over 100 members. Marian and Gladys are also in charge of child welfare which is a very important area of responsibility within the club.

Another generation of Wasps!
Courtesy of Eamonn Smith

Club Juniors at Brussels Grand Prix
M MacDiarmada, L O'Halloran, A Bailey, D Ward, C Rooney, L Dridi

Not content to rest on the success of the senior teams and through the great coaching network set up within the club, Joe set new standards for the junior men and women. Under the tutelage of Brian Mc Donald and Geraldine Reilly the structure has recently begun to produce results. In February 2009 the U 19s won the National cross country title. The following month the club hosted the National inter clubs in Santry and it proved to be an historic day when the Junior men won the title for the first time in 26 years. The full panel consisted of David Fitzmaurice (5th), Eoin Mc Donnell (12th), Jayme Rossiter (17th) Colm Murray (22nd), Larry Brady (27th), Jordan Logue (41st), Tony Kavanagh (43rd) and Conor Mc Guinness (45th). While asking them to emulate the recent achievements of the seniors may be a tall order these young Wasps are surely ones to watch!!

These young athletes are an intrinsic part of the club as they are the future of Clonliffe and must be given every encouragement to stay involved and carry the legend and success of the Wasps in the decades ahead.

Apart from the many successes in the field of competition there have also been a number of "events" connected to the club since the turn of the century :

2001
On 6th June Marie Bremont died in France at the ripe old age of 115 years and 42 days. Marie was the oldest recognised person in the world and the last authenticated person who was alive in the same year that Clonliffe Harriers was founded. She was born on 25th April 1886.

2003
The birth of the Clonliffe Website. This innovation is one of the most important developments in the club's history. For the first time the activities of the members are being documented in full and can be accessed by past and present Wasps from anywhere in the world. Performances covering all age groups from Juvenile to Masters as well as information on all club activities will now be stored for posterity which will no doubt be of enormous benefit to future historians!

2003 Special Olympics World Games at Morton Stadium.
Courtesy of Sportsfile

In 2003 the Special Olympics World Games were held outside the United States for the first time. Several thousand competitors from over 100 countries descended on Dublin and the Morton Stadium was the venue for the athletics events. Hundreds of volunteers helped out for the week and a number of distinguished visitors including Muhammad Ali and Mary Mc Aleese, the President of Ireland, visited the stadium.

2006
TEN THOUSAND WITH TUNNEL VISION

Towards the end of 2006 the largest construction project of the boom years had just been completed. A tunnel linking the city port and the M1/M50 motorways, a distance of five kilometres, was designed to take all the heavy goods vehicles away from the city streets and neighbourhoods. Around this time a certain Padraig Keane had an idea for raising some funds for the club. He suggested Clonliffe should organise a "road" race out one tube of the tunnel and back the other. A committee under the watchful eye of Michael Kearney set about investigating whether it was a possibility. It was reckoned a few hundred might turn up. They were right about the few hundred. They were the stewards !! The idea took off like wildfire and eventually the field had to be capped at no less than 10,000 competitors. It was easily the biggest race ever organised by the club and certainly raised the largest amount of funds for one single event in Clonliffe's history.

From early morning on Sunday 10th December the elite athletes, club runners, social runners, joggers and walkers arrived heeding the organisers request to be in position early. Being a December morning the conditions were somewhat bleak but MC Brian Maguire got the multitudes well warmed up creating a fantastic atmosphere as the wheelchair athletes were sent on their way at precisely 10-45am to the cheers of the ten thousand lined up behind them. Fifteen minutes later the main body was sent off heading downhill for 700 metres to the tunnel entrance. Such were the numbers that it took almost fifteen minutes for the entire field to filter its way into the tunnel and the surreal yellow light and heat generated by the ten thousand bodies.

At the front, an elite group had already formed headed up by Robert Connolly and including Gary O'Hanlon proudly wearing No 1 on his Clonliffe singlet. The first half of the race was very tough as the athletes headed uphill towards the fresh air of the half way point at Santry before heading back into the second tube and returning to the finish line at Dublin Port. Connolly extended his lead to take the win in a time of 30 min 28sec ahead of Martin Conroy (Sligo) and Alan O'Shea (Bantry). Gary finished in sixth place in 31 min 26 sec. The ladies race was won by Sinead Jennings (Donore) in 36 min 24 sec from Barbara Sanchez (Raheny) and Helen Crossan (Unattached). Marcus Costigan (USA) was the first wheelchair home in 31 min 15 sec and was followed by Clonliffe's Patrice Dockery in 33 min 08 sec with Garrett Culleton (Laois) third in 37 min 46 sec.

Thousands continued to cross the line long after the presentations were made to the winners and each finisher was presented with a specially engraved commemorative medallion and souvenir tee shirt. The race made front page news on the following day as many of the participants were competing to raise funds for various charities. The Lord Mayors charity alone raised €50,000. In his post race comments the event director thanked all those who had made the day an unqualified success particularly the juvenile members of the various athletic clubs as well as the Civil Defence, The Dublin Port Tunnel Project and Dublin City Council.

2007
HIRECO.

In 2007, another new departure involved the engagement of the first ever official club sponsor.

Securing the backing of Hireco Dublin Ltd, one of Irelands leading trailer hire companies, has played no small part in helping to alleviate a major part of the financial burden which has been part of the price of recent successes in both track and field and cross country. Their provision of club gear and their support in helping give members access to physio and other related matters has allowed the club to focus more on preparing teams and managing issues like travel and accommodation at national and European club competitions.

2007 National Senior CC Champions.
K Lonergan, C McLoughlin, M Kenneally, S Ciobanu, C Rooney.

This year also saw Clonliffe Harriers voted club of the year at the inaugural Athletics Ireland awards dinner.

2008
Marked the 50th anniversary of the famous summer when world records fell like nine pins at the newly opened Clonliffe Harriers stadium in Santry. On 11th July, almost 50 years to the day of the race, a special gathering was held in the clubhouse. Albert Thomas, who had smashed the world 3 mile record when he ran 13 min 11.80 sec, made a return visit along with his wife Nola and ran a lap of the track before being hosted in the clubhouse where a special presentation was made to him.

On 25th July the Morton Mile meeting attracted one of the biggest crowds seen at an athletics meeting in Ireland for many years. Many international stars competed and one of the most distinguished was world hammer champion Betty Heidler of Germany. Naturally, the centre piece was the Morton Mile and it was won in fine style by American Rob Myers in a time of 3 min 56.23 sec with no fewer than 9 athletes breaking the still magical 4 minute barrier.

Brother At Your Side Schools Cross Country

Back in 1978 club stalwart Lar Byrne had a vision for a Clonliffe Schools Invitation Cross Country event. The first running was held that same year and attracted teams from all over Ireland. St Malachys College Belfast won the first four stagings and the event continued with growing success until 1994 when major reconstruction work was carried out on the Santry Woods area behind the Morton stadium where the event had been held annually since its inception.

Brother At Your Side Schools CC at Santry 2009

The competition was revived in 2009 when club secretary Noel Guiden took up the mantle and held discussions with Sean Sheehan, the CEO of Brother Ireland. The previous year they had generously sponsored the meeting celebrating the fiftieth anniversary of Herb Elliot's world mile record in Santry and Sean agreed that the schools cross country was an event in which his company would be particularly interested. Brother accordingly came on board and the event was rebranded as the Brother at your side Clonliffe Schools Cross Country. The re-incarnation proved to be an immediate success. Fingal County Council have been very supportive in providing the use of Santry Demesne and the now famous Clonliffe race organisation team ensure a fair but testing course and all races run off on time. In 2009 the event was confined to secondary schools only but still attracted a very big field of approximately 700 athletes. In 2010 it was expanded to include fifth and sixth classes in primary schools. By October 2012 there were over 1200 young female and male athletes participating and the competing schools now view the event as the traditional cross country season opener.

The Brother Foundation

Brother Ireland, and Sean Sheehan in particular have proved to be extremely supportive of Clonliffe Harriers in recent years and in keeping with the company ethos of supporting the local community they also, in 2009, established the Brother Foundation. The purpose of the Foundation is to provide assistance for young athletes aged between 16 and 23 in furtherance of their pursuit of excellence. It was set up to provide financial support for young club members at a critical stage in their development.

Brother At Your Side Schools CC 2009

Its aim is to assist them with issues such as travel costs particularly to overseas events or rehabilitation following an injury where the price of treatments like physiotherapy have escalated in recent years. The reasoning being that athletes in this age group will generally still be students, either in secondary school or at third level and the foundation seeks to lessen the financial burden of their participation on their families. All applications must be signed off by the club captain and the athlete's coach.

Brother has provided a substantial amount of support on an annual basis and the foundation is administered by a three man committee consisting of the club secretary together with one of the vice presidents and a club trustee. Thankfully Clonliffe and the Brother Foundation have been in a position to provide this support to date.

2009 European Cross Country Championships

Following the massive success of the Port Tunnel race Clonliffe were then approached by the Athletics Association of Ireland to become part of a tendering process for the hosting of the 2009 European Cross Country Championships. A first class presentation by a committee headed up by then AAI CEO Mary Coghlan and including club president Paddy Marley won the day and thus began a two year preparation for what was to be the biggest event held at Santry since the days of the legendary Billy Morton. It was also the biggest athletic event in Ireland since the World Cross Country at Leopardstown in 2002 when the world got its first sighting of the legendary Kenenisa Bekele as the then 19 year old Ethiopian took gold in the short and long course races

Many months of planning and preparation went into the staging of this event and the Clonliffe organizational machine was not found wanting. All able bodied club members were involved and everything went according to plan. The necessary pieces of the jigsaw were put in place and the big day finally arrived on Sunday 13 December. Unlucky for some but the Clonliffes made their own luck. The first Clonliffe man into action was Tony Murphy. He was designated a place on the drug testing team and had to call to team hotels at 6am to help with the collection of samples. The weather turned out perfect and over ten thousand spectators attended what was a memorable day, not only for Irish Athletics but for the host club, who saw all their months of hard work produce a flawless presentation. To add to the organisational success, Clonliffe was to witness one of its own, Mark Kenneally, run a magnificent race against Europe's best and finish in 8th place overall. Alisdair Cragg (40th) and David Flynn (54th in U/23) also raced for Clonliffe and Ireland that day. The senior ladies race was won by Hayley Yelling (GB) from Rosa Morato (Spain) and Adrienne Herzog (Nederlands). The first man home in the senior event was Alemayehu Bezabeh (Turkey) who was followed by Mo Farah (GB) and Sergiy Lebid (Ukraine).

Mark Kenneally. 2010 National Senior CC Champion.
Courtesy of Sportsfile

Needless to say, that night saw yet another memorable gathering of friends in the Clonliffe bar.

2010 Horan Cup

On Saturday 25th September 2010, the annual club handicap race for the Horan Cup, a race inaugurated in 1908, was won by Trevor Wisdom. Trevor is a grandson of Arthur Wisdom who was a member for more than 60 years from the 1920s until his death. Arthur served as Honorary Treasurer for most of the period from 1931 to 1959 and was still alive and well enough to attend the centenary dinner in 1986. Arthur's brother George was a member of the Clonliffe team which won the 1925 All Ireland Cross Country Championship, a team which included three of the Walker family and was captained by Tommy Burton. George himself actually finished second behind Dan Mc Aleese in the 1921 running of the Horan Cup so Trevor's 2010 win continues a relationship with the club stretching back almost unbroken for over 90 years.

2010 Loki Club Awards Night

The inauguration in 2010 of the club awards night generously sponsored by Loki Sports has provided an opportunity for all club members to get together at the end of the year and reminisce over the happenings of the previous 12 months. It also allows everyone a chance to acknowledge and congratulate those athletes who had either won club or national titles or who had set new records at club or national level. Presentations were made by club president Paddy Marley to the following who had broken club records during 2010 :

Brian Gregan	400 metres	46.21 sec
Matt Field	110 hurdles	15.15 sec.
John Fagan	400 hurdles	52.58 sec.
David Donegan	Pole Vault	5.00 metres
Tomas Rauktys	Discus	52.34 metres
John Fagan, Ciaran Mackey, Brian Gregan, John Laffey	4x400 relay	3.14.07 secs

Presentations were also made to the 2010 National Champions :

Dave Donegan	Pole Vault
Tomas Rauktys	Discus
Sergiu Ciobanu	Marathon and Half Marathon.
Lorcan Cronin, Brian Mac Mahon and Sergiu Ciobanu	Nat Marathon Team Winners

The highlight of the night was the presentation of the club athletes of the year prizes and the inaugural winners were :

Junior Athlete of the Year   Patrick O'Connor
Nat Indoor jnr 60m silver, Leinster Jnr Indoor 200m silver, All Irl Schools 100m gold, 200m silver, Dublin u/18 100&200 gold, Nat u/18 100/200 gold, Tailteann Games athlete of the meeting. Gold 100/200 and 4x100.

Master Athlete of The Year   Mags Greenan
O/50 European and World masters mountain running champion.

Ladies Track &Field Athlete Of The Year   Leah Moore
Leinster 100m gold, Dublin 200m silver, 4th in Nat Snr 200m, and scorer of many valuable points in National league.

Mens Track & Field Athlete Of The Year   Brian Gregan
Ran for Ireland at world indoors in Doha, and at Europeans in Barcelona. Broke club 400 record 3 times during 2010.

Ladies Road/CC Athlete Of The Year   Becky Woods
14th in Nat Snr CC, 4th in Dublin Snr CC, 2nd in Nat Inter Counties u/23, represented Irl at European u/23 CC in Portugal.

Mens Athlete Of The Year   Mark Kenneally
Nat Snr Individual CC Champion, 6th in European Clubs CC in Bilbao

Clonliffe Harrier Of The Year   Stephen Harkness
"Always available for Clonliffe in any event at any distance. Competed in all league and cross country competitions. Whenever called upon Stephen was always prepared to go the extra mile for his club".

Grand Prix Series

Over the decades Clonliffe has promoted many club races some of which date back to the late nineteenth and early twentieth centuries. These events were run as handicaps which encouraged the "ordinary" members to take on, and very often beat, the club "cracks". While there was a drop off in support for some of these races in the 1980s and 1990s they were revitalised again with the introduction of the club grand prix series in 2001. This was designed to incorporate all the club races into an eight/nine month season and would include events on the country, road and track. Going back to the old tradition of the club handicap meant that everyone had an equal chance of prevailing. The cross country races take place in Santry Demense while the track events are held in the Morton stadium and some of the road races in the grounds of Malahide Castle. Since its inception it has proven to be a tremendous success and thanks to the generous sponsorship of various club members the races now have regular fields of 60 to 70 runners. These numbers have been added to in recent years as a result of some races being opened up to invited guests as well as club members.

Club Secretary Noel Guiden takes up the story on this and some other developments of the past decade : "In the year 2000 myself and Pat Bonass along with my father Noel Guiden, now deceased, came up with the idea of a Clonliffe Grand Prix Series. This series began in 2001 and in my view has proved to be an outstanding success for the club. It has provided a race series to keep a lot of master athletes still involved, not only in our sport but in particular in our club. It has also encouraged athletes to join Clonliffe and has provided a good social outlet for about eight or nine months of the year. The Grand Prix Series has also helped to introduce a new body of club members who are willing to roll up their sleeves and help out with the many tasks involved in the successful organisation of the clubs activities. Over the past decade these activities have mushroomed out of all recognition. On an annual basis, in addition to its own internal competitions and open events, the club is involved in hosting events such as the Brother at Your Side schools cross country as well as major inter-club contests like the Dublin and National championships in both cross country and track and field. I would venture to say that were it not for the Grand Prix series, the numbers available to help stage these events would be very thin on the ground indeed.

The main change which I have noted in the club over the last ten years has been the major expansion in two separate sections. Firstly the juvenile section who have benefitted greatly from being able to train on the same night as the seniors. This has created a great buzz in the stadium and this section, comprised of athletes from 9 to 19 years of age form by far the greatest bulk of the club membership. The fact that a lot of these young athletes have blossomed and progressed to the Junior and Senior ranks is down to the excellent guidance provided by the juvenile captain and her team of coaches and assistants.

The other extraordinary feature has been the explosion not only in the sprinter group but in the number of field eventers. Clonliffe has blossomed and grown from its origins as a harrier club into a full blown athletic club. Nowhere has this transformation been demonstrated more than in the five-in-a-row National League titles which would not have been achieved without the major contributions of the field eventers headed by National Pole Vault Champion David Donegan, Junior Pole Vault Champion Ian Rogers, National Discus Champion Tomas Rauktys alongside the high-jumping exploits of Marcin Klinzow".

Masters Athletics

Along with the success of the new generation of Clonliffes, the vets, now rechristened the masters, has been rejuvenated in recent years. This category mainly arose out of the running boom of the 1980s and the early "cracks" would have included many of the "baby boomer" generation who broke on to the national and international scene in the 70s and 80s. The current crop have more than distinguished themselves at county and national level and some of them have earned Irish singlets. In 2007 Gerry Brady and Pat Bonass competed in the world road race championships in Regensburg and Gerry also ran in the world masters mountain running contest. At the 2009 National T&F championships no fewer than 8 medals were taken home by Clonliffe master athletes including Philip O'Doherty (silver 800m), Terry Mee (bronze 800m/silver 1500m), George Maybury (bronze 1500m), Pat Bonass (gold 5000m), Denis Delaney (silver javelin) and Joe Gibbons (bronze in javelin and high jump). George Maybury is a descendent of Clonliffe 1908 High Jump Olympian of the same name.

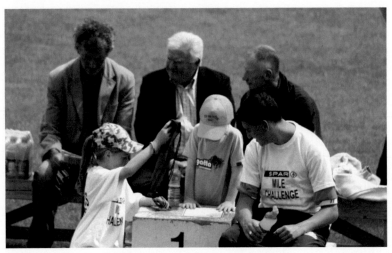

3 old goats and 3 young wasps !!

To show that these performances were not a flash in the pan the following is an extract from the report on the 2011 masters T&F championships in Tullamore - "Philip O'Doherty, who always times things nicely for the nationals was another big winner taking double gold in the V4 400m and 800m. Now that Matt Slattery has rejoined the club it is good to report that, freshly attired in his new Clonliffe singlet, he took gold in the V6 400m and silver in the 800m. Two medals also for big Joe Gibbons with silver in the V4 high jump and bronze in the long jump while Pat Bonass won gold in the V7 5000m".

Masters athletics is now a significant part of club activities and is also one of the best supported categories within the sport in Ireland. It has provided an outlet for former senior athletes to continue competing and in many cases picking up medals which may have been beyond them in earlier years. It also provides the opportunity for members to continue their association with the club and in particular with the many friends they would have made over the years.

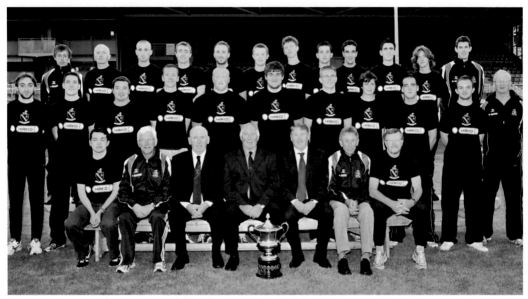

2008 and 2009 National Track And Field League Champions.

Conclusions

Since 1886 the roles played by the two principle officers of the club have been central to its continued success not only in the field of competition but also in the area of administration.

The long history of involvement by various club secretaries such as Joe Ingram (1886-1890), Dan Mc Aleese (1913-1922), Charlie Rothwell (1923-1934), Billy Morton (1942-1969), and Noel Guiden (2005- to present) has helped keep the spirit of the "Wasps" alive and has played no small part in promoting and prolonging the sport of athletics in Ireland. Legendary captains like Tommy Burton (1905-1946) and Harry Cooney (1952-1968) discovered and nurtured new talent during the earlier years and coached many members to national and international level. In more recent times dedicated captains like Paddy Marley (1981-1990), Peter Mc Dermott (1992-2000) and Joe Cooper (2001 to date) have nurtured athletic talent which has kept Clonliffe at the very top of the sport in Ireland.

By the time Clonliffe celebrated its 125th anniversary in 2011, the club stood at the very top of the sport in Ireland. The work begun by "The Lads" in Knotts Cottage in 1886 has continued throughout the decades. The great victories of the early years have inspired successive generations of Wasps to even greater deeds and the results of all the hours of training by the members of this famous club are well documented in the records of Irish athletics. In addition to all the hard work Clonliffe has been extremely fortunate to have had among its members countless numbers of dedicated administrators, coaches, helpers and supporters throughout its long and distinguished history. To all those who have gone before and all those who are still with us it is worth remembering that the overriding memory they have of being a Clonliffe Harrier is not the prizes they have won but the friends they have made and who have remained with them for life

On the occasion of the club's 75th anniversary in 1961, club captain Harry Cooney wrote the following, which I think sums up the philosophy of this great club. "I hope that each generation of Clonliffe Harriers will be able to look back over their time in the club with pride and pleasure and know that they have done something to enable the new generations to look forward with determination to do better and better. Our club motto was well chosen by our founders and if each member lives by it, we are on the high road to further success."

Cinque Mulini 2011 P Marley, N Guiden, J O'Leary, K Lonergan, M Fogerty, G Carr, N Daly

Junior Wasps at Morton Stadium 2009

The famous finishing straight on Clonliffe CC course.

European Clubs Track and Field Championships 2010

CLONLIFFE AT THE OLYMPICS

While men and women take part in many different sporting disciplines for a variety of reasons from keeping fit to competing at local and national level, the ultimate aim of the lucky few is to represent their country. Some will compete in their respective World Cup or World Championships but for track and field athletes that means competing at the Olympic Games.

Ireland has a long and very distinguished association with this quadrennial celebration of the world's finest competitors participating in the world's largest sporting event and has been represented at practically all Olympiads since their revival in 1896. Indeed, Ireland was visited by Baron Pierre De Coubertin, seeking support for this revival, in the summer of 1886, the very year Clonliffe was founded. There were two Irishmen, Dan Bulger of Dublin University and Joe Magee of the Irish Amateur Athletics Association at the meeting when it was decided to revive the Games.

Ireland has had representatives on various IOC committees over the decades and was bestowed with the ultimate accolade in 1972 when Lord Killanin was elected as the sixth President of the International Olympic Committee, a post he held until 1980. Clonliffe Harriers has always been a positive supporter of the Olympic movement and has provided five team managers to different Olympiads over the years and on each of these five occasions a Clonliffe athlete has been a member of the track and field team.

On the competitive front Irish born athletes competed with no small amount of success in the early years of the modern games. Unfortunately, the bulk of them were representing the United States of America. One of the most distinguished was Limerick native John Flanagan who became the first athlete in any discipline to win three consecutive gold medals by taking the hammer title in 1900, 1904 and 1908. Irish natives also took hammer gold in 1912 and 1920 before Pat O'Callaghan did the double in 1928 and 1932.

It was not until 1924 that Ireland was able to enter the Games as an independent nation and among those pioneers in Paris was Clonliffe man Norman McEachern. Our proud record shows that, including 1924, the club has been represented at 15 of the 21 Olympiads up to and including 2012. Clonliffe also holds the record for supplying more Olympians than any other club in Ireland.

The unending commitment to the ideals of the Olympic movement have, in no small way, contributed to the success of our athletes and administrators throughout the past decades and will continue to do so into the future.

Joe Deakin – London 1908 - 3 Mile Relay.

Nicknamed "The Priest", Deakin was the first person to compete in the Olympics who had also worn the Black and Amber of Clonliffe. He served with the British Rifle Brigade in the Boer War and while there he set South African records at both the 880 yards and one mile. After the war he was posted to Dublin where he ran with Clonliffe Harriers. He was third in the National Junior CC Championship in 1901 and later that year he won the 880 yards and one mile senior titles. When he was posted back to England he became a member of Herne Hill Harriers (founded just after Clonliffe in 1889). He continued to show good form and was subsequently selected on the British team for the London Games in 1908. Deakin made the final of the 1,500 metres and finished sixth in 4.07.90. The next morning he led the British team to victory in the three mile team race. After a celebratory lunch, complete with champagne refreshment, he lined up for the heats of the five miles race. Unsurprisingly, Joe was recorded as a DNF! By a strange coincidence, one of his fellow gold winning teammates was Arthur Robertson who was the first Olympian from Birchfield Harriers, one of the great clubs of British athletics. He was also the first Scottish man to win an Olympic Gold. At the age of 82 in 1964, Joe won a five mile road race and continued to compete as a veteran until he ran his last race in 1969 at the age of 90. He died in 1972 just three years after his last outing.

Joe Deakin

George Mayberry – London 1908 – Triple Jump.

Born in Kenmare in 1884 George was a student at Trinity College from where he graduated in medicine. He competed in the high jump at several IAAA Championships and took the silver medal in 1906/07/10 and 1911. He was 4th in 1908 when the 3 competitors in front of him were all Olympians. He subsequently qualified for the London Olympics where he competed in the triple jump. Unfortunately he did not make it out of the qualifying rounds but in later life he became a renowned practitioner in the fight against tuberculosis before the introduction of antibiotics. George passed away in England in 1961.

George Mayberry

Herbert Carmichael Irwin – Antwerp 1920 - 5000 metres.

Born in Dundrum, County Dublin in 1894, Irwin was one of the legends in the early days of Clonliffe. In 1914 at the age of 18, he won the Doran Shield five mile cross country club handicap at Finglas Wood in a time of 26 minutes 10 seconds and in doing so knocked 22 seconds off TJ Downing's course record.

However, it was on the national stage that same year where Irwin completed what is probably still a unique record in Irish athletics. In February he won the

National Junior CC title and one month later in his native Dundrum he won the Individual Senior title and led Clonliffe to the team gold. Later that year he added the national four mile title to his Cross Country victories. At Hampden Park, Glasgow, he finished third in a quadrangular four mile race against England, Scotland and Wales in a time of 20 minutes 01 second.

He represented Ireland on several occasions and was frequently a member of RAF teams in international and inter service events. This situation came about due to Irwin volunteering for the Royal Air Force during the First World War. He competed with great distinction in the UK and was selected on the British team for the 1920 games in Antwerp. He ran in the 5000 metres where he finished second in his heat in a time of 15 minutes 17 seconds. However, he was unable to reproduce that form in the final on the next day and finished in 12th place.

HC Irwin

As well as being a distinguished athlete, Irwin was a notable airman and was captain of the R101 Airship, which was completed in 1929 and was the largest airborne craft ever built up to then. It was built with the purpose of flying from London to India, at that time the furthest outpost in the British Empire, and its longest test flight took it across the Irish sea and over Dublin. While he never ran in a Clonliffe singlet again, Irwin, on returning home from the test flight, wrote to club captain Tommy Burton telling him he had flown over the Finglas fields where he had spent so many memorable days with his fellow Clonliffes.

On its maiden voyage to India in October 1930, the R101 crashed over Beauvais in France and Irwin was one of 48 who lost their lives. However, his story did not end that day. Irwin is the only known Clonliffian to have spoken to the living after his death. Two days after the crash a séance was being conducted by well known psychic Eileen Garrett to make contact with Arthur Conan Doyle who had died that July. However, instead of hearing from Doyle those in attendance heard the voice of Irwin giving details of the manufacturing flaws in the R 101 and why the crash occurred. The narrative was taken down in shorthand and following the official inquiry into the crash, a number of experts confirmed that many of the details recorded as being given to Garrett by Irwin were identical to those in the enquiry.

To add a further twist to this "running story" Sir Arthur Conan Doyle was one of the officials at the famous Olympic marathon in London in 1908 when Dorando Pietri was "officially" beaten by Irishman John Hayes running for the USA. The final sting in the tail from Irwin came in 2008 when he was included in the magnificent Dictionary of Irish Biography a compilation containing biographies of 9000 people representing all areas of Irish life since time immemorial.

Dr. Robert James Rowlette – Medical Advisor - Antwerp 1920, Paris 1924, Amsterdam 1928.

Born in Sligo in 1873 he graduated from Trinity College in 1899 and later became president of the Royal College of Physicians in Ireland as well as holding a number of other medical lecturing positions. While his active athletic career was in the colours of Dublin University Harriers Athletic Club he was a long time vice president of Clonliffe and had the distinction of serving as medical advisor to the GB team (which included HC Irwin) in 1920 as well as the first two Irish teams (including Norman MC Eachern) in 1924 and 1928. During his lifelong involvement in Irish athletics Dr Rowlette served on the management committee of the Irish Amateur Athletic Association and its successor the NACA. He was president of the IAAA from 1908 to 1920. Like many of his fellow Wasps he was actively involved in trying to heal the splits which divided the sport during his lifetime. He was a member of Dail Eireann from 1933 to 1937 and served three terms as a member of the University panel in Seanad Eireann from 1938 until shortly before his death in 1944.

Dr RJ Rowlette
(Reproduced by kind permission of the Royal College Of Physicians Of Ireland).

Norman McEachern – Paris 1924 / Amsterdam 1928 – 800 metres.

Norman J. McEachern has the distinction of being the very first Clonliffe member to represent an independent Ireland at the Olympics. He was born in Edinburgh in 1899. His parents moved to Dublin when he was still an infant and lived in a house in Ballybough no more than half a mile from Knotts Cottage and in close proximity to Clonliffe Road, the home of Joe Ingram one of the club founders. His father Neil was a cabinet maker.

Norman Mc Eachern

Norman Mc Eachern Olympic Commemoration medals

At the age of 16, Norman was spotted by Tommy Burton while training at the Garrison Cricket Grounds in the Phoenix Park. Burton took over his coaching and turned Norman into yet another Wasps legend. During a career that lasted from the late 1910s to the end of the 1920s, McEachern was virtually unbeatable over the half mile. He was Irish quarter mile champion in 1921. He won the half mile title in 1921/'26/'27/'28. At the 1924 Tailteann Games in Croke Park, he beat "All the American and Colonial cracks in the 800 metres". In 1925 he won the half mile at an International meet with England, Scotland and Wales and in 1927 he won the half mile and 4 x 880 yards relay in the annual match between the Irish Universities and Achilles (comprising of the best of Oxford and Cambridge AC). Norman picked up the baton on the last leg a full 10 yards behind the line, and was timed at 1.56.40 seconds, which was .40 seconds faster than the Irish record at the time.

One of the most memorable races of his career was a relay event in London in the same year when a Clonliffe team of McEachern, JV O'Connell, LD Cullen and AW Love took on the cream of English club athletics at the Oval in London. They were surprised to make the final and even more surprised to win the 4 x 880 yards contest with McEachern beating the English half mile champion Cecil Griffiths on the last leg. Norman's time on the final leg was 1.58.20 seconds.

However, like all aspiring athletes, the highlight of his career was his appearance at the Olympic Games. His win at the Tailteann games qualified him for his first Olympics in

Paris in 1924. Having finished second in his heat he was unable to reproduce enough form in the semi final on the following day when he finished in fifth position.

At the Amsterdam games in 1928 he again competed in the 800 metres. He was third in his heat in 1.59.80. His semi final contained Douglas Lowe (GB) who won the title in 1924 and 1928, and then world record holder Otto Peltzer of Germany. Norman set a very brisk pace and despite his best efforts he failed to make the final. He retired from active competition in 1929 and married Wicklow dentist Emily Varian in 1932. He did however maintain his links with the club for the rest of his life and acted as a track judge at all the post war Clonliffe sports meetings.

During his competitive career Norman had moved to live in Wicklow town where he worked for Dublin and Wicklow Manure Ltd, which subsequently became part of Goulding Fertilisers. He was managing director of the Wicklow factory when he retired in 1965. He was a very active participant in local activities and served as Captain, President and Honorary Secretary of Wicklow Golf Club as well as being president of the local tennis club. Norman passed away on 19 February 1986, the centenary year of Clonliffe Harriers.

1928 Olympic Track and Field Team on deck "Orange Nassau" accommodation ship.
Back Row L to R Tom Maguire (coach), Con O'Callaghan (decathlon), Denis Cussen (200m),
Pat O'Callaghan (hammer), Alister Clarke (110 H), Denis Cullen (200m),
Theo Phelan (triple jump),
Front Row L to R Pat Anglim(long jump) Norman Mc Eachern(800m),
Sean Lavin(200/400m), Albert Donnelly(1km cycling time trial),
GM Coughlan (800m/steeplechase)

Charlie Rothwell – Team Manager – London 1948.

Another of the Clonliffe "lifers" Charlie joined in 1909. He was 8th in the National Juniors in 1910 and one month later was a member of the team which saw Clonliffe winning the National Seniors for the very first time. He was also part of the next two triumphs in 1914 and 1923. Charlie served as Hon Treasurer in 1913 and was Hon Secretary from 1923 to 1934. He was later elected club president in 1935, 1948 and 1949. Charlie fought in the British Army in WW1 and during breaks from the front he was proud to show the famous Black and Amber when competing in events in France and Belgium during those turbulent times. At one such event he won a mile race and was approached by a Scottish officer who said "I saw you win a mile in Salford in 1914". Always a modest man, Charlie told him he felt complimented, but that the man he had seen at Salford was a real athlete! It was in fact club champion H.C. Irwin. But the Scottish officer had remembered the famous Clonliffe singlet.

Charlie was one of the kitchen cabinet who kept the club afloat during the turbulent years when money was scarce and hard to get. In his later years he acted as chief official at a large number of sports meetings where his expertise was greatly admired and appreciated. He acted as team manager to the track and field team in 1948. He was one of the longest serving members of the club both as a competitor and as club officer and was deeply involved in organizing the various Clonliffe International sports meetings as well as the plans which resulted in the club finally owning its own permanent home in Santry.

Dave Guiney – London 1948 - Shot Putt.

Born in Kanturk in 1921, Dave was the son of John Guiney who served as MP for North Cork from 1913 to 1918. Having been to school locally, Guiney came to Dublin where he attended Trinity College but left before graduating to take up a post in the Civil Service. However, when he was refused leave of absence to compete in the 1946 European Championships in Oslo, he resigned and turned his talent to journalism.

He was the winner of many national titles at both under age and senior level and when he won the AAA shot put title in 1947, he became the first Clonliffe athlete to win a gold medal at these championships. He retained the title in 1948 becoming the seventh Irishman to win this event going back to Maurice Davin in 1881. His athletic career was wide and varied to say the least. He competed for several different clubs in both the AAU and the NACA and within the former he represented Dublin University, Donore, Civil Service and Clonliffe.

Dave Guiney

It was during his time with Clonliffe that he had his greatest triumphs. These victories enabled Dave to compete at the London Olympics but his throws did not qualify him from the first round. After the Olympics, Guiney continued to compete in Ireland and won several more national championships. His throw of 15.19 metres in 1953 stood as an Irish record until 1961.

It was in the field of sports journalism that Dave became one of the most well known and respected reporters and writers in Ireland for well over 50 years. He was regarded as the foremost Irish authority on the history of the Olympic Games. He also wrote several books on Gaelic Games, golf, soccer and rugby, all of which he had played during his long competitive career. In addition, Guiney was involved in the establishment of the GAA All Stars and player of the month awards.

Dave maintained his links with Clonliffe throughout his life and was the guest speaker at the Centenary Dinner in 1986. He passed away at the age of 79 in October 2000.

John Joe Barry – London 1948 - 1,500/5,000 metres.

John Joe was born in Chicago in 1924. When he was 3 years old his parents returned to Ireland where he grew up on a farm in Tipperary. In 1943 he joined Ballincurry AC and thus began a career which brought him to the top of his sport in Ireland. At one stage he was even being considered as a candidate for breaking the four minute mile. At the age of 21, having already won the Tipperary Minor, Junior and Senior CC titles, John Joe travelled to Dundalk to compete in the NACA National T&F where he won the mile and four mile titles.

Lansdowne Road 1949. JJ Barry being congratulated by C Stone and F Wilt after winning the 3 miles in an Irish record time of 13 min 56 sec.

In July 1946 he ran 4.16.40 in a mile race at the Iveagh Grounds knocking over 2.5 seconds off the Irish record. Among his opponents in that race was Gerry L'Estrange from Mullingar who later served as Fine Gael TD for Longford-Westmeath from 1965 to 1987. In September, Barry ran 9min 18sec for two miles knocking no less than 16 seconds off the existing Irish record. He then took up a job in Dublin and began to "train" in the dance halls around Parnell Square. It was in one of these establishments that he first met Billy Morton who had circled the square in search of his quarry. Billy said to Barry, "If you join my club, I'll get you a job in Dublin Corporation and put your name, Ireland and Clonliffe Harriers on the athletics map forever."

His first race in the Black and Amber was a one mile in Belfast where he only managed to dead heat. Towards the end of 1947 Barry competed in a quadrangular meeting against England, Scotland and Wales and duly won the mile event.

In 1948, Barry, Dolan and Guiney along with fellow Clonliffe stalwart Charlie Rothwell, who acted as team manager, all represented their country at the Olympics in London. Barry had not prepared sufficiently well enough by the time of the games and failed to finish his heat of the 5,000 metres. He finished in eighth place in his 1500 metres heat in a time of four minutes flat.

Despite his Olympic form Barry continued to train and 1949 proved to be his best season to date. He was a regular competitor at the Clonliffe International Sports and was showing the type of form which suggested that he could get close to or even under the four minute mile barrier.

At the nationals in June Barry won the 880 yds (2 min 06 sec) the mile (4 min 39 sec) and the 3 miles (14 min 56 sec). Later that month Billy Morton brought over the then double AAA mile champion Bill Nankeville and Douglas Wilson (1,500 metres in 1948 Olympics) to set up an attack on the four minute mile. A badly run race saw Barry win but his tactics only yielded a time of 4.08.60. It was, however, two tenths inside the Irish record. In June 1949 Barry defeated two of the top American distance runners, Fred Wilt and Curtis Stone in a three mile race in Lansdowne Road. His time of 13.56.20 was more than 30 seconds inside the existing Irish record. Later that summer John Joe won the AAA three mile title in 14 minutes 11 seconds.

In 1950, he began a scholarship program at Villanova which saw him have a mixed career on the indoor circuit before he finally graduated in 1954. He was in top shape in 1952 but due to lack of finance in Ireland, was unable to travel to the Helsinki Olympics.

John Joe's athletic career continued for a few more years before he retired. He spent many more years working in the United States before returning to Ireland where he lived for nearly 20 years before passing away at the age of 70 in 1994.

Billy Morton – Team Manager – Helsinki 1952.
One of 5 Clonliffe men to manage Irish athletic teams at the Olympics. Billy's lifelong career with Clonliffe is documented elsewhere in this publication.

Billy Morton

Paul Dolan – London   1948 - 4 x 100 relay.
Helsinki 1952 - 100/200/400 metres.
Paul was born in Ballyshannon, Co. Donegal in 1927 but spent his working life in the Civil Service in Dublin, much of it in the Department of Justice. He was a top class sprinter who arrived on the scene at national level when he won the 1946 National Championship 100 yards at Lansdowne Road in 10.20 seconds. In 1947 he won the 220 yards in 23.80 seconds and at the 1948 Olympics in London he was a member of the 4 x 400 metres relay team which failed to make it out of their heat.

At the 1949 and 1950 Nationals, Paul won the 440 yards and while he did not feature in 1951, he returned in magnificent form to win the Irish 100, 220 and 440 yards titles in 1952. This is the only time that a Clonliffe athlete has won all three sprints in the same year. His 220 time of 21.60 sec was a new Irish record. These victories qualified him for the Helsinki Olympics where he was entered in the metric equivalent of all three sprints.

Paul Dolan

He finished third in his 100 metre heat in 11.12 seconds. Unfortunately, this time did not qualify him for the quarter finals. In the 200 metres he was second in his heat in 22.04 seconds. In the quarter finals he finished third in 21.90 seconds. While he failed to make the semis, Paul's time was a new Irish record and stood as a Clonliffe club record until broken by Brian Gregan in the summer of 2011. In the 400 metres he was third in 48.81 and failed to make the quarter finals. Qualification in those days was extremely difficult for sprinters as generally only two athletes went through in each round.

Gerry McIntyre – Rome 1960 – marathon.

Gerry spent most of his working life living abroad doing national service. In the mid 1950s he was stationed in Signapore but when he returned home in 1957, he regularly competed for Ponders End in cross country and road races. By 1959, his performances were improving quite substantially and in May of that year he was part of the club team who travelled to Ireland to compete in the Clonliffe 4 x 4.5 mile relay.

In 1960 he joined Clonliffe and decided to have a go at qualifying for the Rome Olympics. At the Irish trial Bertie Messitt won in a new Irish record of 2 hours 28 minutes and along with Willie Dunne, was selected to travel to the games. However, one month later Gerry ran 2 hours 27 minutes and was also selected for Rome. At the games, Messitt stayed with eventual winner Abebe Bikila of Ethiopia for 15 miles before dropping out, while Gerry finished 22nd in another Irish record time of 2 hours 26 minutes. This marathon was famous for the appearance of Bikila, who ran the whole race through the streets of Rome in his bare feet. His winning time was 2.15.16. In 1964 he became the first man to retain the Olympic title when he ran a world best time of 2.12.11.

Gerry continued to run in England during the 1960s but sadly passed away in 2006.

Gerry Mc Intyre and Michael Hoey

Michael Hoey – Rome 1960 - 5,000 metres.

Michael joined the club in September 1956. In 1957 he won the Leinster and All Ireland Schools 1,500 metres Championship. Later that year he became AAU Youths National Champion when he won the mile in 4 minutes 38 seconds. He also competed in the Junior AAAs where his time of 4 minutes 17 seconds got him into the final. At the Clonliffe international meeting in June 1958, Michael ran a PB of 4.12.60 for the mile when finishing 1/10th of a second behind then Olympic champion Ronnie Delaney who won in 4.12.50. Two months later he was the sole Clonliffe athlete in the world record mile race where the first five went under four minutes.

In May 1960 he broke the Irish two mile record with a time of 8 minutes 55 seconds. Michael recalls the race as, "We ran the first mile in 4.25. This was followed by two slow laps and the last two laps were completed in 1.05 and 57.6 seconds respectively." This was followed by victory in the National 5,000 metres Championship where he ran 13 minutes 51 seconds, a time which qualified him for the Rome Olympics. He ran a time of 15.00.52 in Rome, finishing 10th in his heat. The next day he returned home to Dublin to sit his final engineering degree exams in UCD. During his college years he competed regularly at Inter varsity meetings. He retired from track and field competition after winning his second successive Irish three mile title in 1961 but continued to compete on Clonliffe senior cross country teams for several more years. Michael made a brief comeback when he ran the Radio Two Dublin City Marathon in 1980 and 1981 recording a best time of 2 hours 48 minutes.

Michael served on the club committee for most of the period from the mid '60s to the mid '70s. During this time he acted as club delegate to the AAU and was one of those responsible for raising funds to reduce the club debt and building the first Clonliffe Bar and new changing facilities. In 1974 his election as club president made him the first, and to date, the only club member to both compete at the Olympics and reach the highest office in the club.

Frank Murphy – Mexico 1968 – 1500 metres.
Munich 1972 – 800 / 1500 metres.

Frank Murphy

Yet another Clonliffe legend Frank can, without doubt, be rated as one of Ireland's greatest ever track runners. A native of Cork, he was a notable athlete from an early age. As a schoolboy in the mid 1960s, he was not only winning titles but breaking records while doing so. He was equally successful at 800 (National Champion 1970/'72/'76) and 1,500 metres (National Champion 1969/'70/'71). He also won AAU one mile titles in 1966 and 1967.

A scholarship to Villanova where he was coached by Jumbo Elliott soon saw Frank break into the big time. He qualified for the 1968 Olympics in Mexico but, like many other competitors, the altitude had a major effect on his performance and he finished 10th in his 1500 metres heat in 3.54.85. These Games were the first Olympics to be run on a tartan track.

Undaunted, he did well in college and returned to Ireland in the summer of 1969 for probably his greatest season on the track. Having won the National 1500 metres

(3.49.80) he then went on to win the first ever AAA 1500 title in July in a time of 3.40.90 (since its foundation in 1880 this was a one mile event). Buoyed up by these performances he went to the Europeans in Athens in September with high hopes. Having made it to the final, Frank ran a time of 3.39.50 only to be robbed of the gold by one tenth of a second by John Whetton of GB. He became only the second Irish athlete, after Ronnie Delany's bronze in 1958, to medal at these championships.

In 1970 Frank won the Irish 800 and 1500 titles but in August of that year, in the very first Morton Memorial Mile he again lost by the proverbial "thickness of a vest" this time to the reigning Olympic 1500 metres champion Kip Keino. Frank ran 3.59.30 to Keino's 3.59.20.

Frank had a glittering competitive career but he is also a very well respected clubman. He has carried on the proud Clonliffe tradition of passing on the benefits of his own experiences and is fondly spoken of as someone who is never shy about providing encouragement or advice to younger members as they strive to bring further success to the club.

Claire Walsh – Munich 1972 – 800 metres.

Claire Walsh

Claire, along with Ann O'Brien, was one of the first female superstars of Clonliffe Harriers. From Terenure on Dublin's Southside, she was a clerk in Guinness and her early interest was in show jumping. She joined Clonliffe at the setting up of the Ladies Section in 1963 and was the winner of the first ever ladies race organised by the club. In February of 1964, she won the first ever cross country race for Clonliffe ladies, held over a one mile course at Santry. One year later she was a member of the first Clonliffe ladies team to travel to Great Britain for a cross country race.

Once she got into her stride Claire was virtually unbeatable over the sprint distances. Between 1968 and 1973 she won no fewer than 19 track and field national titles. In 1969 and 1971 she won the 100, 200 and 400 Championships as well as doubles in 1970, 1972 and 1973. To show her true versatility, Claire took the Hepthatlon title in 1970. She still holds the club's fastest times over 100/200/400 and 800 metres.

Encouraged by her performances at home Claire went over to the 1970 WAAA championships where she entered the 800 metres. She finished in second place and in doing so she defeated the then Olympic silver medallist Lillian Board and set a new Irish record of 2.04.90. In August 1971 she ran another Irish record of 2.03.40 at the Europeans in Helsinki, which qualified her for the final on the following day where she finished sixth in a time of 2.08.60. At the 1974 Europeans in Rome, she was sixth in the 400 metres quarter final in 54.15 seconds.

Needless to say, all these performances meant it was inevitable that one day Claire would qualify for the Olympic Games. This dream was realised in 1972 when she competed in the 800 metres in Munich. Unfortunately, she only finished seventh in her heat in a time of 2 minutes 09 seconds. But by achieving the ultimate goal of any athlete, Claire again led the way in that she was the first Clonliffe lady to compete at the games. During the latter part of her competitive career, Claire got married and moved for a time to Collooney in County Sligo. Never one to rest on her laurels she soon got involved in organising up to 100 local athletes to compete in the Local and National Community Games. She has since moved back to Dublin where she is still a staunch supporter of the activities of the club.

Danny McDaid – Munich 1972 / Montreal 1976 – marathon.

Danny was one of the true giants not only of Clonliffe but of Irish athletics in general during a stellar career which stretched from the mid 1960s to the mid 1980s. Born in Donegal in 1941, Danny was one of the Donegal mafia who joined Clonliffe in 1967. He soon established himself when he began to win club cross country races and it was not long before he was a regular member of Clonliffe teams at Inter Club events. He was the top cross country man in the club for many years. He had five top ten placings in seven outings in the National Inter Club Cross Country Championships between 1969 and 1975. Unfortunately for Danny, this was a lean period for Clonliffe on the team front as the club had not won a National Inter Clubs Championship since 1955.

His individual brilliance did, however, earn him a total of nine appearances on the Irish team at the World CC Championships. The first of these was Glasgow in 1969 and the last was at Madrid in 1981. He was on the Irish team in 1978 when John Treacy won his first gold medal. Danny was 31st. He was captain of the team on that unforgettable day in Limerick in 1979 when Ireland took the team silver medal and Treacy the individual gold. Danny, at the ripe "old" age of 38, finished an incredible 11th in this race.

In addition to his cross country exploits, Danny was also a top marathon runner and won four national titles in 1970, 1974, 1976 and 1983. In his other four outings at the nationals he placed second in 1969 and 1971, third in 1972 and sixth in 1980. His eight fastest marathons were all under 2hr 20min with his PB being 2hr 13min when he won the national title in a memorable race in Limerick in 1976. In 1983, the 42 year old running machine won his final Irish title in Letterkenny in 2 hr 19 min.

Danny McDaid

He competed in his first Olympics in 1972 where he finished 23rd in 2 hr 22 min. At the Montreal Games in 1976, Danny finished in 46th place in a time of 2 hr 27 min. In 1975 (the year before Clonliffe made their breakthrough at the inter club cross country) Danny returned to Donegal where he worked as a postman and continued to compete for a few more years. His profile in his native county is as prominent as it is in the story of Clonliffe Harriers and indeed the history of Irish athletics generally. The local track has been named after him and a 15k road race named in his honour is held annually which starts and finishes on the Letterkenny track.

Jerry Kiernan – Los Angeles 1984 – marathon.

In October 1971, Jerry, who had just begun his teacher training course in St Patrick's College, arrived up in Santry for the club opening run. One of the first members to meet him was Frank Murphy (Snr) who shook his hand and said to him, "I think you will be a great asset to the club". Frank then ran the first two miles of the opening run with Jerry. Thus began the athletic career of one of the truly great Clonliffians.

During a golden age for Clonliffe in the National Inter Clubs CC, Jerry held the record for the number of appearances (21 from 1974-2001). He finished in the top 10 on 11 occasions and has 10 team gold medals. These records still stand today.

In 1984 he became the first Clonliffe man to win the individual title since Paddy Killeen in 1955. Jerry was equally at home on the track and won the Irish 1,500 metres title at Belfield in 1975 in 3 min 47 sec. He won the 10,000 metres Championship in 1981 in a time of 28 min 55 sec.

Jerry Kiernan

In 1976 he became only the seventh Irishman to break the four minute mile when he ran 3 min 59.02 seconds in London in a race won by Rod Dixon. Jerry was now running well enough to achieve a qualifying time for the Montreal Olympics but circumstances acted against him and as a consequence he then set out on his road running career. This proved to be even more successful and he soon established himself as the top road racer in the country. He became virtually unbeatable over most distances above five miles. His time of 46.15 for 10 miles has yet to be bettered by an Irish athlete.

In October 1982, he ran his first marathon in Dublin. His blistering road form transferred immediately to the ultimate test. Reaching the 10 mile mark in 49.05 he was at the half way point in 63.50 and was on world record pace for almost 24 miles. Suffering severe cramping, he survived to create a new course record of 2.13.45, a time unbeaten for 23 years. This performance convinced Jerry he could again seriously consider the Olympics. In the spring of 1983 he won the Cork City Marathon.

As 1984 dawned, Jerry had an impressive CV. In the National CC he had finished eight in '81, fourth in '82 and third in '83. In February 1984 in Kilmacow, he finally took the gold medal and led his club to their third team title in four years. That week Jerry did 100 miles in training. On the following Sunday he won the Ballycotton 10 mile in a time of 47 minutes 04 seconds. This time still stands as the second fastest for this race. Two weeks later in the National Marathon in Cork, which was also the Olympic trial, Jerry was first across the line in a time of 2 hours 14 minutes. It was now time to focus entirely on Los Angeles. True to form Jerry produced the goods on the day. Details are documented elsewhere but suffice to say it was probably the high point of his athletic career.

Following his Olympic experience Jerry continued competing for his club picking up several more national titles including the 1992 Irish Marathon. Before his retirement from competitive athletics he began coaching young runners and more importantly, he continues to do so to this day. His contribution and commitment to his club is beyond question but, in true Clonliffe fashion, when asked what his greatest achievement was, and is, his reply was "the friends I have made and still have". Jerry Kiernan has truly earned his place at the Clonliffe top table.

Lar Byrne – Team Manager – Los Angeles 1984.

"Laro" was one of the most instantly recognisable members of Clonliffe over the past 50 years. Indeed it could be said that he was more often heard before he was seen as he bellowed words of encouragement to his charges while conducting his training sessions in Santry. A native of Wicklow he went to work in England in the late 1940s where he was employed by Guinness. During his time there he competed in many races particularly over the longer distances and when he returned to work for the company in Dublin in the late 1950s he joined Clonliffe Harriers. While his bronze medal in the national marathon may have been the peak of his competitive career it was a coach, advisor, philosopher and general all round bon viveur that Laro will be best remembered. His coaching career began in Santry in the 1960s and continued for nearly 5 decades. As captain in the early 1970s he oversaw the revival of cross country running within the club which culminated in the historic victory in Ballinasloe in 1976. Many of those Wasps who shared in the team victories accumulated over the following 30 years were coached by Laro. More than a few went on to represent their country where they again found him as their mentor. He was team coach at the European track and field in Prague in 1978, the world cross country in 1978/79 and

81 as well as the world junior T&F in 1990. These international events were among the most successful ever in Irish athletic history. Just as competitive athletes regard selection for the Olympic Games as the pinnacle of their career Laro had the honour of being appointed team manager to the 1984 Games in Los Angeles. It was no coincidence that, under his tutelage, two of the greatest ever performances by Irish athletes ensued, when John Treacy took silver and Laro's own fellow Wasp Jerry Kiernan finished a magnificent 9th in the marathon. No doubt his first words to both of them afterwards would inevitably have been "Fait accompli, par excellence, merci"!!

Lar Byrne Team Manager Los Angeles 1984

While his commitment to the cause of the sport in Ireland was beyond question, Laro was just at home socialising with his protégés and fellow administrators particularly in the club bar on the night of a famous Clonliffe victory. Along with his close friend Frank Behan he would often "winter" in the Canaries before returning home refreshed for the cross country season. He was always willing to impart the wisdom of his years to anyone who sought it out and he had a friend in every corner of Ireland. It was probably best summed up by one club wag when he said "In all my time travelling to races throughout the country with Laro every time we passed a pub he was able to tell me who he had a pint with in it". Sadly, Laro passed away at the age of 80 years in Feb 2009. He left more than a few legacies in the club and among them were the following lines which can probably be addressed to any sports club member :

DO YOU JUST BELONG?

Are you an active member, the kind that would be missed?
Or are you just contented your name is on the list?
Do you attend the meetings and mingle with the flock
Or do you just remain at home, then criticize and knock
Do you take an active part, to help the work along
Or are you just satisfied to be the kind that "Just Belongs"?
Do you ever go to visit a member who is sick?
Or just leave the work to a few and talk about the clique
There's quite a program scheduled that I'm sure you heard about
And we'll appreciate it if you will come and help us out
So come to meetings often and help with hand and heart
Don't be just a member but take an active part
Think it over member you know right from wrong
Are you an active member or do you "just belong"?

Patrice Dockery – Paralympics 1988/'92/'96/2000/'04/'08.

While it is only the very few who manage to win a medal at the Olympics, qualification for the games has to be the ultimate achievement of any athlete. To go there once or twice is remarkable but to qualify for six successive games is indeed outstanding. The time and effort put into achieving qualification is no less arduous for paralympians and in this respect Patrice's record is unique among Clonliffe Olympians.

Patrice Dockery
Photo courtesy of The Irish Wheelchair Association

Born with Spina Bifida she was encouraged by her parents to take an interest in various sports from an early age. When she arrived up to Santry in the early 1980s, she soon realised that she could participate in competitive events and was very soon competing on the international stage. Her first major event was the world juniors in Nottingham in 1986 where she picked up three gold medals. This was to be the start of a long and illustrious career which only ended after the Bejing games in 2008. At the age of 17 and just four months after sitting her Leaving Cert. exams, Patrice competed in her first Games in Seoul in 1988. She came fourth in the 100 metres, a feat she repeated in 1996. By the late 1990s, her sport had become increasingly more competitive and with this in mind she took leave of absence from her job in the Civil Service and did six months of intensive training with the Australian ladies team who, at that time, were the best in the world. As she says herself, "I was in peak form for Sydney and set a new Irish record when finishing sixth in the final of the 5,000 metres. Soon after that I gave the performance of my career at the European Wheelchair Championships in 2001 winning gold at 5,000, silver at 800 and bronze at 100 metres."

In her final games Patrice was given the honour of carrying the Irish flag at the paralympic opening ceremony in Beijing. By an amazing coincidence, the Irish flag at the 2008 Olympics was carried by Ciara Peelo who was representing Ireland in sailing and is a granddaughter of Joe Peelo, a Wasp who was on the teams which won the senior cross country titles in 1923 and 1925.

Anne Keenan-Buckley – Seoul 1988 – 3000 metres.

Ann Keenan Buckley

Anne is only the second lady to represent Clonliffe at the Olympics. In fact she shares the honour with Patrice Dockery who went to the Paralympics in the same year. She has a long and distinguished career in Irish athletics not only as a competitor but as a coach and administrator. Her only track title came in 1987 when she won the 3,000 metres in a time of 9.29.45. By the following year she had improved substantially and qualified for the Seoul Games in 1988 where she finished 13th in her heat in a time of 9.03.10.

However, in 2002 when finishing third in the 5,000 metres at the nationals, Anne recorded a time of 15.47.73 which at that time was a world best for her age group. She competed in the 10,000 metres at the European Track and Field Championships in Munich in 2002.

However, it is undoubtedly in the field of cross country running that Anne has had her best days as a top class athlete. She was Irish Inter Clubs Champion three times in this discipline when she triumphed in 2000/'02/'03. The Inter Counties titles were annexed in 1987/88/2000/'01/'02.

Anne has represented her country at the European and World Cross Country many times. She was 13th at the European long course in 2001 and 10th at the World short course in Dublin in 2002 when Ireland took the team bronze medal. In addition she has been on Irish teams at the World Cross Country Championships on a further nine occasions.

When her racing career was ended, Anne took up coaching and was Irish team manager for the European Cross Country Championships, which were held in Ireland for the first time when they were hosted by Clonliffe in Santry in 2009. Anne has also held posts within the Athletics Association of Ireland and continues to play a prominent role in ensuring a bright future for the sport in this country.

Paddy Marley – Team Manager – Barcelona 1992.

Paddy Marley .Team manager Barcelona 1992.

One of the original Donegal mafia who came to Clonliffe in 1967. Paddy and his fellow journeymen had achieved success at local level and decided to "go up to Dublin in search of an Irish singlet". They got employment working on the building of Sybil Hill nursing home in Killester and when it was completed Paddy became head of maintainence, a job he stayed in until his retirement in 2012. Shortly after arriving in Dublin he went up to Santry and was welcomed with open arms by Billy, Mattie, Sam and Harry. Thus began an association with the club which currently stretches back 46 years and can be ranked among the most distinguished in the long history of Clonliffe Harriers. Paddy and his fellow countyman Danny Mc Daid did achieve their International singlets and also achieved the ultimate goal of going to the Olympic Games. In 1970 he was in the field for the first running of the Morton Mile, alongside his club mate Frank Murphy, in a race won by Kip Keino. During his early years Paddy was a member of club teams which made the breakthrough at the Inter Clubs cross country and also featured on GV Ryan and track and field league panels.

While he had a very successful career as a competitive athlete it was in the field of administration that Paddy excelled. When he was elected captain in 1981 he oversaw the transformation of Clonliffe from one of the top ranked clubs in the country into the most successful club in Ireland at virtually all aspects and disciplines of the sport.

During his 10 years as captain the club won 7 senior cross country titles which included 4 individual winners, in addition to producing 4 Wasps who represented their country at the Olympic Games. He has been a member of various committees of the BLE / AAI over the past few decades and his expertise has been rewarded with his appointment as team manager to the 1998 Europeans in Budapest (which saw Sonia O'Sullivan take gold in the 5000 and 10000 metres) and the 2001 world championships in Edmonton. He was also manager to Irish teams at four world cross country championships. Paddy's great successes at local and international level were justly rewarded in 1992 when he was appointed team manager for the Barcelona Olympics. He continues to-day to be deeply involved in all club activities and his experience is a major asset to Clonliffe. He was elected club president in 2005 and continues in that role to-day. In addition to his duties in Clonliffe Paddy is currently a member of the competitions committee of Athletics Ireland and is one of the most highly regarded members of the sport throughout the country.

Bobby O'Leary – Barcelona 1992 – 20k walk.

Having joined the club in May 1987, Bobby, the son of Johnny, who was himself an international walker, was almost inevitably going to follow the family tradition. After only one year he was selected on the Irish under 23 team which competed against Great Britain and Switzerland in Wales.

In March 1989, he broke the magical 90 minute barrier for the 20k walk and later that year he competed in the IAAF World Cup in Spain finishing in a time of 1 hour 29 minutes 57 seconds.

Having been sidelined with injury in 1990, he started 1991 by seeking the qualifying time for the world championships in Tokyo. Having done a PB of 1 hour 27 minutes 45 seconds for 20k at Clonmel in March, he finished second in the National 10k walk in Cork with a PB of 41 minutes 44 seconds, a time which is still ranked sixth on the Irish all time list.

At the 1991 nationals in Santry, Bobby won the 20k walk in a time of 1 hour 23 minutes 51 seconds. This time still remains the national record for the 20k on the track and it also qualified him for the World Championships in Tokyo where he finished 29th in a time of 1 hour 29 minutes 28 seconds.

Bobby O'Leary

The year 1992 began brightly when he set a new national record of 1 hour 21 minutes 51 seconds when winning a Grand Prix race in the Netherlands. That performance is currently second on the all time best Irish list and qualified Bobby for the Barcelona Olympics. Unfortunately, the race did not go very well as he was disqualified at the 11k point. Over the following years he was plagued with a string of different injuries and finally retired in August 2000.

Niall Bruton – Atlanta 1996 – 1500 metres.

Another product of the "Aidan's Connection". While still at school, Niall came under the watchful eye of Peter McDermott and as a result it was inevitable he would join Clonliffe. During his time with the club he was mainly influenced by Peter, Paddy Marley and "Laro" Byrne and having made contact with former Wasp John McDonnell in Arkansas, Niall set out on a career which saw him become World Student Games 1,500 metres Champion in 1991. The same year he was fourth in the World Indoors 1,500.

He won the NCAA indoor mile in '92 and '93, as well as being awarded the most valuable college athlete at the 1992 Penn Relays.

In 1994 he became the first college student to win the famous Wanamaker Mile when he took the title in a time of 3.58.71. Later in 1994 he ran his fastest mile when he clocked 3.55.10 in Oslo. In 1995, Niall was 11th in the World Championship 1500 metres in Gothenberg and also clocked his fastest 1,500 (3.35.67) in Cologne.

Niall Bruton

These performances gave him the qualifying standard for Atlanta in 1996 and despite the fact that the first round was run at 11.00 am in intense heat, Niall finished third in 3.37.42. Having made the World outdoor final the previous year, he was disappointed to get knocked out in the Olympic semi-final where he placed 12th in 3.42.88.

During his college years Niall returned to Ireland to compete in the National Championships and won the 1,500 title in 1993/'4/'6/'7 with his fastest time being in 1996 when he ran 3.41.68.

Soon after this, persistent injury problems led to his retirement from competition and he is currently the Nike Football Club Business Manager at Arsenal and Manchester United.

Pierce O'Callaghan - Technical Advisor - Beijing 2008 / London 2012.

Pierce is currently the only Irish representative on any of the IAAF technical committees. He has officiated at walking championships around the world extending from world student games to world cup and grand prix finals. He has also worked at the 2009 worlds in Berlin as well as the Beijing and London Olympics. He is also a member of the technical committee of Athletics Ireland.

Pierce O'Callaghan

Alistair Cragg – 5,000 metres 2004/2008/2012.

Born in South Africa in 1980, Alistair went to the Southern Methodist University in Dallas in 1999 where he won the freshmen's 5,000 metres and broke the college record. Following the death of his brother, Alistair dropped out of college for a year but when he decided to return he was recruited by former Clonliffe man John McDonnell into the University of Arkansas. It was here and under the expert eye of McDonnell that Cragg finally began to show his true potential. While a member of the famous Razorbacks, he won NCAA Championships at 1,500, 5,000 and 10,000 metres and was voted college athlete of the year by *Track and Field News* in 2004. In total, Alistair has won seven NCAA titles.

His ancestry allowed him to declare for Ireland and in 2003 he joined Clonliffe. Later that year in his first international outing he placed eight in the European CC Championships. In his first Olympics in 2004 he was 12th in his 5,000 metres heat and did not make the final but the following year he bounced back by taking the gold medal in the European Indoors 3,000 metres in a time of 7.46.32.

He ran an almost identical time when he finished fourth at the World Indoors in 2006 in a time of 7.46.43. Later that year Alistair ran into a bad patch in major championships when he recorded a DNF at the European Outdoors 5,000 metres in

Gothenburg. Similar fates befell him in the 5,000 at the 2008 Olympics in Beijing and the 2010 Europeans in Barcelona.

Alistair Cragg

After these setbacks, Alistair returned to competition in 2011 and ran 60.49 for a new Irish Half Marathon record and 13.03.53 for a new national 5,000 metres record. After finishing 15th in the World 5,000 in Deagu in September, he was third in the Great South Run 10 miler in October in 47 minutes 14 seconds. In 2012 Alistair went to his third Olympics when qualified for the 5000 metres. He finished 17th in his heat in a time of 13 min 47 sec.

He took the silver medal at National Inter Clubs in 2008 and in addition to winning the Irish 1,500 metres title in 2004, Alistair has won the 5,000 metres in 2009/'10/'11. He is the current Irish record holder at 5,000 (13.03.53) and 10,000 (27.39.55).

Mark Kenneally – London 2012 – marathon.

Mark arrived in Santry in 2004 and within 12 months he was the first Wasp home at the national inter clubs cross country. Over the following 5 years he accumulated 1 bronze 3 silver and finally in 2010 he became the twelfth Wasp to win the individual gold at this event.

In 2009 he was the first Irishman home, finishing in a magnificent 8th place at the European cross country championships in Santry. In February 2010 he finished 6th at the European Inter Clubs in Bilbao. The above achievements were duly rewarded when Mark was named AAI athlete of the year for 2010.

In 2011 he won the 10000 metres track title with a time of 28min 58sec. This steady rate of progress was a sure sign of his determination to reach the highest stage. There was one major absentee at the club 125th celebratory dinner on 15 October 2011 and with very good reason. The following morning in Amsterdam Mark ran 2hr 13 min 55sec to achieve the qualifying time for the London Olympics. Mark was in top shape going into the games but having run very well for 17 miles he hit the proverbial wall and was disappointed not to finish higher than 57th in 2 hr 21 min. He has now set his sights on qualifying for the 2016 games in Rio.

Mark Kenneally
Courtesy of Sportsfile

Matt Rudden, Harry O'Gorman, Sean Callen
World record holders for number of International athletics events attended.
Courtesy of Sportsfile

PRESIDENTS 1886-2013

1886	SJ Warry	1929	CF Lonergan	1972	HP Cooney
1887	SJ Warry	1930	CF Lonergan	1973	HP Cooney
1888	SJ Warry	1931	JP Flynn	1974	HP Cooney
1889	SJ Warry	1932	JP Flynn	1975	MJ Hoey
1890	SJ Warry	1933	JP Flynn	1976	A Sweeney
1891	R Trench	1934	JP Flynn	1977	A Sweeney
1892	R Trench	1935	CF Rothwell	1978	A Sweeney
1893	M Butterly	1936	GN Walker	1979	A Sweeney
1894	J Stephen	1937	PJ Lonergan	1980	A Sweeney
1895	J Stephen	1938	J Craigie	1981	A Sweeney
1896	J Stephen	1939	GV Ryan	1982	L Byrne
1897	J Stephan	1940	FJ Ryder	1983	L Byrne
1898	J Stephen	1941	W Morton	1984	CCG Brennan
1899	WC Mc Mahon	1942	ET Galway	1985	CCG Brennan
1900	WC Mc Mahon	1943	ET Galway	1986	D O'Neill
1901	WC Mc Mahon	1944	TP Burton	1987	L Byrne
1902	GF Walker	1945	TP Burton	1988	L Byrne
1903	GF Walker	1946	WW Commiskey	1989	T Griffin
1904	GF Walker	1947	TP Burton	1990	T Griffin
1905	GF Walker	1948	CF Rothwell	1991	T Griffin
1906	GF Walker	1949	CF Rothwell	1992	M Ahern
1907	GF Walker	1950	R Payne	1993	M Ahern
1908	M Horan	1951	R Payne	1994	M Ahern
1909	GF Walker	1952	SJ Gray	1995	M Ahern
1910	JT Graham	1953	SJ Gray	1996	M Ahern
1911	JT Graham	1954	SJ Gray	1997	M Ahern
1912	JL Ryder	1955	SJ Gray	1998	M Ahern
1913	HM Burton	1956	SJ Gray	1999	M Ahern
1914	HM Burton	1957	SJ Gray	2000	M Ahern
1915	CH Caulfield	1958	SJ Gray	2001	M Ahern
1916	CH Caulfield	1959	SJ Gray	2002	M Ahern
1917	H Campbell	1960	SJ Gray	2003	M Ahern
1918	H Campbell	1961	SJ Gray	2004	M Ahern
1919	PJ Lonergan	1962	SJ Gray	2005	P Marley
1920	PJ Lonergan	1963	SJ Gray	2006	P Marley
1921	CF Lonergan	1964	L Reid	2007	P Marley
1922	CF Lonergan	1965	F Hewson	2008	P Marley
1923	CF Lonergan	1966	J Deegan	2009	P Marley
1924	CF Lonergan	1967	F Hewson	2010	P Marley
1925	CF Lonergan	1968	F Hewson	2011	P Marley
1926	CF Lonergan	1969	F Hewson	2012	P Marley
1927	CF Lonergan	1970	F Hewson	2013	P Marley
1928	CF Lonergan	1971	F Hewson		

LADIES CAPTAINS 1963 – 2013

1963	HP Cooney	1980	B Murphy	1997	J Freeman
1964	HP Cooney	1981	F Mansfield	1998	F Mullen
1965	HP Cooney	1982	F Mansfield	1999	F Mullen
1966	O Heaney	1983	J Wyse	2000	J Cooper
1967	O Heaney	1984	J Wyse	2001	J Cooper
1968	U O'Brien	1985	K Walley	2002	J Cooper
1969	F Quinn	1986	F Mansfield	2003	M Greenan
1970	R Keogh	1987	F Mansfield	2004	M Greenan
1971	O Heaney	1988	F Mansfield	2005	M Greenan
1972	O Heaney	1989	M Friel	2006	B Ni Bhriain
1973	O Heaney	1990	B Griffin	2007	B Ni Bhriain
1974	J Appleby	1991	B Griffin	2008	B Ni Bhriain
1975	J Appleby	1992	J Carr	2009	P Cooper
1976	J Appleby	1993	T Coyle	2010	P Cooper
1977	P Moore	1994	T Coyle	2011	P Cooper
1978	P Moore	1995	C Cummins	2012	P Cooper
1979	B Murphy	1996	J Carr/K Davis	2013	P Cooper

MENS CAPTAINS 1886 – 2013

1886	SJ Warry	1929	TP Burton	1972	M Ahern
1887	SJ Warry	1930	TP Burton	1973	L Byrne
1888	SJ Warry	1931	TP Burton	1974	A Sweeney
1889	SJ Warry	1932	TP Burton	1975	C Brady
1890	C Webb	1933	TP Burton	1976	C Brady
1891	T Cuthbert	1934	TP Burton	1977	C Brady
1892	TJ Bergin	1935	TP Burton	1978	C Brady
1893	SJ Warry	1936	TP Burton	1979	J Cronin
1894	PJ Byrne	1937	TP Burton	1980	P Mc Dermott
1895	PJ Byrne	1938	TP Burton	1981	P Marley
1896	SJ Warry	1939	TP Burton	1982	P Marley
1897	PJ Byrne	1940	TP Burton	1983	P Marley
1898	PJ Lonergan	1941	TP Burton	1984	P Marley
1899	PJ Byrne	1942	TP Burton	1985	P Marley
1900	PJ Byrne	1943	TP Burton	1986	P Marley
1901	J Flynn	1944	TP Burton	1987	P Marley
1902	PJ Byrne	1945	TP Burton	1988	P Marley
1903	OH Cunningham	1946	TP Burton	1989	P Marley
1904	PJ Lonergan	1947	HP Cooney	1990	P Marley
1905	TP Burton	1948	J Doran	1991	P Keane
1906	TP Burton	1949	P O'Hara	1992	P Mc Dermott
1907	TP Burton	1950	G Smith	1993	P Mc Dermott
1908	TP Burton	1951	G Smith	1994	P Mc Dermott
1909	TP Burton	1952	HP Cooney	1995	P Mc Dermott
1910	TP Burton	1953	HP Cooney	1996	P Mc Dermott
1911	TP Burton	1954	HP Cooney	1997	P Mc Dermott
1912	TP Burton	1955	J Doran	1998	P Mc Dermott
1913	TP Burton	1956	D Appleby	1999	P Mc Dermott
1914	TP Burton	1957	HP Cooney	2000	P Mc Dermott
1915	TP Burton	1958	HP Cooney	2001	P Mc Dermott
1916	TP Burton	1959	HP Cooney	2002	J Cooper
1917	TP Burton	1960	HP Cooney	2003	J Cooper
1918	TP Burton	1961	HP Cooney	2004	J Cooper
1919	TP Burton	1962	HP Cooney	2005	J Cooper
1920	TP Burton	1963	HP Cooney	2006	J Cooper
1921	TP Burton	1964	HP Cooney	2007	J Cooper
1922	TP Burton	1965	HP Cooney	2008	J Cooper
1923	TP Burton	1966	HP Cooney	2009	J Cooper
1924	TP Burton	1967	HP Cooney	2010	J Cooper
1925	TP Burton	1968	HP Cooney	2011	J Cooper
1926	TP Burton	1969	L Byrne	2012	J Cooper
1927	TP Burton	1970	T Purcell	2013	J Cooper
1928	TP Burton	1971	L Byrne		

HONORARY SECRETARIES 1886 – 2013

1886	J Ingram	1929	CF Rothwell	1972	L O'Reilly
1887	J Ingram	1930	CF Rothwell	1973	L O'Reilly
1888	J Ingram	1931	CF Rothwell	1974	L O'Reilly
1889	J Ingram	1932	CF Rothwell	1975	L O'Reilly
1890	J Ingram	1933	CF Rothwell	1976	M Ahern
1891	SJ Warry	1934	CF Rothwell	1977	M Ahern
1892	SJ Warry	1935	HP Cooney	1978	M Ahern
1893	CH Ewing	1936	HP Cooney	1979	M Ahern
1894	CH Ewing	1937	HP Cooney	1980	M Ahern
1895	CH Ewing	1938	HP Cooney	1981	M Ahern
1896	CH Ewing	1939	HP Cooney	1982	M Ahern
1897	CH Ewing	1940	VJ Walker	1983	F White
1898	CH Ewing	1941	S Farren	1984	F White
1899	JM Hennigan	1942	S Farren	1985	F White
1900	JT Graham	1943	W Morton	1986	M Treacy
1901	JT Graham	1944	W Morton	1987	A Hewson
1902	JT Graham	1945	W Morton	1988	A Hewson
1903	SJ Coates	1946	W Morton	1989	J O'Leary
1904	JT Graham	1947	W Morton	1990	C Milligan
1905	PJ Howlin	1948	W Morton	1991	J Wyse
1906	PJ Howlin	1949	W Morton	1992	J Wyse
1907	PJ Howlin	1950	W Morton	1993	J O'Leary
1908	PJ Howlin	1951	W Morton	1994	J O'Leary
1909	PJ Howlin	1952	W Morton	1995	C Keane
1910	PJ Howlin	1953	W Morton	1996	A Graham
1911	PJ Howlin	1954	W Morton	1997	A Graham
1912	PJ Howlin	1955	W Morton	1998	A Graham
1913	D Mc Aleese	1956	W Morton	1999	A Graham
1914	D Mc Aleese	1957	W Morton	2000	J O'Leary
1915	D Mc Aleese	1958	W Morton	2001	B Ryan
1916	D Mc Aleese	1959	W Morton	2002	B Ryan
1917	D Mc Aleese	1960	W Morton	2003	B Ryan
1918	D Mc Aleese	1961	W Morton	2004	B Ryan
1919	D Mc Aleese	1962	W Morton	2005	B Ryan
1920	D Mc Aleese	1963	W Morton	2006	N Guiden
1921	D Mc Aleese	1964	W Morton	2007	N Guiden
1922	D Mc Aleese	1965	W Morton	2008	N Guiden
1923	CF Rothwell	1966	W Morton	2009	N Guiden
1924	CF Rothwell	1967	W Morton	2010	N Guiden
1925	CF Rothwell	1968	W Morton	2011	N Guiden
1926	CF Rothwell	1969	W Morton	2012	N Guiden
1927	CF Rothwell	1970	CCG Brennan	2013	N Guiden
1928	CF Rothwell	1971	HP Cooney		

HONORARY TREASURERS 1886 – 2013

1886	J Ingram	1929	TE Nolan	1972	CCG Brennan
1887	J Ingram	1930	TE Nolan	1973	CCG Brennan
1888	J Ingram	1931	AJ Wisdom	1974	CCG Brennan
1889	J Ingram	1932	AJ Wisdom	1975	CCG Brennan
1890	J Ingram	1933	AJ Wisdom	1976	J Davis
1891	J Ingram	1934	AJ Wisdom	1977	D Noonan
1892	J Ingram	1935	AJ Wisdom	1978	D Noonan
1893	GF Walker	1936	AJ Wisdom	1979	D Noonan
1894	GF Walker	1937	AJ Wisdom	1980	D Noonan
1895	GF Walker	1938	AJ Wisdom	1981	T Collins
1896	PJ Lonergan	1939	AJ Wisdom	1982	T Collins
1897	JF Lonergan	1940	AJ Wisdom	1983	T Collins
1898	JF Lonergan	1941	AJ Wisdom	1984	F Mansfield
1899	JT Graham	1942	AJ Wisdom	1985	F Mansfield
1900	SJ Coates	1943	AJ Wisdom	1986	F Mansfield
1901	SJ Coates	1944	AJ Wisdom	1987	M Kearney
1902	A Christie	1945	AJ Wisdom	1988	M Kearney
1903	A Christie	1946	AJ Wisdom	1989	M Kearney
1904	PJ Howlin	1947	M Mc Stay	1990	M Kearney
1905	PJ Howlin	1948	M Mc Stay	1991	G Finnegan
1906	PJ Howlin	1949	AJ Wisdom	1992	M Kearney
1907	PJ Howlin	1950	M Mc Stay	1993	M Kearney
1908	J Mc Dermott	1951	M Mc Stay	1994	N Keane
1909	J Mc Dermott	1952	M Mc Stay	1995	N Keane
1910	J Mc Dermott	1953	M Mc Stay	1996	N Keane
1911	A Christie	1954	AJ Wisdom	1997	N Daly
1912	JJ Higgins	1955	AJ Wisdom	1998	N Daly
1913	CR Rothwell	1956	AJ Wisdom	1999	N Daly
1914	TE Nolan	1957	AJ Wisdom	2000	N Daly
1915	TE Nolan	1958	AJ Wisdom	2001	N Daly
1916	TE Nolan	1959	AJ Wisdom	2002	N Daly
1917	TE Nolan	1960	M Mc Stay	2003	N Daly
1918	TE Nolan	1961	M Mc Stay	2004	N Daly
1919	TE Nolan	1962	M Mc Stay	2005	N Daly
1920	TE Nolan	1963	W Morton	2006	N Daly
1921	TE Nolan	1964	W Morton	2007	N Daly
1922	TE Nolan	1965	W Morton	2008	N Daly
1923	TE Nolan	1966	W Morton	2009	N Keane
1924	TE Nolan	1967	W Morton	2010	P Tuite
1925	TE Nolan	1968	W Morton	2011	P Tuite
1926	TE Nolan	1969	W Morton	2012	P Tuite
1927	TE Nolan	1970	T Collins	2013	E Murray
1928	TE Nolan	1971	T Collins		

THE MORTON MILE

Yvonne and Billie Morton alongside Ronnie Delany, Paddy Marley and Noel Daly
at 2012 Morton Mile.
Holding Billy Morton Trophy is race winner Will Leer (USA) whose winning time was
3 min 56.39 sec.
Courtesy of Eamonn Smith.

Amateur 1 Mile World Records.

4 min 55 sec	J. Heaviside	(GB)	Dublin	1.4.1861.
4 min 46 sec	M. Greene	(GB)	Dublin	27.5.1861.
4 min 33 sec	G. Farren	(GB)	Dublin	23.5.1862.
4 min 18 sec	W. George	(GB)	Birmingham	21.6.1884.
4 min 17 sec	T. Conneff	(IRL)	Boston	26.8.1893.

The earliest recorded "professional" world record was 4 min 28 sec run by Charles Westhall (GB) in London on 26 July 1855. On 23 August 1886 Walter George (GB) ran a new world record of 4 min 12.75 sec in London.

Since official IAAF records began for this event in 1913, when American John Paul Jones ran 4.14.40 a total of 23 different athletes have had the privilege of holding the world record for the mile. They have come from 10 different countries. Great Britain top the list with 6 followed by USA (4), New Zealand (3), France, Sweden and Australia (2 each) while Finland, Tanzania, Algeria and Morocco have 1 each.

The shortest time the record was held was Steve Ovetts 3.48.40 on 26 Aug 1981 in Koblenz which was broken 2 days later when Sebastian Coe ran 3.47.33 in Brussels. The longest standing record is the current one (3.42.13) set by Hicham El Geurrouj in Rome on the 7th July1999. This record was set on the same day that Niall Bruton won that year's renewal of the Morton Mile.

The magical mile has for decades been the centre feature of many athletic meetings both local and international. In 1944 the record was less than 2 seconds away from the 4 minute barrier and when World War Two ended and competition resumed there were a number of athletes from various countries striving for immortality. One of the greatest of these "contenders" was Irishman John Joe Barry from Ballincurry in County Tipperary who was a member of Clonliffe Harriers.

When the club began to stage major athletic meetings in Lansdowne Road in the late 1940s and early 1950s John Joe was often the central figure and tens of thousands came to watch him race against the best runners from around the globe. The mile was one of the main events and Barry was among the fastest in the world at the time. Many commentators felt that he would be the one to break the magic barrier but this honour eventually fell to Roger Bannister in May 1954.

After Barry retired, another Irishman Ronnie Delany began to make a career for himself on the indoor circuit in America, where he was also being coached by Jumbo Elliott at Villanova. Indeed it was Billy Morton who persuaded Ronnie to run his first competitive mile which he duly did in an Irish record time of 4.05.80 at the Clonliffe International in August 1955. When Ronnie won the 1500 gold medal in Melbourne in 1956 Billy knew he had his latest big star for the legendary Clonliffe Meetings. When the club built their new cinder track at Santry Ronnie was the main attraction at the opening meeting in June 1958. In August of that year, just 3 years after his first race over the distance, and in front of over 20,000 people Delany competed against the crack Australian and New Zealand athletes in what was, at the time, the greatest mile race ever run.

Following on from Barry and Delany, yet another young star miler was beginning to make a name for himself in the Black and Amber vest. Frank Murphy had set numerous schools records in the mid sixties. Twice 1 mile (1966/67) and three times 1500 metres (1969/70/71) champion of Ireland, Frank came within the proverbial "whisker" of winning the European 1500 metre title in Athens in 1969 where he took the silver medal. Three months later Ireland's "Mr Athletics" passed away. To commemorate Billy and his long and successful association with the mile, the club donated the Morton Trophy and initiated the Morton Memorial Mile.

The first staging was at the Clonliffe International sports on Monday 10th Aug 1970 and even Billy himself could hardly have assembled a more high class line up. Top of the list was then current Olympic 1500 metres gold medallist Kip Keino and Marty Liquori the then USA 1500 metres champion. Marty, at 19 years and 1 month was the youngest ever athlete to compete in an Olympic 1500 metres final when he ran against Keino in the high altitude of Mexico City in 1968. Clonliffe were very strongly represented by European silver medallist Frank Murphy, future club captain and president Paddy Marley and rising young star Tom Gregan.

The line up was as follows :
1. F. Murphy   Clonliffe Harriers
2. P. Riordan   Leevale AC
3. J. Dooley   DCH
4. B. Geraghty   UCG
5   R. Power   Limerick
6. T. Gregan   Clonliffe Harriers
7. P. Marley   Clonliffe Harriers
8. K. Anderson   Sweden
9. K. Keino   Kenya
10. A. Kupczyk   Poland
11. S. Waskiewiez   Poland
12 M. Liquori   USA

The first three across the line were :
Kip Keino   3.59.20
Frank Murphy   3.59.30
Marty Liquori   4.02.10

Start of first Morton Mile at Santry in August 1970.
P Riordan (Leevale), T Gregan (CH), B Geraghty (UCG), P Marley (CH), F Murphy (CH),
R Dixon (NZ/USA).

The following year Frank finished second again, this time to AAA 1500 champion Tony Polhill but ahead of future world record holder and Olympic 5000 silver medallist Dick Quax of New Zealand. The 1981 renewal saw Steve Scott become the only person to win 3-in-a-row when he beat Sydney Maree and the up and coming Dave Taylor. This race was also notable for the fact that Eamon Coghlan lost one of his shoes 450 metres from the line but still managed to break 4 minutes while finishing in seventh position. Coghlan went on to repeat his 1975 win with another victory in 1983.

Financial considerations over the years meant that the Morton Mile did not always take place. Sometimes it featured as part of an international event or was part of a domestic competition including Dublin county board meetings, Donore International Sports and indeed on occasions as a club race. In recent years, however, Clonliffe Harriers have endeavored to hold a stand alone track and field meet with the Morton Mile as the feature event. In 2008 a very successful international meeting was held to mark the fiftieth anniversary of Herb Elliott's world mile record which attracted top class international athletes. The Morton Mile was won on that occasion by Rob Myers (U.S.A.). In more recent years the race has been won by Will Leer (2010/2012) and Jordan McNamara (2011). To mark its 125th anniversary the club promoted the Clonliffe 125 Track and Field Grand Prix. A highly successful International track and field meeting called the Morton Pre-Games took place on the 25th of July 2012 which featured athletes from 16 countries as well as 15 Olympic bound athletes. The highlights included an exciting Morton Mile won by the 2010 Champion Will Leer in 3.56.39 with ten athletes running sub four. A women's International mile was won in a new stadium record of 4.30.65 by Nicole Schappert (USA). Another new stadium record was set in the Albert Thomas mens 3000m by Ben True (USA) when he ran 7.44.40.

It is the intention of the club to continue with an annual international Track and Field meet not only to commemorate the legacy of Billy Morton but to provide top class competition for Irish and International athletes.

Morton Memorial Mile Winners

1970	Kip Keino	Kenya	3.59.20
1971	Tony Polhill	New Zealand	4.00.70
1975	Eamon Coghlan	Donore Harriers	4.02.10
1976	Frank Murphy	Clonliffe Harriers	4.04.54
1977	John Walker	New Zealand	3.52.76
1978	Steve Ovett	England	3.55.70
1979	Steve Scott	U.S.A.	3.56.26
1980	Steve Scott	U.S.A.	3.53.80
1981	Steve Scott	U.S.A.	3.54.70
1983	Eamon Coghlan	Metro	3.53.48
1985	Frank O'Meara	Limerick	3.58.64
1986	Marcus O'Sullivan	Leevale	3.58.50
1987	David Taylor	Clonliffe Harriers	4.01.00
1988	Tommy Moloney	Thurles	4.05.53
1991	Enda Fitzpatrick	Dublin City Harriers	4.03.77
1992	Bobby Farren	Sparta	4.15.10
1999	Niall Bruton	Clonliffe	4.01.36
2002	James Maranga	Kenya	4.00.78
2003	James Nolan	Tullamore Harriers	3.57.70
2004	James Nolan	Tullamore Harriers	3.59.99
2005	Youcif Abdi	Australia	4.01.40
2006	Johan Cronjie	South Africa	4.00.80
2007	Mitch Kealy	Australia	3.58.40
2008	Rob Myers	U.S.A.	3.56.20
2009	Mark Thompson	U.S.A.	4.01.20
2010	Will Leer	U.S.A.	3.56.80
2011	Jordan McNamara	U.S.A.	3.56.80
2012	Will Leer	U.S.A.	3.56.39

THE 2 MILE INVITATION RACE

The Clonliffe Invitation is the oldest club road race in the world and is just one year younger than the Boston marathon which itself is the oldest city marathon in the world. It was first held in 1898 as a "run-in" from The Half Way House Ashtown to the corner of Charleville Road, in Phibsborough, a distance of 2 miles 297 yards. These races would probably have been watched by an 8 year old John Costello, who lived on Charleville Road at this time, and who later went on to become Attorney General to the first free state government and subsequently became Taoiseach on two occasions (1948-1951 and 1954-1957). In 1899 it was held over a course from the entrance gates of the Domville Demense in Santry to Millmount avenue in Drumcondra, a distance of 1.5 miles. The original course was again used in 1900. From 1901 the two mile distance was established when the race started at Floods pub in Finglas village and finished at the Turret (4 O'Clock Gate) at Glasnevin Cemetary.

Tommy Burton Trophy

In 1909, 1910 and 1912 there were 103 competitors which at the time was an Irish record for the number of competitors in a road race. This record was surpassed when 117 turned out for the 1923 renewal. The 2011 race had no fewer than 158 competitors and was won in fine style by David Fitzmaurice of Clonliffe with fellow clubmen Gary O'Hanlon third and Ian Guiden fifth. Ian was also first junior athlete home.

The early years of this race were dominated by Frank Ryder. In 1908 at the age of 18 years he made his club debut in the event. The field of 68 contained 3 internationals and Ryder was hoping to be the first novice home. To everyone's amazement, including Frank's, he won the race after a thrilling battle with three Irish internationals JJ Doyle, Tom Downing and P Buckley. It was the sensation of the day in Irish athletics and the start of Frank's prolific career. Every year from 1908 to 1919, he won the race and his time of 8 min 34 sec set in 1912 stood as a course record for 36 years.

In 1946 Jack Peelo, a club member who had emigrated to the United States in 1904 and brother of Joe, donated the Peelo Cup to be presented to the winner of this race. It was won outright in 1949 by J Mc Guigan of Donore. In 1958 exactly 60 years after he joined Clonliffe and the race was first run the club committee purchased the Tommy Burton trophy to commemorate the man who had been captain for 41 years.

The trophy was a fitting tribute to the man who had initiated the Clonliffe International Sports and who had overseen all the great successes during the first 60 years of the clubs existence.

In 1986, the centenary year of Clonliffe Harriers, sponsorship of this race was taken up by Eugene Kavanagh the current owner of the Gravediggers pub where the race first finished in 1901. Eugene is the third generation of his family to operate this establishment which was also the home of Clonliffe Harriers from 1903 to 1932 and he very generously continues to sponsor the race to this day.

The following accounts of the race are from two different eras in the history of the event and present a picture of the times in which they were staged. The 1909 report describes the weather, the different modes of transport used by the spectators and the "run out" from Glasnevin to the start line at Floods in Finglas. By the time of the 2011 renewal all of the green field lands around Broom Bridge and Finglas Woods had been subsumed into suburban housing estates and competitors were transferred by car directly to the start line at Floods.

Clonliffe Harriers Invitation Race
27th November 1909

The above club brought off on Saturday one of the most successful invitation races held in recent years, from their headquarters, Kavanaghs, Old Gate, Glasnevin.

The rain which fell during the day, luckily cleared off before 3 o'clock, and it was only on the score of early darkness setting in, that any fears existed about the event being brought off on time. Dublin University Harriers wrote, regretting their inability to attend, as they have an engagement near at hand with Edinburgh University.

The muster of 103 runners is the largest that has ever been assembled for an invitation race in Dublin, Clonliffe Harriers turning out 53, Donore 15, City and Surburban 20, Leinster Harriers 5 and Vegetarians 10. There was a large muster of followers of the game, and many old enthusiasts were noticed among the crowd.

As the pack wended it's way from headquarters, the runners were accompanied by sporting enthusiasts on outside cars and tandem bikes for a portion of the outward journey on the road, whence the runners cut into the fields, and cars etc. making straight for upper Finglas to witness the race proper from the starting to the finishing point, at the turret at Glasnevin Cemetary (city end).

Heading off from Kavanaghs Old Gate in 1930s

The pack, paced by T.Burton (capt) followed the trail laid by E.Betts(vice-captain) and H.Egar, over heavy country by the canal to Broom Bridge, King James Castle and Finglas Wood. They entered Upper Finglas shortly after 4 o'clock and lined up opposite "Floods" for the run-in.

Mr.T. Graham despatched the runners to a capital start, the avalanche of colour down the hill being immediately headed by J.Mc Dermott (Clonliffe), who, for the second year, set a cracking pace.

The leaders shortly after leaving Finglas Village were Buckley, Doyle and Downing (City and Suburban), Millington (Donore) with Ryder and Betts (Clonliffe) about 40 yards behind and about 20 yards ahead of the remainder, who were running en masse. At Finglas Golf Club pavilion Ryder came up behind the leaders, with Buckley doing most of the pacing, and Betts and Milligton and now Harris (City and Suburban) forming the connecting link with the pack. Passing the entrance to the Lovers Walk, the order of the leaders was Ryder, Buckley, Downing and Harris. This order remained unchanged until the trying Violet Hill was reached. Some pundit on a tandem shouted that Ryder was faster than Deakin's time at this stage, and as Ryder increased his pace up the hill, the car drivers had to urge on the horses to keep up with the race.

At the top of the hill Ryder had a lead of 40 yards from Harris, and at the entrance gate he started to sprint home in vigorous style, leaving Harris with every stride. He won a magnificent race by 80 yards in the record time of 8 mins 38.4 secs, thus lowering J.F. Deakins (Clonliffe) record of 9 mins and 5 secs which had stood since 1901.

The winner, who has established himself as a great favourite among followers of the sport, came in for a great reception and the result was hailed with a burst of cheering. Previously, Ryder had scored many successes as a boy pedestrian, but acting on the advice of a friend, he took to running, and, gifted with youth, (for he is but 19 years) speed, and stamina to a high degree, he should soon develop into a runner of considerable merit. Sporting events of this nature have become far too rare in Dublin in recent years, and this was the view of many of the spectators, whom formed the interested and enthusiastic crowd that witnessed the finish of this time honoured race, at the Four O'Clock Gate of Glasnevin Cemetary. From the athletes standpoint, this grand old pastime would be given further stimulus, if similar events were promoted by the other Metropolitan Harriers Clubs, and it would eventually benefit them, by creating a larger interest in the sport for their members, as well as affording a possible means of enlarging their active membership roll.

A vote of thanks with acclamation was passed to Mrs. Mc Dermott, who very kindly distributed the medals to the successful runners, and the occasion was availed of to present C.V. Cross with the club gold medal, suitably inscribed, for the best attendance in the club runs during 1908-9.

"Fitzy" wins Clonliffe 2 Mile Invitation (16 June 2011)

Race report filed by club Hon Sec Noel Guiden.

On a perfect night for a road race Clonliffe Harriers hosted the Clonliffe 2 on the traditional Finglas to Glasnevin route finishing outside the Grave Diggers. This year's Clonliffe 2 was an integral part of the Club's 125th celebrations and fittingly the race had its biggest turnout of athletes in many a year. What was particularly notable about last night's race was the number of Clonliffe singlets on the road as the event received tremendous support from the Club members. There was a substantial number of male and female runners representing seniors, juniors, masters and indeed coaches – Messrs. Carr & McDonald take a bow!

Mick Kearney had done a fantastic job in organising the event, with the 160 or so starters being sent on their way at 8.00 p.m. precisely from Finglas Village, down the dual carriageway, past the cemetery – which looked tempting and then swinging left into Prospect Square to finish outside Kavanagh's – which looked even more tempting! The leaders needless to say took off like the proverbial bat out of hell down the hill reaching the first mile in 4 min 25 sec. The front group included the great Vinny Mulvey of Raheny Shamrocks making a very welcome return to this race, and Clonliffe men Dave Fitzmaurice, Gary O'Hanlon and Ian Guiden. On the long uphill section Guiden was dropped as Dave Fitzmaurice applied the pressure, with Mulvey and O'Hanlon hanging on to him. It was then whittled down to Fitzmaurice and Mulvey with young Fitzy prevailing to take a popular win for the host club. Vinny Mulvey was 2nd, as he works his way back towards full fitness. Gary O'Hanlon for Clonliffe came in 3rd with Rathfarnham's Paul Fleming overtaking Ian Guiden to clinch 4th place.

In the Ladies race, Clonliffe had a clean sweep with Ailish Malone, Louise Reilly and Tara Whyte respectively filling the first three places. First Junior Man was Ian Guiden and 1st Junior Woman, also of Clonliffe, was Lorna Begley. Clonliffe also took the mens and womens team races. It is also worth noting that the competitors in the race included 3 generations of the Kavanagh family (Eugene is the race sponsor). The post race presentations and celebrations continued afterwards in the Gravediggers where another great Clonliffian occasion was enjoyed by all. Clonliffe Harriers would like to pay tribute and thank Eugene Kavanagh for his continued sponsorship of this race which began in the club centenary year and has continued unabated for the past quarter of a century. We would also like to thank the members of An Garda Siochana for their presence and assistance in the hosting of the race. Congratulations are also in order to race director Mick Kearney and his team for an excellent event and in particular Clonliffe Harriers would like to thank you the athletes for supporting this famous race in such large numbers.

Clonliffe Invitation Race Winners

1898	P.J Lonergan	Clonliffe Harriers	
1899	F. Curtis	Haddington Harriers	
1900	F. Curtis	Haddington Harriers	
1901	J.E. Deakin	Clonliffe Harriers	9 min 1 sec
1903	H. Muldoon	Haddington Harriers	
1907	F. J. Buckley	Haddington Harriers	
1908	F. J. Ryder	Clonliffe Harriers	8 min 41 sec
1909	F .J. Ryder	Clonliffe Harriers	8 min 38 sec
1910	F. J. Ryder	Clonliffe Harriers	8 min 43 sec
1911	F. J. Ryder	Clonliffe Harriers	8 min 43 sec
1912	F. J. Ryder	Clonliffe Harriers	8 min 34 sec (course record)
1913	F. J. Ryder	Clonliffe Harriers	8 min 45 sec
1914	F. J. Ryder	Clonliffe Harriers	8 min 44 sec
1915	F. J. Ryder	Clonliffe Harriers	9 min 01 sec
1916	F. J. Ryder	Clonliffe Harriers	8 min 45 sec
1917	F. J. Ryder	Clonliffe Harriers	8 min 36 sec
1918	F. J. Ryder	Clonliffe Harriers	9 min 06 sec
1919	F. J. Ryder	Clonliffe Harriers	8 min 46 sec
1920	B. H. Bingham	Clonliffe Harriers	8 min 54 sec
1921	W. Kinsella	Clonliffe Harriers	8 min 51 sec
1922	J. Conaghan	Dublin City Harriers	8 min 38 sec
1923	P. O'Callaghan	Harps A and CC	8 min 46 sec
1924	C. C. Walker	Clonliffe Harriers	8 min 53 sec
1925	G. N. Walker	Clonliffe Harriers	8 min 44 sec
1936	JJ O'Connor	Fearons	8 min 38 sec
1938	E. Jones	Civil Service	8 min 56 sec
1943	E. Jones	Civil Service	8 min 45 sec
1945	P. Haughey	Brownstown	8 min 59 sec
1946	W. Powell	Dublin University	8 min 50 sec
1947	J. Mc Guigan	Clonliffe Harriers	8 min 35 sec
1948	J. Mc Guigan	Clonliffe Harriers	8 min 24 sec (beats Ryders record of 1912)
1949	J. Mc Guigan	Clonliffe Harriers	8 min 31 sec (3rd win he takes J Peelo cup outright)
1952	J Dougan	Donore Harriers	8 min 34 sec

1953	J. Dougan	Donore Harriers	8 min 27 sec
1954	J. Dougan	Donore Harriers	8 min 26 sec
1955	F White	Avondale	9 min 11 sec
1956	P. Melhorn	Civil Service	9 min 07 sec
1957	F White	Avondale	9 min 08 sec
1958	B. Messitt	Donore Harriers	9 min 03 sec
1959	J. Mc Loughlin	Donore Harriers	9 min 19 sec
1960	M. Connolly	Donore Harriers	9 min 18 sec
1961	M. Connolly	Donore Harriers	8 min 57 se
1962	T. O'Riordan	Donore Harriers	8 min 53 sec
1963	T. O'Riordan	Donore Harriers	8 min 54 sec
1964	J. Mc Namara	Donore Harriers	9 min 06 sec
1965	J. Mc Namara	Donore Harriers	9 min 03 sec
1966	T. O'Riordan	Donore Harriers	8 min 57 sec
1967	J. Mc Namara	Donore Harriers	9 min 12 sec
1968	J. Mc Namara	Donore Harriers	9 min 01 sec
1969	E. Spillane	Donore Harriers	8 min 51 sec
1970	T. Gregan	Clonliffe Harriers	9 min 09 sec
1971	J. O'Reilly	Avondale	9 min 06 sec
1972	D. Mc Cormack	Clonliffe Harriers	9 min 10 sec
1973	F. Murphy (jnr)	Clonliffe Harriers	9 min 04 sec
1974	F. Murphy (jnr)	Clonliffe Harriers	8 min 58 sec
1975	F. Murphy (jnr)	Clonliffe Harriers	8 min 55 sec
1976	J. Kiernan	Clonliffe Harriers	8 min 39 sec
1981	N. Harvey	Clonliffe Harriers	8 min 40 sec
1983	N Byrne	Donore Harriers	8 min 51 sec
1984	E. Curran	Clonliffe Harriers	8 min 56 sec
1985	B Horgan	Clonliffe Harriers	8 min 45 sec
1987	R Mulligan	Clonliffe Harriers	8 min 33 sec
1989	B. Downey	Kildare	8 min 48 sec
1990	N Bruton	Clonliffe Harriers	8 min 42 sec
1991	D Wilson	Annadale Striders	8 min 41 sec
1992	N Cullen	Clonliffe Harriers	8 min 32 sec
1995	N Cullen	Clonliffe Harriers	8 min 50 sec
2002	K. Lonergan	Clonliffe Harriers	8 min 44 sec
2003	I. Kimuge	Kenya	8 min 57 sec
2004	P. Fleming	Rathfarnham AC	9 min 12 sec
2005	P. Mc Namar	Athenry	9 min 16 sec
2006	D. Byrne	Tallaght	9 min 32 sec
2007	S. Ciobanu	Clonliffe Harriers	10 min 33 sec
2008	P. Fleming	Rathfarnham	9 min 36 sec
2009	A. Bailey	Clonliffe Harriers	9 min 20 sec
2010	P. Fleming	Rathfarnham	9 min 30 sec
2011	D. Fitzmaurice	Clonliffe Harriers	9 min 04 sec

Heading out from Glasnevin to start of Club 2 mile in 1940s.

Heading out from Glasnevin in 1940s to start of Invitation Race.

A FEW CLUB STINGS !!

Since its foundation in 1886 Clonliffe Harriers has not only produced athletes of all abilities within the sport, it has provided not only competitors at all levels. We have provided administrators etc

Those listed below are some of the famous people who helped to make the club what it is to-day. Their contributions were not only in thletic contests but also as administrators, coaches and advisors, over the decades. Also listed are the names of personalities who achieved fame in other walks of life but had connections with the club.

Don Appleby
One of the most prolific athletes in Clonliffe history, Don won 5 National Inter Club team gold medals in a seven year stretch from 1949-1955. He won the individual title in 1949 and was a silver medallist in 1952/54/55. He was selected on the Irish team for the International Cross Country on nine occasions.

Don was a perennial winner and was habitually followed home by Gerry L'Estrange who never won a title at any distance but who accumulated no fewer than 29 runner up medals. At 1943 nationals Don had to cycle to a race in Naas because of petrol rationing. Gerry had got petrol through political contacts and told Don "To-day I'm afraid you are going to have to take the runner up medal" However Don duly won the race on the last lap.

He was on the Irish team along with John Joe Barry at the world Cross Country Championships at Baldoyle in 1949.

Pat Boone
Famous American singer of the 1950/60 era ran in a Clonliffe Sports as part of a USA relay team.

Cathal Brugha
Born on 18 July 1874. He was an Irish revolutionary who fought in the rising and the war of independence. Cathal ran under his English name Charlie Burgess "for security reasons". He was a member of a Clonliffe Senior Cross Country team which included George Frazer Walker. The family lived on Richmond Road the original home of Clonliffe Harriers. He presided over first meeting of Dail Eireann in Dublin's Mansion House in 1919 during which he became the first person to publicly read the Irish Declaration of Independence. Was Minister for defence from April 1919 to Jan 1922 and was also the first Ceann Comhairle. Died on 7 July 1922 during the civil war as result of fighting near O'Connell St in Dublin.

B.H. Bingham

Graduate of TCD. Died around 1970. He won the National Senior Cross Country title in 1921. He took the individual silver in 1923 and bronze in 1925. Clonliffe won team gold in both these years. In 1921 he finished 3rd in the world cross country championships and led Ireland to the team silver. He finished 18th in 1925 when Ireland again won silver.

GN Walker and C Walker were also on this team.

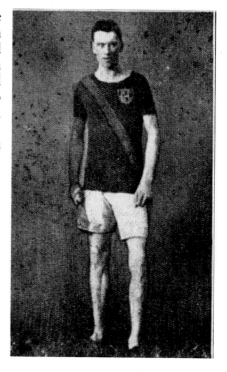

BH Bingham.
Irish CC Champion 1921 and multiple
Irish International.

Michael Byrne

He was one of a group of young athletes which included, among others, Gerry Brady, John and Martin Greene and Derek Carroll who had success at under age level and went on the enjoy many great days in the Black and Amber. Michael was a member of the team which won the National senior XC title in Kilmacow in 1984. He also finished third in the Dublin City Marathon in 1983. Just like fellow Clonliffe man John Mc Donnell in the 1960s, "The Prince" subsequently moved to the United States where he took up a career in coaching. His apprenticeship was served at Iona College where he remained for 24 years. His time there began with the college regularly finishing outside the top 30 at The NCAA Cross Country. In his last five years they had 4 top five finishes. He moved to Wisconsin in 2008 and has only finished once outside the top four. He finally realised his dream when the Badgers took top honours in 2011. Mick is a renowned and very highly regarded coach on the American collegiate circuit and no doubt will see more success in the years ahead.

Patrick Joseph Byrne

Born in Magheracloore Co Monaghan in 1875. Patrick worked in various jobs including solicitors clerk and also in the auctioneering business. He competed in the 880 yards championship of Ireland in 1895 but was unplaced. In 1896 he won the title, leading from gun to tape in a time of 2 min 02 sec. The following year he placed 3rd in the same event.

He was captain of Clonliffe in 1894/5/7/9/1900 and1902.

Patrick J Byrne.
Irish half mile champion 1986.
Club Captain 1894/1902

Chris Cariss

Chris's first run for Clonliffe was at the Nationals in Belfast in 2008 where he scored on the National Senior Cross Country winning team, he followed this up by scoring in 2009 and again in 2010 – three national team medals in a row. Raised in England but with a mother from Waterford Chris came into contact with Clonliffe through a family connection with former president and long serving member Colm Brennan. However satisfying these wins were for Chris it is a miracle that he was able to actually compete in this or any other sporting event. Below, in a letter to the author, is his abbreviated account of a tragic day in Bradford in 1985 and a miraculous day for the Cariss family.

" It is only quite recently that I have been able to talk about the fire.

The match was the final game of the season, in which Bradford City had won the third division championship. It was therefore supposed to be a day of celebration, and it was being shown on local TV. In 1985 my dad owned a fruit & veg shop and on match days my mum used to work in the shop so dad could take my brother Karl and myself to the football. My mother is a sports fan, so whilst in the shop she would tune in to the radio and listen to the match commentary.

Given that the match was on TV and radio people all over Yorkshire could see and hear what was going on. Of course mobile phones were not available back then so many families could only watch and/or listen in horror at the events. I attended the game with my dad Tony, my brother Karl and my Grandad (from Waterford) John. My Grandad watched the match from a small terrace enclosure, which was just to the side of our seats, so we couldn't see each other during the game. The stand was actually due to be demolished after the game. I think it was built in about 1903 and had stood for some 80 years. It took just four minutes for the whole stand to be engulfed in flames. Then we saw people flowing on to the pitch near to the corner flag. The smoke was getting thicker and thicker and my dad decided we better move. The smoke was becoming a real problem and dad grabbed both Karl and me by the scruff of the neck and we made our way to the exit at the back of the stand. This was a mistake as the gates at the back were locked. At this point it was total panic. A man jumped over a fence and landed right on top of me squashing me in the process. I was 10 at the time and in the confusion my dad lost his grip on me. My dad managed to find me and pick me up but by now the situation was becoming desperate. He pushed us out at the back of the stand in between the turnstiles and a door that someone had managed to force open. I can't remember the exact place of my escape due to fact that I could not see because of the smoke. My brother got out just before me and once outside I turned around and the whole roof was on fire. People where running around all over the place, in total panic. My dad must have followed us out at some point. It was the following day before the family were re-united and I had no idea if my father was dead or alive. He never spoke about that day until shortly before he died in the autumn of 2010.

Sadly two children at my school perished, along with their father. In total 56 people died and in excess of 250 people were injured"

During the final months of his fathers life Chris gave up work to look after the person to whom he owed his own life. The bravery of a father on that terrible day in 1985 has, in its own way, made its own contribution to the winning of three national championships for Clonliffe.

Timothy J Carroll

Cleared 6ft 5in (1.94m) at RIC Sports in Kinsale in 1913. This Irish record stood until broken by Brendan O'Reilly in 1954. Carroll won Nationals in 1912-13-14 and 1919. He was a Wasp until 1923 when he moved to Great Britain and joined Polytechnic Harriers.

Sergiu Ciobanu

The following report appeared on the club website in August 2010. "Great news from Longford this afternoon where Sergiu Ciobanu confirmed his status as the most prolific marathon runner in the country with yet another victory. Cork, Belfast, National, Connemara, Longford, Bogtrotters (Strokestown) to name but a few and now yet again another victory in Longford in a time of 2.29.29". His winning time of 2 hr 25 min in Cork in 2010 was a course record. Since arriving in Ireland from his native Moldova Sergiu has blazed a trail in the Black and Amber across the fields and roads of Ireland. He has been equally prolific on either surface and this is borne out by his two National marathon titles (2009/10), six inter club team golds (2007/13) as well as the individual gold at the 2013 National cross country championships. At the Rotterdam marathon in 2012 Sergiu ran a personal best time of 2.15.26 which left him a tantalising 26 sec outside the Olympic qualifying time for London but happily it was inside the time required for the 2013 World Championships where he will represent his country. He has become one of "the lads" in Clonliffe and he describes attending training sessions "like going home".

Sergiu Ciobanu
National Senior CC Champion 2013

Harry Cooney

Harry was one of the legendary Clonliffe men who joined in 1928 and served the club both as a competitor and as an administrator for well over 60 years. He was Hon Sec from 1935 to 1939. In 1947 he succeeded Tommy Burton as club captain and held that position for 19 of the following 21 years, before retiring in 1968. He was a member of the Clonliffe team which won the Dublin Junior title in 1935 alongside Sam Gray, Billy Morton, and Joe Foley. Harry was National marathon champion in 1953 and 1955, the year he set an Irish record. He was also a member of the teams which won four National Cross country titles in the early 1950s. He was a truly dedicated Clonliffe man who was to be seen around the club 7 days a week and made himself available to members young and old. He was one of the inner circle who were responsible for purchasing the lands at Santry and building the stadium.

Harry Cooney wins 1955 Irish marathon title in 2.33.20

Harry was one of the instigators of the ladies section and acted as their captain for the first 4 years. Along with Noel O'Rourke he supervised their training and organised many of their club events as well as travelling with them to fixtures throughout the country. He believed that athletics was there to be enjoyed, and that the club was the mainstay of the sport. To this end he introduced cross country and track and field leagues based on handicapping. A first class handicapper, his idea was to encourage athletes to take part in all events and by using this method everyone had a chance of winning.

The annual Christmas cake race was Harry's idea and his wife Mary made the cake each year, some years making 2 cakes, one for the ladies and one for the men.

Fausto Coppi
World famous Italian Cyclist who won the Giro, Tour De France and World C/ship competed against Shay Elliott on the cycle track at a Clonliffe Sports in 1959. Every Irish Italian Chip merchant turned up for that race.

Martin Crosby
A prominent member of Clonliffe Cross Country teams in the 1940's and 1950's Martin was a well known entertainer for several decades and was the brother of well known teacher Paddy, who was famous for his "School Around The Corner" radio and TV programme. Martin played a number of film roles and was stand-in for Richard Burton during the filming of "The Spy Who Came In From The Cold" which was filmed in Dublin in 1965.

Noel Cullen
Noel was the outstanding club runner of his era. Between 1989 and 2001 he made 13 appearances on Clonliffe Inter Club CC teams which included no fewer than 9 top ten finishes including a bronze in 2000 and 2 silver medals in 1996 and 1999. At the 1993 championships in the Phoenix Park he became the 10th Wasp to win the individual gold. He was only the second athlete, after Donie Walsh, to win individual gold, silver and bronze at the national Cross Country. Noel was equally successful on the road and can count wins in the DCH New Years day 10K, the Rathfarnham 4 mile and the streets of Galway 8K among his many victories. He has run under 48 mins for 10 miles on the road and has also represented Clonliffe and Ireland at the European Inter clubs CC, the European Cup track and field and the world Cross Country Championships.

Noel Cullen

Jack Deegan

At 94 years young Jack, who joined in the 1940s at the end of the Burton era, is the longest living member of Clonliffe. He was a prominent committee man for several decades and was closely associated with all developments during the first 50/60 years in Santry. During his active years he was to be seen officiating at Clonliffe sports meetings as well as national and international events promoted by the organising bodies of athletics in Ireland. Jack was also a long time member of management committees in the AAU, BLE and the AAI and was involved in the negotiations which finally brought about full unity in Irish athletics. He was a member of the inaugural management committee of the newly formed BLE in 1967. Along with Louis Vandendries he was responsible for setting up Tissot and Omega leagues.

Jack Flynn, Jack Deegan and Sam Gray
at 1986 Invitation Race in Kavanaghs

Michael J Dolan

Was a member of club cross country teams during the early part of the 20th century. He was an Abbey actor and later became director of the theatre. He played in many of the famous plays of the early years of the Abbey alongside legendary actors like Eileen Crowe and FJ Mc Cormack.

He wrote to Lady Gregory in 1925 advising her that it was inadvisable to stage an upcoming play by Sean O'Casey called "The Plough and The Stars". When the play premiered in 1926 it resulted in a major riot by the audience over its contents. One of the characters in the play was a prostitute. After similar riots about JM Synge's "Playboy of the Western World", it prompted WB Yeats, a director of the Abbey, to take to the stage and declare : "You have disgraced yourselves again. Is this to be the recurring celebration of the arrival of Irish Genius"?

Sam Gray

One of the Clonliffe "lifers" Sam joined in 1928 and had a very distinguished career in the famous "wasps" vest, winning several club cross country races as well as representing his country in the international championships. He was the undoubted king of the country when it came to club handicaps. His first appearance in the top four was his 3rd place finish in the 1931 running of the Doran Shield. For the next 15 years his record reads :

Irwin Cup	7 fastest times	11 top 4 finishes
Doran Shield	8 fastest times	9 top 4 finishes
Horan Cup	8 fastest times	11 top 4 finishes
O'Connor Cup	5 fastest times	4 top 4 finishes

In a further example of Tommy Burton's expertise in "knowing his man" Sam only got his name on the Irwin Cup and the Doran Shield once, and the Horan Cup twice. Sam did however, through these victories, amass one of the largest collection of Clonliffe gold medals in Clonliffe history. At the national cross country championships Sam finished 6th in 1937 and 1938, 5th in 1939 and 1940 and 3rd in 1943. Unfortunately these were lean times on the team front and Sam never added an inter club medal to his collection. He did represent Ireland at the world cross country in 1938 and 1939. The Second World War meant this event was postponed and Sam's career was over by the time it resumed. He did however continue to serve Clonliffe and Irish athletics for the rest of his life and was a member of the inner circle which purchased the lands at Santry and built the world famous stadium. Sam served as club president from 1952 to 1963 and in his later years was a highly respected member of the club whose company and advice was much sought after.

Noel Guiden

Joined in the early 1980s and was a regular member on Cross Country teams. While his own athletic career did not reach the stellar heights of some of his contemporaries Noel has been one of the main driving forces behind the club's most recent successes. Since becoming Honorary Secretary in 2006 he has overseen many new innovations including the Brother at Your Side schools cross country. This event, very generously sponsored by Brother sewing machines, attracts well over 1000 male and female athletes from 8 to 18 years of age to Santry every October. He has also been responsible for obtaining the very significant and much appreciated sponsorship of Hireco Trailer Rentals which has played a major part in the continued success of club athletes in all age groups and disciplines. Noel is a partner in Behan and Associates Legal Cost Accountants who are also a major club sponsor. To quote the man himself…"as if I had'nt enough to do" he also coaches the club juvenile athletes which not only involves managing training sessions but also the endless task of attending competitions up and down the country as well as following Clonliffe teams as they represent Ireland in European club competitions. It was under his stewardship that Clonliffe won their first ever National Track and Field Club title in 2008 and this has put extra pressure not only on club finances but also on time resources. Noel however has never shirked in any of his duties and is a fitting successor to people like Tommy Burton and Billy Morton who have kept the club at the very top of Irish Athletics. Indeed Clonliffe were the first winners of the Athletics Ireland Club of the year award in 2008. Despite all these accolades and achievements his proudest moments to date have probably been watching the progress of his son Ian graduate from the juvenile ranks to recently being honoured with an Irish under 23 vest.

Cub Hon Sec Noel Guiden pictured with Eamon Coghlan, Eileen O'Keeffe and Ronnie Delaney at launch of Morton Games.
Courtesy of Sportsfile

Noel Harvey

One of the leading lights in what many regard as the golden age of Irish athletics over the past 50 years, Noel arrived up in Santry as a 13 year old in 1974. He was influenced and encouraged by many of the older members in particular Laro Byrne, Padraig Keane and Paddy Marley. At 16 years of age he competed in his first 20 mile road race but lack of heavy milege told on him that day.

While he ran well during his first few years, it was not until he was 18/19 that he began to "come out of the pack".

He went to Trinity College and despite failing to get one of the first Cospoir sports grants, Noel proceeded to regularly beat all before him on the Inter Varsity circut setting records at 5000, 10000 and steeplechase.

In 1981 Laro "included" Noel on the Irish team alongside fellow clubman and Clonliffe legend Danny Mc Daid for the Mallusk cross country race near Belfast.

In a field that included Steve Ovett and was won by Barry Smith of England, Noel ran a blinder, beating Danny in the process.

That same year he made his first appearance on the Clonliffe cross country team and over the next 8 years he collected no fewer than 6 team medals (3 gold and 3 silver).

During these years the standard of competition in the club and throughout Ireland generally was very high. Training sessions were very tough and if athletes were to succeed they too had to be very tough and many adopted a "no prisoners" approach to their training and racing. There was a single minded approach to their sport and no distractions were tolerated.

Feb 1986.
Noel Harvey wins National Senior Cross Country at Santry in club centenary year.
Photo by B Tansey

In 1986, the club centenary year, the national Inter Clubs Cross Country Championships were staged on Clonliffe's home ground in Santry.

In a never to be forgotten afternoon, Noel, who was only ranked as our number 3 man, ran one of his greatest races to come out of the pack in the last mile and take the individual title. To cap it all, he also led Clonliffe to the team gold.

He regards his run in the following years European Clubs as his best at this event.

In 1981(Madrid) and 1983 (Gateshead) Noel was selected on the Irish team for the world cross country championships.

Throughout the 80s Noel was a regular winner both as an individual and as part of club teams which won many national titles on the road, on the track and in the country. At the Cork City Sports in 1986 he ran the 5000 metres in 13 mins 38 secs, which at the time ranked him in the top ten and currently ranks him 29th in the Irish all time best performances for the distance.

In September 1986, he emigrated to the United States to complete his post graduate studies and while there he competed with great success in all distances on the road. He travelled all over the country and one of his more "notable" events was the Sacramento marathon, where he was in the lead at 19 miles, hit the wall at 20, walked the final 6, and still finished in 2 hrs 21 mins

Noel ran his last race in 1990, and is currently living in Galway where he lectures in Business studies at GMIT. He was one of the iron men of Clonliffe and Irish athletics and this is exemplified in the bare fact that he never once failed to complete a race. He still runs 5 miles every morning at 7am and has not missed a day for several years.

Despite all his many successes, at national and international level, Noel says his greatest memories are of being with his fellow Clonliffe clubmen, whether in Ireland or abroad at European club competitions.

Fred "Mattie" Hewson

Born in Dublin in 1917, Mattie went to school in Synge Street where one of his classmates was multiple Irish high jump champion Dick O'Rafferty of Donore Harriers. He joined Clonliffe in 1933 and remained a lifelong stalwart of the club for over 40 years. A shop manager for General Distributors Ltd, Mattie was, along with his fellow Wasps, one of the founder members of the Irish Amateur Athletic Union when it was set up in 1937. Along with TJ Miller of Donore Mattie was responsible for setting up the graded meetings in the early 1950s which are still in existence to-day. This was a major innovation in club athletics as it allowed everyone from the "novice" to the top club runner to compete at the same meeting. Standards were set for each grade so that when a competitor achieved the standard they were "promoted" to the next highest level. In addition it allowed athletes compete at different levels in different events so for example an athlete could be grade A in 200 metres but only grade C in the high jump. This system allowed many "ordinary" level athletes to compete against people of the same ability but incentivised them to raise their own standard and compete at a higher level. It has stood the test of time and over 60 years later is still as popular as ever. More than anything else Mattie was Billy's right hand man and probably spent more time with him than any of his fellow club members. He served as club President from 1968 to 1971.

Padraig Keane

The man from Ballinlough in county Roscommon is one of the best loved people not only in Clonliffe but in all of Irish athletics. As a teenager he tasted success in junior road races at locations as diverse as Ballyhaunis, Swinford and Sligo. This was in the days before multinational sports conglomerates and high tech shoes and Padraig likes to relate the story of how he won these races wearing brown suede shoes ..."Elvis had his blue suede shoes and I had my brown suede shoes".

Padraig leads them out at Quinlan Cup in Tullamore

In 1970 he was introduced to Laro and joined Clonliffe on the same day as Gerry Finnegan, yet another of the baby boomer breakthrough brigade of the 1970s. Padraig recalls his first club race in Santry as " Incredible. I was running against 5 Irish internationals including 1 Olympian, all from the one club". It did not take long for Padraig himself to make his mark. In 1971 he won the national junior cross country title leading Clonliffe to the team title and Dublin to the inter county championship. In doing so he created what is probably a unique record of winning 3 gold medals in the same race. This victory also made him the first Clonliffe man to win a BLE title. He was selected on that year's Irish Junior team at the world championships in San Sebastian. From then on Padraig became a fixture on club teams at the national inter clubs and road relay championships. He was now racing alongside his fellow baby boomers and when Clonliffe won their first Inter clubs of the modern era in 1976 Padraig, at 24 years of age, was the oldest man on the team. He went on to win 2 more team golds at this event as well as adding 15 Dublin senior and 9 national road relay team golds to his collection. Having made his senior debut at the world cross country in 1972 Padraig was again selected in 1977 when he finished in 21st position in a race won by Carlos Lopez. He won his third and final senior vest in Rome in 1982. In one of his many displays of affection for the club he loves to tell of the day in 1981 in Mullingar when he was on the Clonliffe "B" team which finished second to the Clonliffe "A" team at the road relays. Outside of the championship events Padraig was a regular participant in all the major open races in a career which extended over 3 decades. He was one of the leading athletes in Clonliffe during a golden age of road running and relates how training runs of 10 miles in 53 minutes were classified as "easy". Runs from Santry down through Coolock and Raheny, over the hill of Howth and back to Santry, a distance of 20 miles, were done in 2hr 05mins and classified as "mild". Having won the national vets cross country at the age of 43 Padraig retired from competitive athletics. He does however continue to run on a daily basis. Apart from his athletic endeavours Padraig is a devoted supporter of all club activities and attends all the major races of the current generation. He is undoubtedly the greatest raconteur in Clonliffe over the past few decades. An hour with Padraig in the club bar on the night of a big Clonliffe victory is a better tonic than any doctor could prescribe. He is as much loved in athletic circles outside the club as he is inside and his contribution towards making Clonliffe the top athletic club in Ireland has been immeasurable.

Killian Lonergan

Killian first attempted to join Clonliffe at 9 years of age but was rejected as the club only accepted members of 12 and over at that time. That same year he entered his first 10K race setting himself a target of 40 min. He ran 41 min and this led to his parents encouraging him to join Greenfield AC. This club was subsequently subsumed into Clonliffe and thus began a career in the black and amber which ranks alongside any of those of the past quarter century. In his first cross country race he finished 4th in the under 10 Dublin championships and was on the team which placed 4th in the Dublin 4x100 relays. He later finished 2nd in the National under 17 CC championship and this was the forerunner to a very successful senior career. Killian then pursued an academic career in America but his running was not abandoned and in 1996 he first broke 14 mins for 5000 metres. This time was later improved to 13 min 48 sec in 2002. Following the retirements of many of the leading lights of the Marley and McDermott eras, Killian broke into the senior CC team in 1998 when he was fourth Clonliffe man home in 22nd overall. The team took bronze. Over the following decade he only once finished outside the top ten at the National Senior Inter Clubs CC winning individual bronze in 2006 and taking home 5 gold and 3 team silver medals. These performances also resulted in International vests at the FISEC games in 1991 (a team that also contained fellow Wasps Gary O'Hanlon, Cian McLoughlin and Rory Byrne), the World Juniors in 1993, and the World Senior CC in 2004. He also represented Ireland at the Europa Cup 3000m in 2002.

Killian Lonergan (Mr Statistics)
Bronze medallist at 2006 Nat Snr CC and multiple team medallist.
Courtesy of Sportsfile

In addition to his competitive career Killian has served on the club committee for many years as well as acting as coach to many club athletes and teams. Since 2007 he has been the club statistician and part of his enormous array of information can be found elsewhere in this publication. He has also been part of the team which has compiled the most comprehensive list of Irish athletics statistics ever assembled.

Tom Maguire

Tom Maguire first competed for Clonliffe at a meeting in College Park in 1910. He was Irish Long Jump champion. He subsequently volunteered for service in WW1. Tom took part in running events on the front, which were organised by the Commanding Officer when there was a lull in the fighting. He later won the military medal at Passchendale.

After the war he joined the RIC and when they were disbanded in 1922 he became a coach in Trinity College, where he remained for over 30 years and became a legend in College Athletics. Tom died in 1954

Dan Mc Aleese

Dan was a member of the famous all conquering Clonliffe team of 1914 which won the Irish Southern Counties and national Inter Clubs cross country championships. He was a winner of the Doran Shield and Horan Cup in 1921. Joined the civil service at the foundation of the state and retired in 1955 as head of the Revenue Commissioners. He was succeeded in that post by another "Wasp" Sean Reamonn.

John Mc Donnell

As a young man in his early twenties, John came to Dublin from his home in County Mayo and took up a job driving a bread van and delivering to housing estates on the northside of the city. He lived in Marino, and having a liking for athletics, he joined the Clonliffes. Indeed, he was known to disappear for a couple of hours on a Saturday afternoon when he drove his van into a nearby laneway and did his training on company time!!

John was a very disciplined individual who took his running very seriously and this dedication manifested itself in cross country and track events.He finished 11th in the National Senior Cross Country championship in 1962 and was first Clonliffe man home in 8th place the following year. The club won team silver on both occasions. In 1962 he also won the Irish 1 mile title in 4.09.50 and repeated the win in 1963 in a time of 4.14.90. He also added the 3000 steeplechase title in 1962. In 1963 he won a scholarship to Emporia State College in Kansas where his training sessions are still remembered with fondness by those who survived them.

In his mid twenties John decided to seek his fortune in the United States where he became a six time all American at Track and Cross Country. He coached at New Providence and Lafayette high schools before taking up the job of cross country coach at the university of Arkansas in 1972. He subsequently added the post of track and field coach in 1978.

Over the next 30 years John annexed no fewer than 42 NCAA Championships (19 Indoor Track, 12 Outdoor Track, and 11 Cross Country) to become the most successful coach in the history of American College Athletics. He has coached 23 Olympians over 3 decades spanning six different games including Gold, Silver and Bronze medallists. Although he officially retired in 2008, John still keeps an eye on the activities at the Mc Donnell track at the University Of Arkansas.

Jim Norton

Well known stage actor was also a member. He had a brief "career" as a sprinter before progressing to become one of Irelands top stage and screen actors. He played the role of Bishop Brennan in the Fr Ted TV series and also had parts in Harry Potter and the Chamber of Secrets as well as The Boy in The Striped Pyjamas. On the stage he has won a Tony and an Olivier Award for his part in The Seafarer, an Irish play set in Baldoyle a suburb of Dublin where many Clonliffe Harriers competed many years ago.

Ann O'Brien

A founder member of the ladies section in 1963 Ann went on to become one of the leading lights in Clonliffe and Irish athletics. During a career which spanned over more than a decade she became a true pioneer for her sport in Ireland. Ann stands 2nd in the all time list of National Cross country champions with four straight wins from 1968 to 1971. In doing so she has led Clonliffe to 3 Inter Club titles in 1966/67 and 1970. She has also tasted numerous victories in Dublin senior and Inter County championships. Equally versatile on the track Ann has no fewer than 18 National Senior titles ranging from 400 to 3000 metres. She has also won an Irish high jump title. In October 1965 Ann became the first Clonliffe member (male or female) to break a world record when she ran 9 miles 1133 yards (14,428 metres) in 1 hour in Santry. In 1966 she became the first Irishwoman to break the 5 minute mile barrier when she clocked 4 mins 59.20 sec when winning the AAU title in Santry. Less than an hour later Ann won the 880 yard title in 2min 16 sec. In 1967 in Barry (Wales) Ann donned the Irish vest for the first time where she finished 7th in the home countries International. The following year she was 2nd in the WAAA 1500 metres in 4 min 25 sec. In 1969 she won the same event in 9 min 47 sec which was a British all comers record and the second fastest time ever for the distance up to then. Ann added a third WAAA title in 1970 with a time of 9 min 34 sec.

Ann O'Brien wins 1964 Irish 800 metres title.

1969 also saw her become the first Clonliffe lady to compete at a major track championship when she ran the 1500 metres at the Europeans. Ann ran 4.34.40 to finish 11th in her heat.

Gary O'Hanlon

Joined the club in 2001. Gary was a very successful athlete at schools level and won national titles from 800 to 3000 metres.

After several attempts by Joe Cooper to sign him up Gary finally became a Wasp in 2001. His first breakthrough came when he was a member of the team which won the Inter clubs at Roscommon in 2004. He has been on the winning team in 9 of the last 10 years and was in the scoring four on 3 occasions. His successes at home have seen him compete on a number of teams at the Euro Inter clubs and Gary regards these races as among his most cherished memories. His biggest influences on joining the club were Killian Lonergan and Joe Cooper. In the more recent past Gary has added the marathon and half marathon to his "to do" list and, like his fellow Wasp Sergiu, he has become something of a pot hunter when it comes to accumulating road races. It is not unknown for him to compete in 3 races on a weekend and his tally must now put him at or near the top when it comes to club appearances.

A very much loved Wasp Gary has been known to bring on severe medical palpitations to the club captain at very tense times in the minutes before the start of a big race. One of the most memorable of these incidences was at the Inter Clubs at Santry in 2012 when Gary was missing a shoe 30 secs before the off. Joe managed to locate it. Gary then went on to take the individual bronze in addition to adding yet another team gold.

Joe Peelo

Born in Dublin in 1897 the third youngest of 10 children (5 boys and 5 girls). His father John was a carpenter as were most of his brothers. Joe joined the post office as a messenger boy at the age of 14 in 1911. He not only maintained a detailed diary of his athletic career but also recorded many of his experiences while employed by the post office. He remembers the day at Easter 1916 when he went into the GPO to report for duty and was promptly told to go home without being given any explanation. Joe later recorded in his diary that "some crowd or other" had taken over his work place. As he progressed in his career Joe was later given responsibility for installing telephones. This would have mainly been in business premises or state offices. On one occasion he was called to Dublin Castle to install a phone in the office of Michael Collins The "Big Fella" was in the middle of a meeting and was moving at speed around the room while Joe fitted the apparatus.

Joe joined Clonliffe in 1918 and began a career which ranks him as one of the top Clonliffe runners of his era. He won the last race run under the old IAAA and was on the club team which was the first team to win the senior inter clubs under the NACA in 1923. Joe also holds the distinction of being the only Wasp to appear on Pathe News when he won the 1922 Dublin Juniors at Baldoyle racecourse.

Barry Raftery

Barry was probably the youngest person ever to start "training" in Clonliffe Harriers. As a young boy growing up in 1950's Dublin, Barry lived directly across the road from the Morton Stadium. He is remembered by older athletes as a small boy of 5-6 years of age, playing in the long jump pit. There is at least one record of him being told "stop throwing the sand onto the (cinder) track. I'm trying to run intervals here".

In later life Barry went on to become one of Ireland's most distinguished academics, culminating in 1997 when he became only the fifth person to hold the professorship of Celtic Archaeology at University College Dublin. Before taking up this post, Barry had been visiting professor of European prehistory at universities in Munich, Kiel, and Vienna. In addition he had published substantial works on all aspects of Irish archaeology. He was also a good Clonliffe man and competed in many club races as well as running the first 2 Dublin City Marathons in 1980 and 1981. In April 2010 a Festschrift entitled "Relics Of Old decency" was published. Barry sadly passed away at the age of 65, after a long illness, in August 2010.

Sean Reamonn

Was a prominent club member in the 1930s and 1940s. He competed in all club events and in addition to winning the O'Connor Cup in 1942, he finished 1st in the Horan Cup in 1939 and 1942 as well as being first man home in the "Grand National" for the Irwin Cup in 1934.

He finished 3rd in this race in 1941 and 1942. Sean succeeded his fellow club man Dan McAleese as head of the Revenue Commissioners and following Billy Morton's passing he was responsible for initiating some of the fundraising schemes to help reduce the debt.

Frank (FJ) Ryder

For the sheer breath of his achievements, Frank Ryder was most probably, the greatest athlete in the history of the "Wasps".

Indeed he was one of the greatest and most successful runners that Ireland has ever produced.

He was a champion at nearly all distances from the half mile to 10 miles and was equally proficient over track, road, and cross country, though most of his victories were on the track.

Tommy Burton and Frank Ryder at Clonliffe Sports RDS 1913

He first came to notice in 1904, when at the age of 14, he entered the 1 mile walk for boys under 17 at the Dublin Tramway Sports. Not only did he triumph at his first attempt, he went on to win it 3 times in 4 years, finishing 3rd on the fourth occasion.

Almost inevitably, the legendary Tommy Burton spotted Frank and persuaded him to join Clonliffe and turn his attention to running.

"Give up that walking, it will get you nowhere, you have the legs and shoulders of a distance runner" Tommy told him, " join Clonliffe and we'll make a champion of you in 3 years."

In 1908 at the age of 18 years he made his club debut in the famous Clonliffe 2 mile invitation from Finglas to Glasnevin. The field of 68 contained 3 internationals and Ryder was hoping to be the first novice home. To everyone's amazement, including Frank's, he won the race after a thrilling battle with the 3 internationals JJ Doyle, T Downing and P Buckley. It was the sensation of the day in Irish athletics and the start of Frank's prolific career.

Every year from 1908 to 1919, he won that Invitation race, always from big fields. In 1910 there were 103 starters. His time of 8 mins 34 secs set in 1912 stood for 36 years.

In his 11 years on the circuit, Frank competed all over Ireland and Great Britain.

In 1918 he ran 15 mins 27.80 secs at Lansdowne Road to break the Irish 3 mile record (this was on a grass track with 5 laps to the mile).

Frank was the first Clonliffe man to win the individual Senior CC Title in 1911 and was on many all conquering teams of this period.

Singlet worn by FJ Ryder when winning 1911
Senior CC Championship.

David Taylor
National Senior CC Champion 1987/88

David Taylor

One of the most outstanding athletes to come to the club in the 1980s was Dave Taylor. He first established himself with Dundrum AC at under age when he finished fifth in the National Junior Cross Country in 1978.

He was selected for the Irish team which competed in Glasgow in the same year. At the 1978 Junior Track and Field championships he won the 1500 metres in 3 min 52 sec and it was here that he first met former Clonliffian and then Arkansas coach John Mc Donnell who persuaded both Dave and Frank O'Meara to take up a scholarship with the Razorbacks. In his first year Dave ran 3 min 44 sec to become the fastest freshman on the American college scene. In the 1981 Morton Mile he finished third behind Steve Scott and Sydney Maree and in doing so became the first Irishman to beat Eamon Coghlan at this distance.

It was Frank White who persuaded Dave that his athletic future lay with the Wasps and the move proved to be correct when he finished fifth behind Noel Harvey at the 1986 Inter Clubs. He then went on to win the individual title at Killenaule in 1987 and Ballyhaise in 1988.

His victory at Killenaule in 1987 was also a red letter day for Irish athletics as it marked the first appearance on the national stage of Sonia O'Sullivan when she won her first senior title. Taylor rounded off his Wasps career with a bronze medal at Limerick in 1990. Dave was a very versatile athlete and had as much success on the track and road as he did over the country. He was Irish 5000 metre champion in 1986 in a time of 13 min 50.91 sec and the following year he won the national 1500 metres in 3.47.94.

Eamonn Tierney

Joined in 1975. Early influences included Denis Noonan, Padraig Keane, Paddy Marley, The 3 Gerrys, Peter Mc Dermott, Mick Murphy, The Greenes, Mick Byrne, Martin Treacy.

PBs		
	1500	3.51
	5000	14.07
	10000	29.20
	Half Marathon	64.00
	Marathon	2.16.05

1976	Won National Junior 5000
1979	Won Clonliffe Invitation
1987	5th in Amsterdam and 1st in Glasgow marathons
1994.	Won National marathon

In addition Eamonn won 2 Nat CC team medals and 7 Nat road relay medals as well as several Dublin road championships over 5K, 10K and 10 miles. He competed for Ireland at the world cup marathon in Milan in 1989.

He has the unique distinction of winning the last race on the old cinder track and the first race on the new tartan track in Santry.

George Blennerhasset Tincler

The first Clonliffe member to win an Irish championship. He won the mile title in 1892 (4.39.20) and 1893 (4.33.20). Following these victories Tincler turned professional and ran many races in England and Scotland before moving to America where he became one of the greatest athletes of the late 19th and early 20th centuries.

When he first appeared on a track he set everyone laughing with his peculiar gait. He was tall and lanky with an unusual long neck and sloping shoulders. His awkward gait in which there was a marked role earned him the nickname "The Gander".

He subsequently held the world record for the one, two and three miles. In a time trial in the USA in the 1890s Tincler ran a mile in 4 min 8 sec, a time which stood until broken by New Zealander Jack Lovelock 35 years later. At his peak, he had no equal, and was the greatest mile runner the world of his time had ever seen. Possessed of a puckish sense of humour, he was known to "romp home" well ahead of the field, juggling the corks he sometimes carried to help him keep his hands closed.

In 1897-1898 he won 40 of the 41 races he entered and continued racing until he retired in 1916 at the age of 41. At the age of 48 he ran a mile in under 5 mins for a wager.

This is from article on Tommy Conneff of Clane, who was a famous runner of the late 19th century and won several IAAA championships. reproduced courtesy of "Le Cheile"

In 1896, he turned professional and ran a series of matches with F.E. Bacon at the Old Worchester Oval. In 1897 he met George Tincler over a mile, and although in poor condition and defeated, he forced Tincler to run 4min 15.2sec. He was now thirty one and far past his best. That race settled Conneff who, however, was full of praise for his adversary, saying 'I never knew how to run a mile 'til today. Tincler is the greatest runner I have ever met and I think he is capable of running the mile in 4:10. I ran as well as I ever did and I am satisfied with the result'

Tincler's best mile in a race was against Conneff at Worcester on 21-8-1897 when he clocked 4 mins 15.2 secs, then the 2nd fastest official mile ever behind Walter George's 4 mins 12.3 secs in 1886.

GB Tincler

Tincler, who was the son of a solicitor, had an elder brother Samuel who was a barrister and who acted as part of the defence team for the men who took part in the Phoenix Park murders in 1882.

"Tincler's Path" just off the main road of the Phoenix Park was, for many years, used by many Wasps and other club athletes for interval training.

In 1899, a greyhound named "George Tincler" beat Wild Night, Peregrine Pickle, and Dick Burge before losing to eventual champion Black Fury in the semi final of the Waterloo Cup. "Tincler's" prize money of £15-00 was probably his smallest ever !!!!

Tincler died in Johannesberg SA in Jan 1938 at the age of 62.

Walker Family

This family have a unique association not only with Clonliffe but with Irish athletics itself. The story of their involvement precisely reflects the contribution made by Clonliffe Harriers to the survival of the sport in Ireland. It is probably safe to say that no other family has had the continued association with and success in our sport.

The story began with George Frazer Walker who joined the club in 1893 and was a member of the first Clonliffe team to win a national CC title when they took the junior in 1895. He won individual bronze in the same event the following year.
GF was president of Clonliffe between 1902 and 1907 and again in 1909.

His four sons George Noel, Charles, Albert (Bertie) and Vincent were all members of Clonliffe and made their own contributions to the success of the club.
George, Charles and Albert were members of the 1925 National Senior Cross Country winning team.
George (23rd) and Charles (24th) were on the Irish team which took silver behind England in the International CC championships (the forerunner of the present World CC) at Baldoyle in the same year.
George was on the Irish team again in 1926 and was elected club president in 1936.
Vincent served as club Hon Sec in 1940.

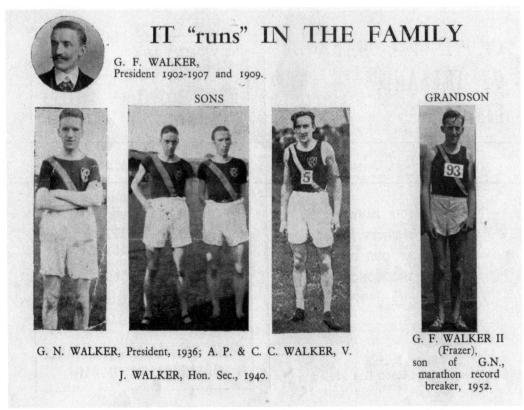

IT "runs" IN THE FAMILY

G. F. WALKER,
President 1902-1907 and 1909.

SONS

GRANDSON

G. N. WALKER, President, 1936; A. P. & C. C. WALKER, V.

J. WALKER, Hon. Sec., 1940.

G. F. WALKER II
(Frazer),
son of G.N.,
marathon record
breaker, 1952.

Three generations of the Walker family.

In 1924, GF had the unique distinction of watching his 3 sons, AP, GN, and CC compete in the Horan Cup 6 miles club handicap.

The trophy was won by AP while GN took third place as well as fastest time.

CC subsequently got his name on the cup in 1928 when he won from scratch and also had the fastest time.

CC (1924) and GN(1925) were also winners of the Clonliffe 2 mile invitation.

The present generation is represented by George Frazer Walker, son of George Noel.

Frazer has continued the remarkable performances of his antecedents. Like his father and grandfather he was on a Clonliffe team which won National CC titles when he was a member of the 1953 Senior team. He was also on Irish teams at the International CC championships in 1955 and 1958. In addition he won the Irish marathon title in 1957,1958 and 1959

Frazer's brother Reggie was assistant Sec to Billy Morton during many of the difficult years when the club struggled to overcome financial challenges during the 1950sand 1960s. While he did not aspire to the great athletic achievements of his brother, Reggie was a loyal servant of Clonliffe and played no small part in the establishment of our home in Santry.

In 1966 the family presented the club with the Walker Cup which is a 4 mile track handicap race run each September. Thankfully it is still taking place and is generously sponsored each year by Frazer.

The Walkers indeed have a long and very proud association, not only with Clonliffe Harriers, but also an unbroken link with Irish International athletics for over 100 years.

OUTSIDE LANE

Quips and Tales By and About Clonliffe Harriers

"Fellow Wasp

In view of the championship next Saturday I shall be glad if you will turn up at Kavanaghs on to-morrow (Tuesday) between 8-15 and 9pm for a rub down".

Letter to Joe Peelo dated 12-2-1923 from Club Captain Tommy Burton.
(Clonliffe duly won the Junior title)

***

Call to arms for the 1923 National Junior CC.

"Fellow Wasps.

The hour of battle is drawing nigh as we are due to meet the opposing forces on the plains of the Phoenix Park racecourse to-morrow in worthy combat for National junior honours. I trust you will put up a fight characteristic of the Clonliffes of the past, who carried the black and amber to victory in this race in 1895 and 1903 and who on each occasion inflicted a defeat on Cork City Harriers.

Words of advice.

Retire to bed early this evening. Let your breakfast be a hearty and substantial one. Have no dinner until after the race, but instead partake of a cup of Bovril (tea or coffee) and toast between 12 and 1pm but not later than 1-10pm. Blacklead your shoes (soles and uppers) well, as this will help to keep them dry during the run".

Tommy Burton 2-3-1923.
(and they won)

***

The final call to battle which saw Clonliffe add the senior team cross country title to the junior.

"Fellow Wasp

The last of our engagements will be fought to-morrow at 3-30 sharp when a stirring conflict lasting nearly an hour will finally establish once and for all, who are the All Ireland senior cross country champions of 1923.

"Stand by our motto – we never despair

E'en when the "crack" from Celbridge is there

He may be a champion, but senior he's not

For he'll never beat Bingham and our little lot"

We shall again prove invincible and complete a wonderful year's work by winning the last of the season's "classics".

Don't miss the last charabanc from O'Connell Bridge at 2-15".

Yours Sincerely
Thomas P Burton (Captain) 23-3-1923.

***

"Clonliffe has always given attention to novices. The secret of turning crocks into cracks is 'A Clonliffe shirt makes all the difference.'"

F.J. Ryder, 7 December 1946.

***

John Joe Barry: "Billy, let's go. I'm ready to join your club."

Billy: "Good. Sign this form and I'll call the boys." (What Billy really meant was a press conference!).

***

"You can do it, man, I know you can. Man, you can run 3.55. If I had you in California for just three months, I could make you the greatest miler in the world."

Mal Whitfield (Olympic 800 metre champion 1948 and 1952) to John Joe Barry.

***

"Cross Country runner would like to meet girl working in laundry."

SPEED DATING (from "Clonliffe News" 1947).
***

"'War will be declared during the track season this summer.' The belligerent individual is the usually mild mannered Captain Paddy O'Hare and the enemy is 'dirty shorts and singlets in open competitions'."

Clonliffe Newsheet May 1950.
***

"I could never train on a Friday as I had to stay home and do the family ironing."

Olive Heaney, one of the founders and captains of Ladies Section.
***

"I say to you young members, 'Don't be misled by people who set themselves up as "coaches". The club has officials from the captain down who will advise you properly. Don't read too many books on athletics because all these would-be coaches are only reading books themselves. Don't join the club and think you will be a Ronnie Delaney in a month. It is no easy road. It takes hard training, plenty of patience, guts and will power.'"

- Billy Morton.

"I say to you young members, 'the future of our club and stadium is in your hands. You are the athletes and officials of the future. Next year our club will be 75 years old and we are already planning the biggest programme ever of athletic and social events to mark this wonderful occasion.'"

- Billy Morton, 1960.
***

"Billy Morton said it was his dream to bring the best athletes in the world to Ireland. As a coach, it is my dream to produce the best athletes here in Ireland."

- Laro Byrne.
***

"The club's action in presenting a Clonliffe gold medal to the popular music singer Dickie Rock is deplorable, and can only be comparable to that of the British Labour Party awarding the Order of Member of the British Empire to the Beatles!"

- Ted Collins, 1966.

***

"So, without expressing any wish or being asked to join the club, I found myself at the age of 15, a member of Clonliffe Harriers as a few days later, I received a demand to pay my subscription!"

- Norman McEachern, Olympian 1924/'28 and Half Mile Champion of Ireland.

***

"P.J. Lonergan of the Clonliffe Harriers, today swam across the bay at Kilkee, a distance of two miles, in 31 minutes!"

Anglo Celt 14 September 1904.

***

"After far too long on the sidelines, I had managed to accomplish an athletic goal first set over 20 years before – to run faster for the 10,000 metres than Emil Zatopek."

- Killian Lonergan on his 10k PB of 28.37.05 in 2007. (Zatopek's world record was 28.54.20)

***

"In case I get a flat!"

- Padraig Keane (when asked by a spectator why he was carrying a spare set of spikes).

***

"The match was poorly attended and both beneficiaries lost cash on it. In addition, our expenses were further increased by two large bottles of whiskey and five bottles of beer being consumed by the match officials."

- Billy Morton (on outcome of fundraiser between Coventry City and Glenmore at Dalymount Park in 1964.)

***

"This is Drumcondra."

> - Opening salvo in phone call from Archbishop's Palace after first Clonliffe ladies race in 1963.

***

Training note to club captain Harry Cooney

The strength seems to have run out of the legs.

You are not really in the dire straits you think you are. Don't let this seeming lack of strength bring on a hypnosis which takes command of your mind as well as your body. Now is the time for the real you to take over with will and determination.

Veto passivness and be more aggressive.

***

"Keep the meetings for Liberty Hall."

> - Joe Cooper (to chattering volunteers building course for European XC, December 2009).

***

"Gary would give you a heart attack. He was always missing a shoe, a sock, or shorts. I often wondered, 'Is he an adult, should I even give him his number?'"

> - Joe Cooper.

***

"His mother reckons there's a full time minder following him around."

> - Joe Cooper (again on Gary).

***

"You know me better than I know myself."

> - Tim Hutchins to Gary O'Hanlon after being given his splits for the last two laps at World CC.

***

"He's the fastest hedgehog I've ever seen."

- Laro' on Padraig.

***

"This Clonliffe team, they are the Kerry of athletics."

Club team being introduced at boiler race in Dundalk.

***

"The new Santry Stadium is a monument to the industry of Billy Morton and his Clonliffe colleagues."

- M. V. Cogley, *Irish Independent*, 1 August 1958.

***

"My friend here is so well known that he needs no introduction from me."

- Billy Morton (when introducing a prominent sports star whose name he had forgotten).

***

"They huddled around the boiler to witness the burning of unmentionable correspondence to a chorus of Nil Desperandum"

(Description of 1960s committee meeting dealing with letters demanding payment !)

***

"My wish for 1966 is that all national sporting associations will commence consideration of all the problems relating to the next Olympics in 1968, whether to do with training, selection, finance or administration."

- Lord Killanin (President IOC 1972-1980).

Lord Killanin at 1956 OG: "Who Won?"
Prince Phillip sitting in front of him: "Your Man."

***

"My wish for 1966? Is there any need to ask me? Somewhere, somehow, the money must be found to pay the debts on Santry Stadium. Somewhere there must be someone who could substantially help the progress of athletics in Ireland. It would be wonderful to get £14,000.00 and clear the debt."

- Billy Morton.

***

"Coming back in the train, at customs in Dundalk, Frank Murphy's copy of The Carpetbaggers by Harold Robbins was confiscated!"

- Tom Quinn, member of All Ireland winning 4 x 110 yards relay title in Belfast August 1964.

***

"If Billy Morton was a blood donor, it would come out black and amber and put into a blood group labelled.."Only for members of Clonliffe Harriers"

Mac in Evening Mail 1959.

***

"What the club offers is a sense of belonging to a family of like-minded individuals, the majority of who desire to escape from the ongoing stresses and strains of life by pursuing a healthy and active lifestyle. For others like myself, the club can become a competitive and dedicated means of reaching goals and with some luck, seeing some of your dreams come true."

- Mary Donohoe (National CC Champion 1986).

***

"Women in shorts upsetting the men of Ireland."

Newspaper headline following one of early ladies Cross Country races.

***

"In the late '60s and early '70s when groups were brought together for International team training, the athletes often knew more than the coaches and the coaches thought they knew more than the athletes."

- Anon.

***

"I am doing my shopping here. Now kindly turn that music off."

- Ted Collins to Leydens C&C staff when purchasing supplies for a
Clonliffe meeting.

***

*"Discus technique was taught by Harry Cooney to the strains of the Blue
Danube Waltz."*

- Anon.

***

"Clonliffe Captain Drops Runner for Walker."

Newspaper headline on selection of Frazer Walker for Club team.

***

"Germany calling, Germany calling !!

*Irish walkers going through Brandenburg Gate. Chinese and Russian walkers
falling back. RTE, lift the censorship of Irish athletics. Over and out"*

-Message left on Jerry Kiernan's answering machine by Padraig Keane who was
at World Championships in Berlin in 2009. Olive Loughnane won silver. Event was
not covered by RTE.

***

*"The dressing room doors kept opening, revealing far too much information
for passers by!"*

- Maurice McCrohan.

***

*"One day I was on the bus to Dublin Airport. I decided to sit on the upper
deck and do some sightseeing. As the bus drove past Morton stadium I saw the
track. The next day I got on my bicycle and cycled from Crumlin to Santry"*

Sergiu Ciobanu (Twice Irish marathon champion and 2013 Inter Clubs Cross
Country champion)

***

A Santry Scandal!

The environs of Santry have distinction, charm and seclusion: it is moreover a high class residential district where I have my house. A few years ago it was subjected to a monstrous inundation of vulgarity, when a gang of skinny thullabawns, who call themselves the Clonliffe Harriers purported to open a stadium there. (Dictionary: "HARRIER – one who harries or pillages, a name for several species of Hawks").

Last Tuesday we carried a report of a "banquet" held to launch a campaign for the building there of a grandstand, seating 2,400 persons and costing £12,000. If this stand is built (complete with money swallowing turnstiles, of course), local residents may look forward to the periodic influx of fruit and ice cream peddlers, conmen, crooked bookies and catpurses. Assaults, robberies and housebreakings will be the order of the day and a recurrent high tide of drunkenness is certain. Some vigorous local action should be taken to confine these harriers to their own localities and make them aware that gentlemen require neither their company nor their physical proximity: still less do they crave the visitations of their bowsie following.

I wish, however, to offer comment on a broader basis. This cult of the body has, around Dublin, risen to the status of a dementia: it is pagan, injurious and evil, almost inevitably, making addicts into morons for life. The ancient philosophers unanimously condemned it, and roundest denunciation of it may be found in the fragmentary Autolycus Of Euripides.

True, many of the primitive athletes such as gladiators or boxers wearing the caestus (a strap affair about the fist containing metal), were not regarded as human beings at all. I would scarcely concede that standing to certain athletes and ball players of today whom I have met and tried to converse with, clearly they have been debauched by so called clubs, promoters and trainers (who themselves train on whiskey). They have been deprived of their minds and the right to earn the living which would otherwise be theirs.

It is quite in order that those in school should be invited to take part in ball games and that sort of thing, since physically, they are in the formative state. It is preposterous, however, that they should continue ball games after they leave school, and think nothing of getting into white knicks when they are already going bald. This grotesque perversion entails prolonging adolescence to 40 and over, remaining preoccupied with childish problems and "competitions" and thinking reluctantly of marriage when 55. It is fashionable nowadays to be concerned with the soundness of the race, this manic devotion to what is called sport is a form of genusuicide. It should be controlled, if not stopped, and ball games in the field sense, should be prohibited absolutely in the universities. I say this because of the disquieting fact that many university chaps who continue playing rugby, take up the study of medicines. Fat good it will do a man with a serious disease to know that his physician is a first-class wing forward.

The continuance of games after leaving school can cause serious moral deterioration. The murderous assaults occurring in the course of GAA games as reported weekly in the provincial press, proves this. It may be true that similar assaults take place in soccer, but soccer is not strictly a game, but a profession, and is to that extent defensible as the occupation of middle-aged and elderly men. Boxing could be defended for the same reason.

I wish I could compile and print here a map of the "sports grounds" which exist in Dublin and district. I think readers would find it staggering and demand to know why such open spaces should not be available as public parks to the Plain People.

Why should soccer, rugby and the GAA have enormous separate enclosures instead of combining to use one?

Lansdowne Road would scarcely do because the lease prohibits playing games there on the Sabbath. Croke Park should therefore be expropriated by law and turned over to a council comprising all codes.

I mentioned moral deterioration. Several decades ago I invented and promoted an event which I called the "Bray Walk". It was a great success, entailing not "sport" but wholesome exercise. Last year the Clonliffe Harriers, without a word to me, or even an invitation to attend, stole this idea of mine and promoted an identical fixture. I can now look forward to the robbery of my orchards at Santry!

> - Lord Santry (aka Myles Na Gopaleen)
> From Cruiskeen Lawn,
> *Irish Times* 1960.

***

III Electrical Retaliation

The Limerick below is taken from, *An Illustrated Collection Of Limericks For Engineers and Physicists* written by club member (Annraoi De Paor, "perfesser" as Morton named him), Harry Power who is Professor of Electrical Engineering in UCD and the founder of the Rehabilitation Engineering Laboratory at the National Rehabiltation Institute in Dun Laoighaire. He was also a co-founder of the Centre for Disability Studies in UCD and has completed extensive work on deep brain stimulation.

When Clonliffe Harriers moved to Santry, the humorist Myles na gCopaleen complained that they were invading the privacy of his estate, disturbing the peacocks on his lawns! Here he plants electrical traps in retaliation.

"At Santry the volatile Myles
Saw runners on top of his stiles.
At the flick of a switch,
They were down in the ditch.
Winked Myles, 'My electrical wiles!'"

(Another Of Harry's outpourings on a 19th century sporting first.)

The world's first wireless coverage of a sporting event, by Marconi himself, was of a yacht race in Kingstown now Dún Laoghaire, 21 July 1898.

"Marconi, perplexed, exclaimed, 'Queer-ah!
This place where my signals came clear-ah,
Was Kingstown, I'd swear
Yachts raced over there
They tell me I'm now in Dún Laoghaire!'"

***

A YEAR IN THE LIFE – BY NOEL GUIDEN

With the turn of the year and before the 2012 action gets underway *clonliffeharriers.com* looks back over the clubs 125 celebration year month by month – 2011 another excellent year in the history of Clonliffe Harriers A.C.

January:

The 125 celebrations kicked off on the 2nd of January with the club cross country championships with over sixty club athletes taking part. The women's 2011 champion was Becky Woods, Senior Men's champion was Lorcan Cronin, master men Phillip O'Doherty and junior men Ian Guiden. January 11th marked the rescheduled inaugural club athletics awards which saw Stephen Harkness being awarded the prestigious Clonliffe Harrier of the year for 2010. At the Dublin Masters Cross Country on the 16th of January Pat Bonass took the O/65 title with Phillip O'Doherty taking bronze in the O/50. On the 22nd of January at the Woodies DIY Indoor Games there were wins for Ciaran Mackey in the 400 metres and Snezana Bectina in the women's 200. At the National Masters Indoor Championships in Nenagh on the 23rd of January Phillip O'Doherty took double gold in the 400m and 800m, George Maybury took O/55 800 silver and 400 bronze. At the Raheny 5 mile on the 30th of January Declan Power was first Master, the same day Keith Pike took Leinster Indoor junior 60m gold.

February:

Brian Gregan was out of the blocks like lightening winning the 400 at the Vienna Indoor Classic in a time of 46.82 and in the process getting the European Indoor QT. The senior men travelled to Milan along with a large travelling contingent for the European clubs cross country in conjunction with the Cinque Mulini, an extraordinary event on a course which literally ran through two mills and a farmyard housing hens, ducks and cattle. The Clonliffe team finished a credible 10th of the twenty-one teams in action led home after a superb performance by Cian McLoughlin in 37th place. At the National Intermediate and Masters Cross Country held the same day at ALSAA there was individual silver won by Pat Bonass in the O/65 race. On the 16th of February Clonliffe played host to the Aviva Irish Schools Leinster Cross Country Championships putting on an excellent Meet which received universal acclaim. On the 20th of February at the National Indoor Championships at the Odyssey Arena, Belfast the club produced two national champions as Dave Donegan retained his indoor pole vault with Ian Rogers 3rd and Brian Gregan taking the 400 title. Marcin Klinkzow took bronze in the high jump with a 2.00m clearance. On the 26th of February Clonliffe played host to the National Cross Country Championships where they again put on an outstanding event which really was a great tribute to the members of the club who turned out in force over the two days to mark the course, act as marshals on race day and produce an event worthy of a National Championships. The event was dominated by DSD who swept the boards winning all four team races. From a Clonliffe perspective there were good performances in particular from Sergiu Ciobanu in 6th place as the team finished 3rd.

March:

Brian Gregan travelled to Paris for the European Indoors but unfortunately he failed to progress to the semi-finals. The club also embarked on a juvenile athletics spring series with Raheny Shamrocks, Skerries A.C. and Lusk A.C. with races in March on the track in Santry, the grass at St. Annes (hosted by Raheny) and finally on the beach in Skerries hosted by Skerries A.C. The other big news in early March was Sergiu Ciobanu winning the prestigious Ballycotton 10 in a PB of 49.37. On the 20th of March at the European Masters Cross Country in Ghent Pat Bonass was on the O/65 Irish team that took silver. The same day young Megan Coomber won the National Juvenile U/16 Indoor long jump. On what was an excellent weekend for Clonliffe Harriers at the New York City half marathon Alistair Cragg set a new Irish record of 60:49 in finishing 6th. There was also a first international vest won by Ian Guiden on the Irish men's junior team taking part in the home countries cross country in Antrim on the 26th of March and on the 27th of March Mark Kenneally won the prestigious Dunboyne 4 Mile.

April:

Andrew Heeney won the U/17 National Indoor title in Nenagh with a winning jump of 1.96. Fionnuala Doherty had a superb win in the Connemara marathon on the 10th of April. On the 14th of April David Flynn got the European U/23 QT at the Mount Sac relays running a time of 8.52.26 for the 3000 SC. Mark Kenneally was on target for the London marathon QT in Vienna until he had a problem with cramping and dehydration finishing in a time of 2:17.22. Also that day, April 17th, the ladies senior team did the club proud by winning the first ladies national team road relay medal for many years with the team of Eleanor Alexander, Becky Woods and Ailish McDermott winning bronze. That same weekend a large contingent of the club's young juvenile athletes travelled to Wales and performed superbly at the Deeside College Stadium.

May:

On the 1st of May Brian McMahon won the Limerick half marathon in a time of 69:46 with Lorcan Cronin 3rd. At the graded meet held on the 4th of May Thomas Rauktys got his season off to a record breaking start by setting a new club shot putt record, while Stateside David Flynn won at conference in the 3000 SC in Colorado. The club's ever popular Grand Prix Series also got underway in May as did the Dublin juvenile league. Gary O'Hanlon took to the roads in May winning the Dundalk half marathon and Kildare half marathons. The club track and field championships again proved to be one of the highlights of the year once again being held in superb sunshine on the 22nd of May in the Morton Stadium with athletes from the juvenile, junior, senior and masters sections all participating. A fantastic day of athletics superbly organised once again by the club captains where once again the highlight was the men's 800 which was won by Stephen Harkness in 1.56.9. The senior men then travelled to Belgrade for the European inter clubs where a weakened team finished in 8th place overall. There were however two club records set by Matt Field in the 110 hurdles and John Fagan in the 400 hurdles.

June:

The month got off to a positive start with the news of David Flynn's selection for the Irish team for the European team championships. On the 6th of June Sergiu Ciobanu won the Cork City marathon. Lorcan Cronin was in 2nd place for all but the last couple of miles when he 'suffered a bad day at the office' finishing 5th. That same day there were medals won by our athletes at the Leinster Championships. Phillip O'Doherty winning 400, 800 and 1500 O/50 gold, John Hartnett winning O/35 400 gold and 200 silver, Stephen Harkness won the senior 800, Conor McCrossan won the 110 H and Keith Pike took bronze in the 100. On the 11th of June at the Diamond League Meet in New York Alistair Cragg finished 8th in the 5000 in an excellent 13.12.21, while on the 12th of June the defence of the national track and field title got off to a solid start in Sligo. Over the course of the same weekend the club's juvenile athletes had considerable success at the Dublin Track and Field Championships where approximately 40 medals were won over the course of the wet weekend in Santry. June 16th was the night of the 120th Clonliffe 2 mile invitation race on the traditional Finglas to Glasnevin course. An excellent race with over 160 starters was led home by Clonliffe's own Dave Fitzmaurice in a time of 9 min 04sec.

July:

At the Cork City Sports on the 2nd of July Pat O'Connor was 6th in the 100 A race and won the 200 B race in a time of 22.72. John Fagan was 4th in the 400 H and Ian Rogers joint 3rd in the pole vault. Over in the UK Matt Field again lowered the 110 hurdles club record with a time of 14.77 sec. There was a most successful outing by our road racers to the Achill Half marathon with Fionnula Doherty winning the ladies race with Tara Whyte finishing 3rd and Marie Byrne 5th. Mark Bermingham was 3rd in the men's race. July 8th was the date of the Clonliffe 125 Track and Field Grand Prix featuring the Morton Mile. An excellent night of athletics was served up in the Morton Stadium the highlight of which was a thrilling Morton Mile won by Jordan McNamara (U.S.A.) in 3:56.83. In doing so he led no fewer than seven athletes under the magical four minutes including for the first time Ciaran O'Lionaird and Paul Robinson. Other highlights on the night included a magnificent sprints double from Jason Smyth (City of Derry), an excellent 3000 metres won by Michael Mulhare and a most entertaining pole vault won by Geoff Coover (U.S.A.) with a vault of 5.3m. A new stadium record of 11.49 sec was set by Amy Foster in the 100 metres and there were also some superb IMC 800 metre races. That same weekend at the National Juvenile Championships in Tullamore there was double sprint gold from Patrick O'Connor U/19 100 and 200 metres, Andrew Heeney 2nd U/17 high jump, Ian Guiden silver U/18 3000m, bronze also for Elaine Begley U/18 300 H and for Simon Galligan U/17 hammer. Manuel Calvo-Curry won gold in the U/18 hammer with gold also for Keith Pike in the U/18 100 metres. Clonliffe athletes Ryan Whelan and Andrew Heeney were selected for the Aviva Irish Schools International. Speaking of internationals there was also of course the small matter of Brian Gregan winning European U/23 silver in a new PB of 46.12! On the 23rd of July the National juveniles saw more success for Clonliffe athletes with Ryan Cleary capturing silver in the U/17 3000 race walk and Ryan Whelan taking U/17 javelin gold by a margin of over 4 metres. The month was rounded off with the news of both Ryan Whelan and Ian Guiden's call up to the Irish team for the Celtic Games to be held at the Antrim Forum.

August:

The month got underway with the news that Keith Pike had also been added to the Irish team for the Celtic Games in the 4 x 100 relay. The National track and field took place over the weekend of the 6th and 7th of August with probably the most successful outcome from a club perspective in many a year. On the opening day Mark Kenneally took a superb National 10,000 metre title while Brian Gregan decided that he would shatter the club 200 metre record, not once but twice lowering the time to 21.09 as he took bronze. Also on day one Tomas Rauktys took silver in the shot putt and Marcin Klinkzow took high jump bronze. The following day the highlight was the 5,000 metres with a Clonliffe one two courtesy of Messrs Cragg and Kenneally. This was followed by an unbelievable 13th National title for Dave Donegan in the pole vault with Ian Rogers again 3rd. Gold also for the big man Tomas Rauktys in the discus. Paul Marry took javelin silver to round off a superb weekend for the club. Overseas Brian Gregan continued his exploits at the world student games in China powering his way into the final with a semi-final win in a new club record of 46 dead. The following day he finished 5th in the final as he went sub 46 for the first time with an incredible 45.98. What a season. Things got better and better from a club perspective when on the 20th of August the men and women's team finished double top in the National League. The men retaining for the fourth year in a row the premier title with some truly inspirational performances whilst an emotional day was completed by the ladies last gasp victory winning the 4 x 400 and in the process winning division one and gaining promotion to the premier. Champagne all round!! The Masters athletes were in action for the National Masters Track and Field where once again Phillip O'Doherty took double gold in the 400 and 800. There was treble gold from Kathryn Walley in the 100, 200 and 400. There were also gold medal performances from Matt Slattery in the 400 and Pat Bonass in the 5000.

September:

At the National half marathon championships the senior men's team of Gary O'Hanlon, Michael McDiarmada and Declan Power finished 2nd. At the world track and field championships in Daegu Alistair Cragg exceeded expectations in making in the world 5,000 metres final where he placed 15th. That same weekend Mark Kenneally ran an excellent 48:15 in a ten mile road race in the Netherlands. Also this month at the world mountain running championships there were very good performances from Clonliffe athletes Brian McMahon and James Kevan on the senior men's team, Sarah McCormack on the senior women's team and Louise Hill-Sterling in the Junior women's team. On the 16th of September there was an unbelievable performance from Alistair Cragg at the Diamond League Grand Prix 5000 in Brussels when he set a new Irish record of 13.03.53. On the 24th of September Louise Hill-Sterling won bronze in the British and Irish mountain running championships in Wales and led the Irish team to team bronze. Fintan Doherty also picked up a team bronze in the boys race.

October:

On the 1st of October the Clonliffe opening run took place. There was also a club photograph taken of an estimated 150/160 club members ranging in ages from eight to ninety as part of our 125 celebrations. The following day Jayme Rossiter won his biggest race to date winning the Dublin novice cross country and leading the men's team of Conor McGuiness 3rd, Brian Tobin 7th and Mark McDonald 8th to the team title. On the same day Mark Kenneally was 4th in the Great Edinburgh 10k road race in a time of 29 min 23 sec.The 12th of October was the date of the third annual Brother at your side Clonliffe Schools Invitational Cross Country. This event has now grown into the biggest Clonliffe promotion currently on the calendar with 1100 athletes taking part in races for primary and secondary schools. There were wins for Clonliffe athletes Ruth Bergin in the primary girls, Morcheen Leonard in the primary boys and Ian Guiden in the senior secondary boys. On the 15th October over 300 hundred past and present members gathered together for the 125th anniversary Gala Dinner in the Crowne Plaza hotel in Santry. A memorable night of reminiscing and celebrating was enjoyed by all as young and old Wasps marked yet another landmark in the history of Clonliffe harriers. The following day in Amsterdam Mark Kenneally reached the promised land as he was 65 seconds inside the London Olympic Marathon QT with a time of 2:13.55. At the Jerry Farnan festival on the 23rd of October there were excellent runs by Brian McMahon, David Flynn, Jayme Rossiter and Dave Fitzmaurice in the men's race while Ian Guiden took the boys U/18 Dublin title as the Clonliffe lads took team silver. Both Declan Power and Pat Bonass were selected for the British and Irish Masters. Later in the month Alistair Cragg finished 3rd in the great south run in Portsmouth in a time of 47:14 whilst at the British Columbia Cross Country Championships in Canada Michael McDiarmada was 7th in the men's race and Becky Woods 10th in the women's race. At the Dublin City Marathon on Oct 31st Sergiu Ciobanu, with a time of 2 hr 20 min 56 sec, was the club's top finisher finishing 2nd having put up a sterling defence of his national title. A great run in this race on his marathon debut from Gary O'Hanlon finishing 5th in the National Marathon in 2:26.3. These two along with Mark Bermingham running a PB of 2:48.47 took the National team title.

November:

Clonliffe hosted the Dublin Cross Country Championships at Santry Demesne on the 6th of November. In the juvenile championships the U/10 girls took team gold with the U/14 boys taking team bronze. In the junior men's race the Clonliffe team finished 3rd. The senior women also took 3rd place whilst the senior men with Dave Flynn 3rd, Brian McMahon 4th, Eoin Pearse 16th, Dave Fitzmaurice 17th, Lorcan Cronin 33rd and Brian Tobin 35th took team silver. At the annual Athletics Ireland awards night on the 12th of November Brian Gregan was named U/23 athlete of the year. The following day the juvenile athletes were back in action at the Dublins in Marley Park with some excellent performances by the U/19 boys team of Ian Guiden 1st, Fintan Doherty 5th, Johnny Bradley-Ward 13th and Eoin McCullogh 14th taking team gold. On the 20th of November the intermediate men picked up team silver at Tymon Park with a fine run by Mark McDonald in 2nd place, David Krinjik was 6th, Brian Tobin 14th and Stephen Harkness 20th. Good news from overseas was the performance of Wisconsin in winning the NCAAs coached of course by Mick 'The Prince' Byrne. The club's annual general meeting took place on the 22nd of November with Paddy Marley being returned as club president. On the 27th of

November the National Inter counties took place on a very difficult course in Sligo. An inspirational run by Gary O'Hanlon in the senior race saw him finish in an excellent 11th place. Superb runs also by Dave Fitzmaurice and Jayme Rossiter. At the end of November the Grand Prix series came to a conclusion with Colm Hickey taking the spoils from long time leader Paddy Tuite with Phillip O'Doherty 3rd. News also of Declan Power scoring on the Irish O/40 team that took bronze and Pat Bonass scoring on the O/65 team that also took bronze at the British and Irish International in Glasgow. The month concluded with the selection of David Flynn and Dave Fitzmaurice on the Irish U/23 for the European cross country championships.

December:

On the 1st of December the club athletes of the year awards took place. The Clonliffe Harrier of the year was Snezana Bectina. The junior athlete of the year was Patrick O'Connor, master athlete Phillip O'Doherty, women's track and field Ciara McCallian, women's cross country Ailish Malone, men's track and field athlete Brian Gregan and men's road/cross country Mark Kenneally. At the European Cross Country in Slovenia Dave Fitzmaurice finished 81st with Dave Flynn 84th on a memorable weekend for Irish athletics as Fionnuala Britain took gold in the women's race. On December 18th a new event took place in the Morton Stadium. The Christmas Cracker 5K was an outstanding success particularly having regard to the challenging weather conditions on the day and in an excellent race Joe Warne (Doheny A.C.) took the spoils from Emmett Dunleavy (Sligo A.C.) with Conor Healy (Clonliffe) in 3rd place. Sara Treacy was a runaway winner of the ladies race. The final events of a very successful Clonliffe 125 were the seasonal Christmas cake races. First off were the juveniles on a rain sodden Morton Stadium on the 20th of December with the U/12 race won by Gavin O'Brien and the girls equivalent won by Ella Bergin. The U/15 boys race was won by Sean Carrig and the winner of the girls race was Sally Aherne. The senior races on the 22nd were won by Roisin Leahy and Mark McDonald bringing the curtain down on 2011.

KILLIAN'S CORNER

The tables listed here were compiled by club statistician Killian Lonergan. While endeavouring to get as much of the information as complete and as current as possible it should be remembered that this project is very much a work in progress. Future updates will be listed on the club website clonliffeharriersac.com

LIST OF NATIONAL CHAMPIONS 1886-2013

Number	Year	Event	Men/Women	Type	Athlete	Performance
1	1892	1 Mile	Men	Outdoor	GB Tincler	4.39.20
2	1893	1 Mile	Men	Outdoor	GB Tincler	4.45.00
3	1896	880 yds	Men	Outdoor	PJ Byrne	2.02.20
4	1901	1 Mile	Men	Outdoor	JE Deakin	4.33.00
5	1901	4 Miles	Men	Outdoor	JE Deakin	20.36.00
6	1903	100yds	Men	Outdoor	JC Healy	12.40
7	1903	220yds	Men	Outdoor	JC Healy	24.40
8	1904	100yds	Men	Outdoor	JC Healy	10.20
9	1904	220yds	Men	Outdoor	JC Healy	23.40
10	1908	3 Mile Walk	Men	Outdoor	JJ Reid	23.11.40
11	1910	220 yds	Men	Outdoor	William Murray	23.80
12	1910	Long Jump	Men	Outdoor	Tom Maguire	6.42
13	1911	100yds	Men	Outdoor	William Murphy	10.20
14	1911	220yds	Men	Outdoor	William Murphy	23.80
15	1911	XC	Men	XC	Frank Ryder	45.47.2
16	1912	880yds	Men	Outdoor	Jim Hill	2.02.00
17	1912	4 Miles	Men	Outdoor	James Murphy	20.25
18	1913	440yds	Men	Outdoor	Jim Hill	57.20
19	1913	880yds	Men	Outdoor	Jim Hill	2.08.6
20	1913	High Jump	Men	Outdoor	Tim Carroll	1.60m
21	1913	Mile	Men	Outdoor	Frank Ryder	4.47.6
22	1913	4 Miles	Men	Outdoor	Pat Flynn	21.59.40
23	1913	Triple Jump	Men	Outdoor	Tim Carroll	12.75m
24	1914	4 Miles	Men	Outdoor	HC Irwin	20.52.8
25	1914	High Jump	Men	Outdoor	Tim Carroll	1.84m
26	1914	XC	Men	XC	HC Irwin	48.59
27	1919	4 Miles	Men	Outdoor	Frank Ryder	21.38.6
28	1919	Mile	Men	Outdoor	Frank Ryder	4.30.4
29	1920	120yds Hurdles	Men	Outdoor	Thomas George Wallis	17.00
30	1920	Long Jump	Men	Outdoor	Sgt Major Miller	6.35
31	1920	XC	Men	XC	Tim Crowe	46.25
32	1921	120yds Hurdles	Men	Outdoor	Thomas George Wallis	16.40
33	1921	4 Miles	Men	Outdoor	HC Irwin	22.31.8
34	1921	440yds	Men	Outdoor	Norman McEachern	54.40
35	1921	880yds	Men	Outdoor	Norman McEachern	2.02.8
36	1921	Mile	Men	Outdoor	HC Irwin	4.38.4
37	1921	XC	Men	XC	BH Bingham	47.43
38	1922	120yds Hurdles	Men	Outdoor	Thomas George Wallis	16.40
39	1922	High Jump	Men	Outdoor	Tim Carroll	1.70m
40	1922	Shot Putt	Men	Outdoor	Michael O'Halloran	11.01m
41	1923	10 miles	Men	Outdoor	BH Bingham	55.43.0
42	1923	56lbs dist	Men	Outdoor	PJ Bermingham	7.88m
43	1923	56lbs over	Men	Outdoor	PJ Bermingham	4.19m
44	1923	Discus	Men	Outdoor	PJ Bermingham	39.06m
45	1923	High Jump	Men	Outdoor	Tim Carroll	1.75m
46	1923	Javelin	Men	Outdoor	Michael O'Halloran	35.99m
47	1924	880yds	Men	Outdoor	Norman McEachern	2.00.6
48	1926	10 miles	Men	Outdoor	BH Bingham	NT
49	1926	880yds	Men	Outdoor	Norman McEachern	1.58.4
50	1927	880yds	Men	Outdoor	Norman McEachern	1.57.6
51	1928	880yds	Men	Outdoor	Norman McEachern	1.59.8
52	1931	100yds	Men	Outdoor	W Burke	10.20
53	1932	100yds	Men	Outdoor	W Burke	10.20

Number	Year	Event	Men/Women	Type	Athlete	Performance
54	1933	10 miles	Men	Outdoor	JJ O'Connor	60.15.2
55	1933	100yds	Men	Outdoor	W Burke	10.20
56	1934	10 miles	Men	Outdoor	JJ O'Connor	57.11
57	1935	10 miles	Men	Outdoor	JJ O'Connor	55.32
58	1935	4 Miles	Men	Outdoor	JJ O'Connor	20.46.0
59	1935	XC	Men	XC	JJ O'Connor	NT
60	1936	Marathon	Men	Outdoor	Billy Morton	2.48.27
61	1938	Long Jump	Men	Outdoor	L Carroll	6.83m
62	1939	100yds	Men	Outdoor	Stan De Lacy	10.00
63	1940	100yds	Men	Outdoor	Stan De Lacy	10.40
64	1940	220yds	Men	Outdoor	Stan De Lacy	23.00
65	1940	Long Jump	Men	Outdoor	L Carroll	6.48m
66	1941	Long Jump	Men	Outdoor	L Carroll	6.57m
67	1946	100yds	Men	Outdoor	Paul Dolan	10.20
68	1947	220yds	Men	Outdoor	Paul Dolan	23.80
69	1947	800yds	Men	Outdoor	JJ Barry	2.06.4
70	1947	Hammer	Men	Outdoor	Maurice Curtin	43.38m
71	1947	Mile	Men	Outdoor	JJ Barry	4.39.4
72	1948	880yds	Men	Outdoor	JJ Barry	1.59.7
73	1948	Mile	Men	Outdoor	JJ Barry	4.32.6
74	1948	Shot Putt	Men	Outdoor	Dave Guiney	14.88m
75	1948	Shot Putt	Men	Outdoor	David Guiney	14.88m
76	1949	3 miles	Men	Outdoor	JJ Barry	14.50.5
77	1949	400yds	Men	Outdoor	Paul Dolan	51.00
78	1949	800yds	Men	Outdoor	JJ Barry	2.06.4
79	1949	Mile	Men	Outdoor	JJ Barry	4.25.1
80	1949	Pole Vault	Men	Outdoor	Maurice Furlong	3.05m
81	1949	Shot Putt	Men	Outdoor	David Guiney	13.50m
82	1950	100yds	Men	Outdoor	Louis Crowe	10.20
83	1950	220yds	Men	Outdoor	Louis Crowe	22.60
84	1950	3 miles	Men	Outdoor	Don Appleby	15.05.7
85	1950	440yds	Men	Outdoor	Paul Dolan	50.00
86	1950	Discus	Men	Outdoor	Ronnie Taylor	40.34m
87	1950	Mile	Men	Outdoor	JJ Barry	4.20.1
88	1950	Pole Vault	Men	Outdoor	Maurice Furlong	3.35m
89	1951	100yds	Men	Outdoor	Ronnie Plant	10.20
90	1951	220yds	Men	Outdoor	Ronnie Plant	23.50
91	1951	Discus	Men	Outdoor	Kevin Healy	38.96m
92	1951	Pole Vault	Men	Outdoor	Maurice Furlong	3.30m
93	1952	100yds	Men	Outdoor	Paul Dolan	10.20
94	1952	200yds	Men	Outdoor	Paul Dolan	22.60
95	1952	440yds	Men	Outdoor	Paul Dolan	49.20
96	1952	Discus	Men	Outdoor	Kevin Healy	39.47m
97	1952	Pole Vault	Men	Outdoor	Maurice Furlong	3.35m
98	1953	100yds	Men	Outdoor	Louis Crowe	10.20
99	1953	3 miles	Men	Outdoor	Frank White	14.49.6
100	1953	Discus	Men	Outdoor	Kevin Healy	38.07m
101	1953	Marathon	Men	Outdoor	Harry Cooney	2.43.15
102	1953	Triple Jump	Men	Outdoor	JJ Higgins	12.87m
103	1954	3 miles	Men	Outdoor	Frank White	14.34.5
104	1954	440yds H	Men	Outdoor	M McGarry	60.70
105	1954	Discus	Men	Outdoor	Kevin Healy	39.31m
106	1954	Shot Putt	Men	Outdoor	Jim Byrne	14.22m

Number	Year	Event	Men/Women	Type	Athlete	Performance
107	1954	Triple Jump	Men	Outdoor	JJ Higgins	13.36m
108	1955	220yds	Men	Outdoor	Gary Dempsey	22.80
109	1955	6 Miles	Men	Outdoor	Don Appleby	32.13.8
110	1955	Discus	Men	Outdoor	Kevin Healy	42.11m
111	1955	Marathon	Men	Outdoor	Harry Cooney	2.33.20
112	1955	XC	Men	XC	Paddy Killeen	52.36
113	1956	220yds	Men	Outdoor	Gary Dempsey	22.50
114	1956	Hammer	Men	Outdoor	Bert Healion	52.70m
115	1957	220yds	Men	Outdoor	Gary Dempsey	23.10
116	1957	440yds	Men	Outdoor	Gary Dempsey	50.80
117	1957	Marathon	Men	Outdoor	Frazer Walker	2.39.58
118	1958	Marathon	Men	Outdoor	Frazer Walker	2.32.42
119	1959	Marathon	Men	Outdoor	Frazer Walker	2.40.47
120	1960	3 miles	Men	Outdoor	Michael Hoey	13.51.0
121	1961	3 miles	Men	Outdoor	Michael Hoey	13.56.0
122	1961	Long Jump	Men	Outdoor	Noel Hoffman	6.81m
123	1962	3000m st	Men	Outdoor	John McDonnell	9.21.6
124	1962	Decathlon	Men	Outdoor	Noel Hoffman	5582pts
125	1962	Long Jump	Men	Outdoor	Noel Hoffman	6.90m
126	1962	Mile	Men	Outdoor	John McDonnell	4.09.5
127	1963	Mile	Men	Outdoor	John McDonnell	4.14.9
128	1964	Long Jump	Men	Outdoor	Noel Hoffman	6.68m
129	1965	100yds	Men	Outdoor	Dan Kennedy	10.10
130	1965	2 mile Walk	Men	Outdoor	John O'Leary	15.02
131	1965	200yds	Men	Outdoor	Jimmy Jordan	23.00
132	1965	Long Jump	Men	Outdoor	Noel Hoffman	6.54m
133	1966	100yds	Men	Outdoor	B Whitney	10.20
134	1966	100yds	Men	Outdoor	Brian Whitney	10.20
135	1966	3k Walk Track	Men	Outdoor	John O'Leary	14.49.6y
136	1966	400m H	Men	Outdoor	F O'Cuinneagain	58.20
137	1966	Mile	Men	Outdoor	Frank Murphy	4.09.2
138	1966	Mile	Women	Outdoor	Ann O'Brien	5.04.2
139	1967	1500m	Men	Outdoor	Frank Murphy	3.50.1
140	1967	Mile	Men	Outdoor	Frank Murphy	4.09.4
141	1967	880yds	Women	Outdoor	Ann O'Brien	2.29.7
142	1967	High Jump	Women	Outdoor	Ann O'Brien	1.40m
143	1967	Mile	Women	Outdoor	Ann O'Brien	5.32.0
144	1968	120yds Hurdles	Men	Outdoor	Paul Griffin	15.60
145	1968	1500m	Men	Outdoor	Frank Murphy	3.45.0
146	1968	Long Jump	Men	Outdoor	Hugo Duggan	6.81m
147	1968	Shot Putt	Men	Outdoor	Gerry Downes	14.81m
148	1968	440yds	Women	Outdoor	Ann O'Brien	59.40
149	1968	880yds	Women	Outdoor	Ann O'Brien	2.12.7
150	1968	Mile	Women	Outdoor	Ann O'Brien	5.04.7
151	1968	XC	Women	XC	Ann O'Brien	13.56
152	1969	110m H	Men	Outdoor	Paul Griffin	15.50
153	1969	1500m	Men	Outdoor	Frank Murphy	3.49.8
154	1969	3000m st	Men	Outdoor	Des McCormck	9.22.2
155	1969	Mile	Men	Outdoor	Frank Murphy	4.01.5
156	1969	100m	Women	Outdoor	Claire Walsh	12.50
157	1969	1500m	Women	Outdoor	Ann O'Brien	4.32.2
158	1969	200m	Women	Outdoor	Claire Walsh	25.40
159	1969	400m	Women	Outdoor	Claire Walsh	56.60

Number	Year	Event	Men/Women	Type	Athlete	Performance
160	1969	800m	Women	Outdoor	Ann O'Brien	2.12.5
161	1969	XC	Women	XC	Ann O'Brien	14.51
162	1970	1500m	Men	Outdoor	Frank Murphy	3.50.4
163	1970	2 Mile	Men	Outdoor	Danny McDaid	9.14.2
164	1970	3000m st	Men	Outdoor	Des McCormck	9.10.8
165	1970	800m	Men	Outdoor	Frank Murphy	1.48.9
166	1970	Long Jump	Men	Outdoor	Hugo Duggan	7.22m
167	1970	Marathon	Men	Outdoor	Danny McDaid	2.22.13
168	1970	1500m	Women	Outdoor	Ann O'Brien	4.38.6
169	1970	200m	Women	Outdoor	Claire Walsh	24.30
170	1970	400m	Women	Outdoor	Claire Walsh	55.40
171	1970	800m	Women	Outdoor	Claire Walsh	2.10.6
172	1970	Pent	Women	Outdoor	Claire Walsh	3837p
173	1970	XC	Women	XC	Ann O'Brien	14.41
174	1971	1500m	Men	Outdoor	Frank Murphy	3.46.4
175	1971	200m	Men	Outdoor	Claire Walsh	24.60
176	1971	400m	Men	Outdoor	Claire Walsh	54.40
177	1971	Long Jump	Men	Outdoor	Hugo Duggan	6.94m
178	1971	Mile	Men	Outdoor	Frank Murphy	4.03.5
179	1971	100m	Women	Outdoor	Claire Walsh	12.20
180	1971	1500m	Women	Outdoor	Ann O'Brien	4.29.8
181	1971	400m	Women	Outdoor	Claire Walsh	54.40
182	1971	XC	Women	XC	Ann O'Brien	14.20
183	1972	15 miles	Men	Outdoor	Danny McDaid	75.24
184	1972	800m	Men	Outdoor	Frank Murphy	1.50.6
185	1972	Long Jump	Men	Outdoor	Hugo Duggan	7.10m
186	1972	Mile	Men	Outdoor	Frank Murphy	4.05.5
187	1972	200m	Women	Outdoor	Claire Walsh	24.60
188	1972	400m	Women	Outdoor	Claire Walsh	55.40
189	1973	100m	Women	Outdoor	Claire Walsh	12.20
190	1973	200m	Women	Outdoor	Claire Walsh	24.30
191	1974	10k Walk track	Men	Outdoor	John O'Leary	49.42.4
192	1974	2 Mile	Men	Outdoor	Denis Noonan	NT
193	1974	20k Walk	Men	Outdoor	John O'Leary	1.34.06
194	1974	5000m	Men	Outdoor	Tom Cregan	14.25.8
195	1974	Marathon	Men	Outdoor	Danny McDaid	2.19.03
196	1974	800m	Women	Outdoor	Padraigin O'Dwyer	2.12.8
197	1975	10k Walk	Men	Outdoor	Tommy Griffin	50.53.7
198	1975	1500m	Men	Outdoor	Jerry Kiernan	3.47.2
199	1975	400m	Women	Outdoor	Padraigin O'Dwyer	56.50
200	1975	800m	Women	Outdoor	Padraigin O'Dwyer	2.07.9
201	1976	20k Walk	Men	Outdoor	John O'Leary	1.42.46
202	1976	800m	Men	Outdoor	Frank Murphy	1.54.2
203	1976	Marathon	Men	Outdoor	Danny McDaid	2.13.06
204	1977	1500m	Women	Outdoor	Jean Appleby	4.22.7
205	1977	3000m	Women	Outdoor	Kathryn Davis	9.24.6
206	1978	20k Walk	Men	Outdoor	John O'Leary	1.36.21
207	1978	XC	Women	XC	Kathryn Davis	17.46
208	1981	10000m	Men	Outdoor	Jerry Kiernan	28.55.9
209	1984	XC	Men	XC	Jerry Kiernan	37.00
210	1986	5000m	Men	Outdoor	David Taylor	13.50.91
211	1986	XC	Men	XC	Noel Harvey	36.20
212	1986	10k Walk	Women	Outdoor	Pamela Reynolds	58.56

Number	Year	Event	Men/Women	Type	Athlete	Performance
213	1986	3000m	Women	Outdoor	Mary Donohue	9.16.06
214	1986	XC	Women	XC	Mary Donohue	17.51
215	1987	1500m	Men	Outdoor	David Taylor	3.47.94
216	1987	XC	Men	XC	Dave Taylor	33.44
217	1987	3000m	Women	Outdoor	Ann Buckley	9.29.45
218	1988	XC	Men	XC	Dave Taylor	41.25
219	1989	10000m	Men	Outdoor	Richard Mulligan	30.14.09
220	1990	10000m	Men	Outdoor	Richard Mulligan	30.06.52
221	1991	20k Walk	Men	Outdoor	Bobby O'Leary	1.23.51
222	1992	5k Walk	Men	Indoor	Bobby O'Leary	19.32.4
223	1992	Marathon	Men	Outdoor	Jerry Kiernan	2.17.19
224	1993	1500m	Men	Outdoor	Niall Bruton	3.50.93
225	1993	XC	Men	XC	Noel Cullen	37.02
226	1993	Half Marathon	Women	Outdoor	Cathy Shum	74.34
227	1994	1500m	Men	Outdoor	Niall Bruton	3.42.27
228	1994	Marathon	Men	Outdoor	Eamonn Tierney	2.27.30
229	1994	200m	Women	Outdoor	Marisa Smith	24.36
230	1994	Half Marathon	Women	Outdoor	Cathy Shum	72.48
231	1995	High Jump	Men	Indoor	Stephen Dowdall	2.03m
232	1995	Marathon	Men	Outdoor	Richard Mulligan	2.27.11
233	1995	60m	Women	Indoor	Emer Haastrup	7.95
234	1996	1500m	Men	Outdoor	Niall Bruton	3.41.68
235	1996	200m	Women	Indoor	Marisa Smith	25.02
236	1997	1500m	Men	Outdoor	Niall Bruton	3.42.77
237	2003	800m	Men	Indoor	Brendan O'Shea	1.55.01
238	2003	Pole Vault	Men	Indoor	David Donegan	4.65m
239	2003	Half Marathon	Men	Outdoor	Cian McLoughlin	66.14
240	2004	800m	Men	Indoor	Brendan O'Shea	1.50.58
241	2004	Triple Jump	Men	Indoor	Michael Wyss	14.43m
242	2004	1500m	Men	Outdoor	Alistair Cragg	3.44.37
243	2005	XC - Short Course	Men	XC	Mark Kenneally	12.12
244	2006	Pole Vault	Men	Indoor	Anthony McCreery	4.60m
245	2006	Marathon	Men	Outdoor	Cian McLoughlin	2.22.37
246	2006	Pole Vault	Men	Outdoor	David Donegan	4.60m
247	2007	Pole Vault	Men	Indoor	Anthony McCreery	4.55m
248	2007	Half Marathon	Men	Outdoor	Sergio Ciobanu	69.05
249	2007	Pole Vault	Men	Outdoor	Anthony McCreery	4.90m
250	2008	Pole Vault	Men	Indoor	David Donegan	4.75m
251	2008	1500m	Men	Outdoor	Colm Rooney	3.58.74
252	2008	Pole Vault	Men	Outdoor	David Donegan	4.75m
253	2009	Pole Vault	Men	Indoor	David Donegan	4.83m
254	2009	10000m	Men	Outdoor	Josphat Boit	29.44.55
255	2009	5000m	Men	Outdoor	Alistair Cragg	13.52.15
256	2009	Marathon	Men	Outdoor	Sergio Ciobanu	2.22.06
257	2009	Pole Vault	Men	Outdoor	David Donegan	4.91m
258	2010	Pole Vault	Men	Indoor	David Donegan	4.85m
259	2010	5000m	Men	Outdoor	Alistair Cragg	14.04.64
260	2010	56lbs dist	Men	Outdoor	Tomas Rauktys	7.89m
261	2010	Discus	Men	Outdoor	Tomas Rauktys	51.68m
262	2010	Marathon	Men	Outdoor	Sergio Ciobanu	2.19.33
263	2010	Pole Vault	Men	Outdoor	David Donegan	4.70m
264	2010	XC	Men	XC	Mark Kenneally	34.37
265	2011	400m	Men	Indoor	Brian Gregan	47.01

Number	Year	Event	Men/Women	Type	Athlete	Performance
266	2011	Pole Vault	Men	Indoor	David Donegan	4.80m
267	2011	10000m	Men	Outdoor	Mark Kenneally	28.58.39
268	2011	5000m	Men	Outdoor	Alistair Cragg	13.48.03
269	2011	56lbs dist	Men	Outdoor	Tomas Rauktys	8.40m
270	2011	Discus	Men	Outdoor	Tomas Rauktys	52.06m
271	2011	Pole Vault	Men	Outdoor	David Donegan	4.70m
272	2012	Pole Vault	Men	Indoor	David Donegan	4.60m
273	2012	3000m st	Men	Outdoor	David Flynn	9.06.58
274	2012	56lbs dist	Men	Outdoor	Tomas Rauktys	8.73m
275	2012	Discus	Men	Outdoor	Tomas Rauktys	53.40m
276	2012	Pole Vault	Men	Outdoor	David Donegan	4.70m
277	2013	200m	Men	Indoor	Brian Gregan	21.33
278	2013	60m	Men	Indoor	Keith Pike	6.92
279	2013	60m H	Men	Indoor	Matt Field	8.20
280	2013	Pole Vault	Men	Indoor	David Donegan	4.60m
281	2013	XC	Men	XC	Sergio Ciobanu	38.26

CLUB RECORDS AT 30.6.2013

MENS OUTDOOR RECORDS

Event	Record Holder	Record	Year	Venue
100m	Alagie Faye	10.79	2007	Donnas
200m	Brian Gregan	21.05	2013	Santry
400m	Brian Gregan	45.53	2013	Heulva
800m	Frank Murphy	1.47.40	1969	New Jersey
1500m	Niall Bruton	3.35.67	1995	Cologne
Mile	Niall Bruton	3.53.93	1996	Oslo
3000m	Alisdair Cragg	7.32.49	2007	Monaco
5000m	Alisdair Cragg	13.03.53	2011	Brussels
10000m	Alisdair Cragg	27.39.55	2007	Palo Alto
Marathon	Jerry Kiernan	2.12.20	1984	Los Angeles
3000s/c	Des McCormack	8.46.20	1970	New York
20K Walk	Bobby O'Leary	1.21.51	1992	Oedonrode
110m H	Matt Field	14.44	2012	Bedford
400m H	John Fagan	52.38	2011	Belgrade
4x100	Mc Hale, Woods, Penco, Regazzoli	41.90	1987	Mardyke
4x400	Laffey, Mackey, Fagan, Gregan	3.14.07	2010	Bern
Shot Putt	Gerry Downes	17.55	1969	Alpine
Javelin	Paul Marry	58.35	2008	Antrim
Hammer	James Russel	63.06	1988	Boston
Discus	Tomas Rauktys	55.77	2013	Dublin
Long Jump	Hugo Duggan	7.20	1968	Santry
Triple Jump	Marco Mattiuzzo	14.45	2009	Dubnica
High Jump	Simon Phelan	2.14	2013	Loughborough
Pole Vault	David Donegan	5.00	2010	Cork

LADIES OUTDOOR RECORDS

Event	Record Holder	Record	Year	Venue
100m	Claire Walsh	11.90	1972	Munich
200m	Claire Walsh	24.10	1973	Cork
400m	Claire Walsh	53.70	1973	London
800m	Claire Walsh	2.03.40	1971	Helsinki
1500m	Jean Appleby	4.19.00	1977	Belfield
Mile	Ann O'Brien	4.51.00	1968	Santry
3000m	Ann K Buckley	9.00.88	1988	Belfast
5000m	Sara Mc Cormack	15.49.03	2012	Bedford
10000m	Mary Donohoe	33.25.32	1993	Rotterdam
Marathon	Cathy Shum	2.38.14	1993	Dublin
3000 S/C	Becky Woods	11.23.40	2013	Cork
100m H	Paula Carthy	14.67	1990	Santry
400m H	Joanne Heffernan	62.61	1990	Santry
4x100	Moore, O'Neill, Walsh, Other	47.30	1973	Santry
4x400	Moore, O'Neill, Walsh, Cummins	3.45.80	1970	Crystal Palace
Shot Putt	Clare Wheeler	9.89	n/a	n/a
Javelin	Denise Byrne	41.89	2013	Tullamore
Hammer	Caoimhe Morris	42.36	2013	Santry
Discus	Caoimhe Morris	35.59	2013	Dublin
Long Jump	Paula Carthy	5.73	1996	Santry
Triple Jump	Fiona Mullan	12.04	1999	Santry
High Jump	Fiona Mullan	1.65	1999	Santry
	Agne Liadova	1.65	2009	Antrim
Penthathlon	Claire Walsh	3837 pts	1970	Santry

MENS INDOOR RECORDS

Event	Record Holder	Record	Year	Venue
60m	Keith Pike	6.92	2013	Athlone
200m	Brian Gregan	21.27	2013	Athlone
400m	Brian Gregan	46.07	2013	Athlone
800m	Frank Murphy Snr	1.51.10	1969	Detroit
1500m	Niall Bruton	3.40.77	1997	Paris
Mile	Alisdair Cragg	3.55.04	2006	Fayetville
3000m	Alisdair Cragg	7.38.59	2004	Fayetville
5000m	Alisdair Cragg	13.28.93	2003	Fayetville
60m H	Matt Field	8.13	2013	Eton
Pole Vault	David Donegan	4.85	2010	Belfast
High Jump	Stephan Dowdall	2.03	1995	Nenagh
Long Jump	Michael Wise	6.75	2004	Belfast
Triple Jump	Michael Wise	14.43	2004	Belfast
Shot Putt	Tomas Rauktys	14.92	2010	Belfast

LADIES INDOOR RECORDS

Event	Record Holder	Record	Year	Venue
60m	Leah Moore	7.61	2013	Athlone
200m	Leah Moore	24.93	2012	Vienna
400m	Marisa Smith	55.40	1996	Birmingham
800m	Claire Walsh	2.07.40	1972	Sofia
3000m	Becky Woods	10.00.32	2011	Nenagh
60m H	Paula Carty	9.20	1990	Nenagh
High Jump	Paula Carty	1.50	1990	Nenagh
Long Jump	Paula Carty	5.39	1990	Nenagh
Triple Jump	Fiona Mullen	12.04	1999	Nenagh
Shot Putt	Paula Carty	8.73	1990	Nenagh

TOP 10 PERFORMANCES(Men)

	100m			110m H			200m	
1	10.79	Alagie Faye	1	14.44	Matt Field	1	21.05	Brian Gregan
2	10.81	Paul Whelan	2	15.39	Jeremy Lyons	2	21.74	Paul Dolan©
3	10.88	Pat Woods	3	15.66	John Fagan	3	21.78	Patrick O'Connor
4	10.89	Daniel Kavanagh	4	15.72	Ian Graham	4	21.97	Chris Russell
5	10.93	Keith Pike	5	15.75	Paul Griffin	5	21.98	Paul Whelan
6	10.96	John Laffey	6	15.79	Conor McGrossan	6	22.02	John Laffey
7	10.96	Patrick O'Connor	7	15.93	Ben McIlroy	7	22.03	Mark Penco
8	11.00	Mark Penco	8	16.15	Chris Minn	8	22.05	Daniel Tobin
9	11.07	Vincent Regazzoli	9	16.27	Conor Keegan	9	22.06	Pat Woods
10	11.12	Paul Dolan	10	16.64	TG Wallis©©	10	22.07	Robert Ryan

	400m			400m H			800m	
1	45.53	Brian Gregan	1	52.38	John Fagan	1	1.47.3	Frank Murphy Sr©
2	47.60	Anthony Foran	2	53.04	Jeremy Lyons	2	1.48.16	Brendan O'Shea
3	47.84	John Laffey	3	54.91	Matt Field	3	1.48.20	Niall Bruton
4	48.35	Daniel Tobin	4	54.93	John Connolly	4	1.49.48	Eugene Curran
5	48.35	Paul Dolan©	5	55.60	John Murray	5	1.49.89	Conor Healy
6	48.62	Ciaran Mackey	6	55.98	Chris Minn	6	1.50.16	Andrew Walker
7	48.90	Robert Ryan	7	56.05	Harry Sydner©©	7	1.50.5	Tom Gregan
8	49.10	Karl Kennedy	8	56.20	Glen Carroll	8	1.50.8	Philip Byrne
9	49.15	Frank Murphy Snr	9	56.61	Terry O'Neill	9	1.50.80	Colm Rooney
10	49.15	Dominic Branigan	10	57.10	Michael Kennedy	10	1.50.81	James Nolan

	1500m			Mile			3000m	
1	3.35.67	Niall Bruton	1	3.53.93	Niall Bruton	1	7.32.49	Alistair Cragg
2	3.36.18	Alistair Cragg	2	3.55.04	Alistair Cragg	2	7.54.62	Niall Bruton
3	3.37.58	Dave Taylor	3	3.56.97	Dave Taylor	3	7.54.70	Jerry Kiernan
4	3.38.5	Frank Murphy Sr	4	3.58.1	Frank Murphy Sr	4	7.54.82	David Taylor
5	3.40.36	Andrew Walker	5	3.58.54	Eugene Curran	5	7.56.92	Josphat Boit
6	3.40.49	James Nolan	6	3.58.96	Andrew Walker	6	7.59.08	Mark Kenneally
7	3.41.9	Jerry Kiernan	7	3.59.12	Jerry Kiernan	7	7.59.81	James Nolan
8	3.42.0	Tom Gregan	8	4.00.60	Tom Gregan	8	8.00.02	Noel Cullen
9	3.42.97	Neville Davey	9	4.01.02	James Nolan	9	8.01.10	Eugene Curran
10	3.43.13	Colm Rooney	10	4.01.11	Neville Davey	10	8.01.2	Frank Murphy Sr

	5000m			10000m			3000m Steeple	
1	13.03.53	Alistair Cragg	1	27.39.55	Alistair Cragg	1	8.46.2	Des McCormack
2	13.27.42	Josphat Boit	2	28.33.12	Mark Kenneally	2	8.49.20	David Flynn
3	13.32.71	Jerry Kiernan	3	28.37.05	Killian Lonergan	3	8.51.4	Noel Harvey
4	13.32.93	Dave Taylor	4	28.50.7	Brian Dunne	4	9.01.6	John McDonnell
5	13.36.22	Noel Cullen	5	28.53.38	Richard Mulligan	5	9.06.8	Brian Dunne
6	13.36.71	Mark Kenneally	6	28.53.64	Noel Harvey	6	9.09.5	Jim Cleary
7	13.38.88	Noel Harvey	7	28.55.9	Jerry Kiernan	7	9.13.38	Cronan Gantley
8	13.46.06	Brian Dunne	8	29.05.6	Gerry Finnegan	8	9.16.04	Paolo Doglio
9	13.47.99	Killian Lonergan	9	29.16.0	Martin Green	9	9.16.16	Jayme Rossister
10	13.49.42	Richard Mulligan	10	29.20.19	Noel Cullen	10	9.20.5	Padraig Keane

	Marathon			High Jump			Long Jump	
1	2.12.20	Jerry Kiernan	1	2.14	Simon Phelan	1	7.38	Hugo Duggan
2	2.13.55	Mark Kenneally	2	2.09	David O'Mahony	2	7.18	Noel Hoffman
3	2.15.27	Sergiu Ciobanu	3	2.06	Stephen Dowdall	3	7.01	Ian Graham
4	2.16.07	Eamonn Tierney	4	2.00	Marcin Klinkosz	4	6.88	Colm O'Neill
5	2.17.12	Danny McDaid	5	2.00	Andrew Heaney	5	6.83	L Carroll
6	2.18.08	Mick Byrne	6	1.95	Thomas Quinn	6	6.78	T Sheil
7	2.18.42	Noel Cullen	7	1.95	Graham Woodcock	7	6.75	Michael Wyss
8	2.18.49	Cian McLoughlin	8	1.87	Hugo Duggan	8	6.72	Philip Moore
9	2.19.46	Chris Cariss	9	1.86	Tim Carroll	9	6.70	R Coady
10	2.20.19	Martin Green	10	1.86	Ian Graham	10	6.67	John Murray

	Triple Jump			Shot Putt			Discus	
1	14.45	Marco Mattiuzzo	1	17.55	Gerry Downes	1	55.64	Tomas Rauktys
2	14.43	Michael Wyss	2	17.28	Tomas Rauktys	2	46.36	Martin Nutty
3	13.65	Aidan Hayes	3	15.65	Martin Nutty	3	45.36	Hugh O'Callaghan
4	13.44	E O'Dwyer	4	15.39	Ronnie Taylor	4	45.36	Brendan Kelly
5	13.41	Tomas Dorina	5	15.05	Luke Mangan	5	43.66	Kevin Healy
6	13.41	JJ Higgins	6	14.92	Dave Guiney	6	42.28	David McDonnell
7	13.41	Alex Anyaegbunam	7	14.60	Jim Byrne	7	41.10	Conor Farron
8	13.28	Ian Graham	8	14.49	Christophe Enjorlas	8	41.03	Ronnie Taylor
9	13.25	Hugo Duggan	9	13.61	Eugene Divney	9	41.00	James Russell
10	13.22	Philip Moore	10	13.09	Kevin Healy	10	40.80	Conor Mulcahy

	Hammer			Javelin			Pole Vault	
1	63.06	James Russell	1	58.35	Paul Marry	1	5.00	David Donegan
2	57.86	Kevin Cardiff	2	57.94	Arthur Pollock	2	4.90	Anthony McCreery
3	57.06	Martin Hunt	3	54.83	Denis Delaney	3	4.80	Ian Rogers
4	54.80	Conor Mulcahy	4	54.10	Marcin Klinkosz	4	4.50	Michal Strzelczyk
5	53.79	Bert Healion	5	53.81	Ryan Whelan	5	4.00	Dirk Feil
6	53.26	Martin Nutty	6	51.65	C Ryan	6	3.96	Michael Kennedy
7	52.61	Christophe Enjorlas	7	48.71	David Guiney	7	3.80	Ben McIlroy
8	52.34	Colm Flynn	8	47.62	N McDermott	8	3.65	Myles Fitzgerald
9	49.82	Paul McCauley	9	45.13	ER Cantwell	9	3.52	Maurice Furlong
10	48.56	David McDonnell	10	44.38	J Travers	10	3.00	Stephen Dowdall

© = Coverted from hand timing
© © = Coverted from hand timing and yards

TOP 10 PERFORMANCES (Women)

	100m			100m H			200m	
1	11.90	Claire Walsh	1	14.67	Paula Carty	1	24.10	Claire Walsh
2	11.97	Marisa Smith	2	15.11	Shauna Furman	2	24.23	Marisa Smith
3	12.02	Leah Moore	3	15.63	Cathy Winters	3	24.59	Leah Moore
4	12.06	Emer Haastrup	4	16.00	Elaine Begley	4	24.67	Emer Haastrup
5	12.25	Emer Diskin	5	16.25	Sarah Doyle	5	25.01	Sophia Ellis
6	12.38	Audrey Farrelley	6	16.32	Aoibhean Kearney	6	25.04	Padraigin O'Dwyer ©
7	12.41	Sharon Kilduff	7	16.34	Jenny Corcoran	7	25.49	Paula Carty
8	12.44	Therese Deeprose ©	8	16.84	Emer Diskin©©	8	25.52	Ciara McCallion
9	12.47	Barbara McDonnell	9	17.04	Claire Walsh©©	9	25.61	Joanne Heffernan
10	12.55	Ciara McCallion	10	17.87	Fiona Mullen	10	25.64	Therese Deeprose ©

	400m			400m H			800m	
1	53.70	Claire Walsh	1	62.21	Joanne Heffernan	1	2.03.4	Claire Walsh
2	54.57	Michaela Monaghan	2	64.20	Paula Carty	2	2.07.6	Jean Appelby
3	54.70	Marisa Smith	3	64.64	Elaine Begley	3	2.07.6	Padraigin O'Dwyer
4	55.30	Padraigin O'Dwyer	4	64.86	Sarah Woods	4	2.09.2	Nicola Fallon
5	55.41	Ciara McCallion	5	66.58	Fiona Scully	5	2.09.9	Jean O'Neill
6	56.46	Joanne Heffernan	6	68.62	Sarah Doyle	6	2.10.3	Ann O'Brien
7	56.90	Geraldine Keogh	7	69.50	Shauna Furman	7	2.10.8	Kathryn Davis
8	57.10	Jean O'Neill	8	69.80	Jenny Corcoran	8	2.11.04	Siobhan Browne
9	57.40	Adrienne O'Hara	9	70.67	Sandra Byrne	9	2.11.3	Anne Buckley
10	57.40	T Moore	10			10	2.11.64	Eleanor Alexander

	1500m			Mile			3000m	
1	4.19.0	Jean Appelby	1	4.51.0	Ann O'Brien	1	9.00.88	Ann Buckley
2	4.20.34	Anne Buckley	2	5.03.8	Jean Appelby	2	9.03.15	Mary Donohue
3	4.20.77	Mary Donohue	3	5.15.61	Emma Cooper	3	9.24.6	Kathryn Davis
4	4.23.61	Patricia Appelby	4	5.18.21	Becky Woods	4	9.29.6	Patricia Appelby
5	4.25.2	Kathryn Davis	5			5	9.34.4	Ann O'Brien
6	4.25.6	Ann O'Brien	6			6	9.34.8	Amanda McAleenan
7	4.26.78	Eleanor Alexander	7			7	9.47.30	Mary Friel
8	4.28.75	Amanda McAleenan	8			8	9.55.0	Frances Nic Reamoinn
9	4.30.90	Becky Woods	9			9	9.57.29	Louise Reilly
10	4.33.69	Louise Reilly	10			10	10.00.32	Becky Woods

	5000m			10000m			3000m Steeple	
1	15.49.03	Sarah McCormack	1	33.25.32	Mary Donohue	1	11.23.40	Becky Woods
2	16.36.13	Mary Donohue	2	34.31.52	Sara McCormack	2		
3	16.51.80	Frances Nic Reamoinn	3	34.38.59	Cathy Shum	3		
4	17.30.4	Ann O'Brien	4	36.06.4	Ann O'Brien	4		
5	17.57.82	Ailish McDermott	5	37.31.20	Louise Hill-Stirling	5		
6	18.04.98	Louise Reilly	6			6		
7	18.07.51	Louise Hill-Stirling	7			7		
8	18.36.0h	Emma Cooper	8			8		
9	18.57.0	Joyce O'Hare	9			9		
10			10			10		

	Marathon				High Jump				Long Jump	
1	2.38.14	Cathy Shum		1	1.65	Fiona Mullen		1	5.73	Paula Carty
2	2.48.02	Ann Archbold		2	1.65	Agne Liadova		2	5.65	Megan Coomber
3	2.50.09	Ailish Malone		3	1.63	Cathy Winters		3	5.58	Mary Davitt
4	2.51.35	Caroline Dobbyn		4	1.53	Claire Walsh		4	5.51	V Murphy
5	2.57.25	Anne Kearney		5	1.50	Aisling Jordan		5	5.43	Claire Walsh
6	2.58.35	Ann O'Brien		6	1.50	Paula Carty		6	5.41	Fiona Mullen
7	3.00.01	Aisling Coppinger		7	1.50	Siobhan Browne		7	5.13	Seanna Reilly
8	3.03.00	Amanda McAleenan		8				8	5.04	Snezana Bechtina
9	3.05.56	Fionnuala Doherty		9				9	4.93	Therese Deeprose
10				10				10	4.80	Debbie Kenny

	Triple Jump				Shot Putt				Discus	
1	12.04	Fiona Mullen		1	9.89	Clare Wheeler		1	35.59	Caoimhe Morris
2	10.80	Orna McGinley		2	9.54	Rachel Callaly		2	29.80	Olive Heaney
3	10.55	Deirdre Mullen		3	9.14	Sinead Hartnett		3	29.79	Frances Mansfield
4	10.32	Aoibhean Kearney		4	9.03	Agne Liadova		4	27.59	Rachel Callaly
5	9.97	Snezana Bechtina		5	8.73	Paula Carty		5	23.46	N Burke
6				6	8.17	H O'Connor		6	22.21	Denise Byrne
7				7	8.02	T Byrne		7	21.71	T Redmond
8				8	7.92	Claire Walsh		8	19.95	Nadine Lattimore
9				9	7.78	P Quinn		9	19.21	Ruth Farrelly
10				10	7.78	Frances Mansfield		10	18.90	Eileen Farrell

	Hammer				Javelin				1500m Walk	
1	42.36	Caoimhe Morris		1	41.71	Denise Byrne		1	7.15.0	Pam Reynolds
2	19.06	Frances Mansfield		2	38.84	Clare Wheeler		2	7.57.4	Ciara Heneghan
3	17.58	Rachel Callaly		3	33.76	Ruth Farrelly		3	8.26.36	Bronagh Ni Bhrian
4				4	26.26	Pamela Cooper		4	8.31.1	A Woods
5				5	26.04	Monica Squires		5	9.45.20	Snezana Bechtina
6				6	25.52	Ursala O'Brien		6	10.11.22	Margaret Perdin
7				7	24.88	Jean Brady		7	10.16.1	Ann Marie Burns
8				8	23.90	J Dunne		8	10.55.22	Kate Purcell
9				9	22.35	T O'Brien		9	11.31.56	Pamela Cooper
10				10	21.79	Ant O'Brien		10		

© = Coverted from hand timing
© © = Coverted from hand timing and yards

INDIVIDUAL WINNERS OF CROSS COUNTRY CHAMPIONSHIPS

SENIOR MEN

1911	Booterstown	Frank Ryder
1914	Dundrum	Herbert C Irwin
1920	Baldoyle	Tim Crowe
1921	Baldoyle	BH Bingham
1935	Thurles	JJ O'Connor
1955	Finglas	Paddy Killeen
1984	Kilmacow	Jerry Kiernan
1986	Santry	Noel Harvey
1987	Killenaule	David Taylor
1988	Ballyhaise	David Taylor
1993	Phoenix Park	Noel Cullen
2010	Phoenix Park	Mark Kenneally
2013	Tullamore	Sergui Ciobanu

SENIOR LADIES

1968	Ann O'Brien
1969	Ann O'Brien
1970	Ann O'Brien
1971	Ann O'Brien
1978	Kathryn Davis
1986	Mary Donohoe

JUNIOR MEN

1955	Noel Jenkins
1962	Richard Burke
1971	Padraig Keane
1973	Jerry Kiernan
1974	Frank Murphy
1983	David Dunne
1993	Derek Walters

WINNING MENS SENIOR TEAMS

1910 - Clonskeagh	Pl	1914 - Dundrum	Pl	1923 - Phoenix Park	Pl	1925 - Baldoyle	Pl
Tom Downing	2	Bertie Irwin	1	Billy Bingham	2	Billy Bingham	3
Frank Ryder	4	Frank Ryder	2	Harry Walters	6	Charles Walker	6
B Parker	6	Sam Pearson	7	William Kinsella	7	George Walker	8
P Kelly	7	Fred Guthrie	12	Joe Peelo	8	Archie Cassidy	17
Sam Pearson	25	Dan McAleese	19	Archie Cassidy	11	???	23
G Johnston	31	John Cronin	25	George Walker	12	???	24
Tommy Burton	37	Charlie Rothwell	28	Charlie Rothwell	13		
J Malone	38	George Wisdom	30	Norman McEnchern	16		
M Wilson	43	C Gross	32	C Kenna	25		
Charlie Rothwell		William Barden	36				
C Gross		Tommy Burton	40				
JJ Higgins		J Monaghan	43				
J Quigley							

1952 - Garristown	Pl	1953 - Finglas	Pl	1954 - Finglas	Pl	1955 - Santry	Pl
Don Appleby	2	Don Appleby	5	Don Appleby	2	Don Appleby	2
Larry Reid	5	Frank White	6	Larry Reid	4	Larry Reid	4
Doug Roe	6	W McAuliffe	7	Frank White	5	Frank White	5
F Sherwin	8	Doug Roe	9	Frazer Walker	7	Frazer Walker	7
Joe Dempsey	9	Jack Leech	11			Jack Leech	11

1976 - Ballinasloe	Pl	1977 - Ennis	Pl
Gerry Finnegan	9	Padraig Keane	4
Jerry Kiernan	12	Jerry Kiernan	5
Frank Murphy Jr	14	Gerry Finnegan	18
Padraig Keane	19	Tony Murphy	20
Denis Sherry	24	Denis Sherry	23
Dennis Noonan	28	Martin Green	24
John Green	37	John Green	25
Paddy Marley	47	Denis Noonan	27
Martin Green	57	Frank Murphy Jr	33
Gerry Brady	58	Paddy Marley	65
Paddy Darling	64	Alex Sweeney	66
Alex Sweeney	82	Gerry Brady	69
Frank McDaid	85	Pat Halpin	93
Sean Cronin	113	Paddy Darling	105
Hugh Durin	130	B Harvey	108

1980 - Phoenix Park	Pl	1981 - Killeshin	Pl	1982 - Mullingar	Pl	1984 - Kilmacow	Pl
Gerry Finnegan	9	Jerry Kiernan	8	Jerry Kiernan	4	Jerry Kiernan	1
Jerry Kiernan	18	Noel Harvey	9	Padraig Keane	8	Gerry Brady	13
Denis Noonan	23	Gerry Brady	15	Brian Dunne	12	Noel Harvey	16
Eamonn Tierney	24	Peter McDermott	20	Gerry Finnegan	14	Denis Noonan	37
Peter McDermott		Denis Noonan	21	Peter McDermott	19	Padraig Goragley	42
		Martin Treacy	79	Eamonn Tierney	20	Mick Byrne	53
				Martin Treacy	92	Peter McDermott	71
						Greg Shiel	73
						Loughlin Campion	75

1986 - Santry	Pl	1987 - Killenaule	Pl	1988 - Ballyhaise	Pl	1989 - Killenaule	Pl
Noel Harvey	1	Dave Taylor	1	Dave Taylor	1	Richard Mulligan	6
Dave Taylor	5	Jerry Kiernan	8	Jerry Kiernan	4	Jerry Kiernan	9
Eugene Curran	15	Eugene Curran	15	Noel Harvey	24	Gerry Brady	16
Dermott Redmond	20	Eamonn Tierney	25	Gerry Finnegan	27	Gerry Finnegan	28
Gerry Finnegan	28	Noel Harvey	47	Padraig Keane	31	Noel Cullen	30
Eamonn Tierney	31	Gerry Finnegan	48	Gerry Brady	36	Dermott Redmond	33
Padraig Keane	42	Padraig Keane	54	Liam Marley	39	Loughlin Campion	50
Gerry Wyse	46	Dermott Redmond	62	Richard Mulligan	41	Denis Noonan	53
Denis Noonan	48	John Murphy	66	Gerry Wyse	62	Martin Treacy	65
Liam Marley	56	Martin Treacy	89	Martin Treacy	75	Padraig Keane	70
David Dunne	61	Liam Marley	107	Ken Harris	86	Gerry Wyse	75
Martin Treacy	63	Loughlin Campion	112	Jim Cleary	119		
Jim Cleary	68	Jim Cleary	148				
Jim McGlynn	81						
John Murphy	83						
Loughlin Campion	87						
Noel Guiden	132						
Dermott Higgins	134						
J Hyland	164						

1991 - Limerick	Pl	1992 - Santry	Pl
Richard Mulligan	2	Richard Mulligan	4
Noel Cullen	7	Noel Cullen	8
Dermott Redmond	14	Jerry Kiernan	9
Gerry Brady	24	Dermott Redmond	25
Kevin Heffernan	56	Keiran Tumbleton	28
Loughlin Campion	59	Kevin Heffernan	33
Martin Treacy	61	Gerry Brady	36
Larry Molloy	67	Padraig Keane	50
Tommy Griffin	85	Martin Treacy	71
Pat O'Grady	89		
Liam Marley	101		

2000 - ALSAA	Pl	2004 - Roscommon	Pl	2005 - Santry	Pl	2006 - Santry	Pl
Noel Cullen	3	Killian Lonergan	5	Mark Kenneally	2	Killian Lonergan	3
Cian McLoughlin	5	Cian McLoughlin	7	Killian Lonergan	9	Mark Kenneally	6
Paolo Doglio *	6	Paolo Doglio	12	Aidan Bailey	26	Gary O'Hanlon	12
Niall Bruton	13	Rory Byrne	17	Paolo Doglio	28	Cian McLoughlin	16
Nigel Brunton	18	Gary O'Hanlon	19	Cian McLoughlin	30	Aidan Bailey	21
Colin Coyne	53	Colm Rooney	38	Robert Malseed	35	Colm Rooney	28
Gerry Brady	57	Kevin English	41	Gary O'Hanlon	37	Ed Coughlan	32
Jerry Kiernan	61	William Stafford	64	Nigel Brunton	43	Nigel Brunton	43
				Ed Coughlan	55		
				David Brennan	80		
				William Stafford	89		
				Tom Monks	100		

2007 - Sligo	Pl	2008 - Belfast	Pl	2009 - Santry	Pl	2010 - Phoenix Park	Pl
Mark Kenneally	2	Alistair Cragg	2	Mark Kenneally	2	Mark Kenneally	1
Killian Lonergan	8	Chris Cariss	5	Chris Cariss	6	Chris Cariss	8
Colm Rooney	9	Sergiu Ciobanu	9	Sergiu Ciobanu	10	Sergiu Ciobanu	9
Cian McLoughlin	13	Brian MacMahon	13	Killian Lonergan	12	John Heneghan	15
Sergiu Ciobanu	19	Cian McLoughlin	16	Cian McLoughlin	15	Brian MacMahon	16
Aidan Bailey	34	Paolo Doglio	19	Aidan Bailey	18	Gary O'Hanlon	21
Robert Malseed	41	Colm Rooney	21	David Flynn	21	Lorcan Cronin	30
Gary O'Hanlon	50	Aidan Bailey	22	Gary O'Hanlon	24	Michael MacDiarmada	39
		Gary O'Hanlon	30			Ernie Ramsey	70
		Niall Sherlock	46			Nigel Brunton	88

2012 - Santry	Pl	2013 - Tullamore	Pl
Sergiu Ciobanu	2	Sergiu Ciobanu	1
Gary O'Hanlon	3	Michael MacDiarmada	8
Brian MacMahon	4	David Flynn	11
James Keevan	16	Gary O'Hanlon	16
John Heneghan	18	John Heneghan	20
Jayme Rossister	19	Pat Davoren	54
Cian Delaney	49		
Ernie Ramsey	58		
Conor Delany	79		
Eoin Murray	106		
Gerard Kirwan	112		

WINNING LADIES TEAMS

1966	PL	1967	PL	1970	PL	1976	PL
Rita Keogh	2	Ann O'Brien	2	Ann O'Brien	1	Padraign O'Dwyer	6
Ann O'Brien	4	Rita Keogh	4	Claire Walsh	6	Jean Appleby	10
Nuala O'Brien	5	Mary Norton	6	Mary Byrne	12	Kathryn Davis	12
M Norton	8	Betty Norton	9	Rita Keogh	16	Patricia Appleby	14
B Norton				Ursula O'Brien	25		
Felicia Farrelly				P. O'Dwyer	36		
K Keogh							
P O'Dowd							

WINNING JUNIOR TEAMS

1955	PL	1956	PL	1957	PL	1962	PL
N Jenkins	1	Mick Kelly	2	Michael Hoey	3	Dick Burke	1
J McNamara	2	P Rafter	4	P Toomey	5	???	10
G Taylor	8	M Kealy	7	Mick Kelly	8	???	12
???	12	???	12	M Kinsella	14	???	13
???	22						

1971	PL	1973	PL	1974	PL	1983		2009	PL
Padraig Keane	1	Jerry Kiernan	1	Frank Murphy	1	David Dunne	1	David Fitzmaurice	5
Tom Gregan	12			David Carroll	6	Sean McGuirk	9	Eoin McDonnell	12
B Fox	18					Kieron Tumbleton	15	Jayme Rossiter	17
B McGuire	25					G Byrne	24	Colm Murray	22
B Maguire	35					Eugene Curran	27	Larry Brady	27
Derek Reilly	59							Jordan Logue	41
Matt Slattery	65							Tony Kavanagh	43
Derek Carroll	101							Conor McGuinness	45

APPEARANCES AT SENIOR CROSS COUNTRY CHAMPIONSHIPS

Athlete	Active Senior Years at National XC Championships	National XC Appearances for Clonliffe	National XC Individual Winner	National XC Individual Medal Winner
Jerry Kiernan	1974 - 2001	21	1	2
Gerry Brady	1976 - 2001	20		
Padraig Keane	1971 - 1994	18		
Martin Treacy	1981 - 1999	14		
Noel Cullen	1989 - 2001	13	1	4
Cian McLoughlin	1996 -	13		
Gerry Finnegan	1975 - 1990	13		
Peter McDermott	1973 - 1985	11		
Gary O'Hanlon	2002 -	10		1
George McIntyre	1961 - 1974	10		
Richard Mulligan	1988 - 2002	9		1
Killian Lonergan	1998 -	9		1
Larry Reid	1947 - 1959	9		
Don Appleby	1950 - 1959	9		4
Denis Noonan	1974 - 1984	8		
Nigel Brunton	1999 -	8		
Paddy Marley	1970 - 1979	8		
Sean Cronin	1965 - 1978	8		
Sergiu Ciobanu	2007 -	7	1	2
Noel Harvey	1981 - 1988	7	1	1
Dermott Redmond	1985 - 1992	7		
Loughlin Campion	1984 - 1991	7		
Christie Brady	1962 - 1970	7		
Charlie Rothwell	1911-1924	7		
Sam Gray	1933-1943	7		
Maurice Ahern	1964-1971	7		
Danny McDaid	1969 - 1974	6		
Charles Walker	1924 - 1933	6		
Frazer Walker	1954 - 1959	6		
Eamonn Tierney	1978 - 1995	6		
Tony Murphy	1972 - 1979	6		
Liam Marley	1988 - 1995	6		
Ray Heffernan	1962 - 1971	6		
Mark Kenneally	2005 -	5	1	4
Billy Bingham	1920 - 1925	5	1	3
Paolo Doglio	2000 -	5		
Aidan Bailey	2005 -	5		
Tommy Burton	1908 - 1914	5		
Harry Cooney	1933 - 1948	5		

CLONLIFFE TEAMS AT EUROPEAN CROSS COUNTRY CHAMPIONSHIPS

Year	Venue	Competed	Place	Athlete	Club	Times/Points
31.01.1981	Varese, ITA	Yes	9	Clonliffe Harriers	IRL	78
			16	Jerry Kiernan	Clonliffe Harriers	28.13
			25	Noel Harvey	Clonliffe Harriers	28.42
			37	Denis Noonan	Clonliffe Harriers	29.21
			49	Gerry Brady	Clonliffe Harriers	29.47
			58	Eamon Tierney	Clonliffe Harriers	30.20
30.01.1983	Lyon, FRA	Yes	5	Clonliffe Harriers	IRL	66
			7	Jerry Kiernan	Clonliffe Harriers	
			8	Noel Harvey	Clonliffe Harriers	
			19	Gerry Finnegan	Clonliffe Harriers	
			32	Denis Noonan	Clonliffe Harriers	
03.02.1985	Acoteias, POR	Yes		Clonliffe Harriers	IRL	???
			ET	Eugene Curran	Clonliffe Harriers	
			ET	Sean McGuirk	Clonliffe Harriers	
			ET	Billy Horgan	Clonliffe Harriers	
01.01.1987	Clusone, ITA	Yes	8	Clonliffe Harriers	IRL	162
			9	Noel Harvey	Clonliffe Harriers	32:26:00
			38	Eugene Curran	Clonliffe Harriers	33:28:00
			55	Gerry Finnegan	Clonliffe Harriers	34:00:00
			60	Eamonn Tierney	Clonliffe Harriers	34:12:00
			71	Dermott Redmond	Clonliffe Harriers	34:39:00
			83	Martin Treacy	Clonliffe Harriers	35:52:00
05.02.1989	Acoteias, POR	Yes		Clonliffe Harriers	IRL	???
			ET	Gerry Brady	Clonliffe Harriers	
			ET	Noel Harvey	Clonliffe Harriers	
			ET	Eamon Tierney	Clonliffe Harriers	
04.02.2001	Villamoura, POR	Yes	9	Clonliffe Harriers	IRL	???
			16	Killian Lonergan	Clonliffe Harriers	
				Noel Cullen	Clonliffe Harriers	
				Cian McLoughlin	Clonliffe Harriers	
				Colin Coyne	Clonliffe Harriers	
				Nigel Brunton	Clonliffe Harriers	
				Paolo Doglio	Clonliffe Harriers	
05.02.2005	Mantova, ITA	Yes	8	Clonliffe Harriers	IRL	160
			19	Mark Kenneally	Clonliffe Harriers	29:16:00
			27	Killian Lonergan	Clonliffe Harriers	29:28:00
			54	Cian McLoughlin	Clonliffe Harriers	30:42:00
			60	Gary O'Hanlon	Clonliffe Harriers	31:00:00
			74	Nigel Brunton	Clonliffe Harriers	31:36:00
			83	Paulo Doglio	Clonliffe Harriers	31:50:00
05.02.2006	Caceras, ESP	Yes	5	Clonliffe Harriers	IRL	92
			10	Killian Lonergan	Clonliffe Harriers	30:16:00
			24	Mark Kenneally	Clonliffe Harriers	31:03:00
			26	Cian McLoughlin	Clonliffe Harriers	31:07:00
			32	Gary O'Hanlon	Clonliffe Harriers	31:29:00
			56	Colm Rooney	Clonliffe Harriers	32:57:00
			62	Aidan Bailey	Clonliffe Harriers	33:30:00
04.02.2007	Istanbul, TUR	Yes	10	Clonliffe Harriers	IRL	185
			17	Colm Rooney	Clonliffe Harriers	30:43:00
			36	Cian McLoughlin	Clonliffe Harriers	31:42:00
			59	Aidan Bailey	Clonliffe Harriers	32:40:00
			73	Kevin English	Clonliffe Harriers	33:44:00
			76	Michael Mac Diarmada	Clonliffe Harriers	33:51:00
			85	Gary O'Hanlon	Clonliffe Harriers	34:34:00
02.02.2008	Acoteias, POR	Yes	7	Clonliffe Harriers	IRL	162
			29	Colm Rooney	Clonliffe Harriers	31:13:00
			36	Gary O'Hanlon	Clonliffe Harriers	31:31:00
			47	Cian McLoughlin	Clonliffe Harriers	31:56:00
			50	Brian MacMahon	Clonliffe Harriers	32:14:00
			52	Paulo Doglio	Clonliffe Harriers	32:18:00
			62	Aidan Bailey	Clonliffe Harriers	32:49:00

Year	Venue	Competed	Place	Athlete	Club	Times/Points
01.02.2009	Istanbul, TUR	Yes	9	Clonliffe Harriers	IRL	161
			15	Mark Kenneally	Clonliffe Harriers	33:07:00
			39	Sergui Ciobanu	Clonliffe Harriers	34:29:00
			53	David Flynn	Clonliffe Harriers	35:05:00
			54	Cian McLoughlin	Clonliffe Harriers	35:08:00
			62	Aidan Bailey	Clonliffe Harriers	35:23:00
			75	Gary O'Hanlon	Clonliffe Harriers	36:19:00
07.02.2010	Bilbao, ESP	Yes	9	Clonliffe Harriers	IRL	169
			6	Mark Kenneally	Clonliffe Harriers	32:49:00
			37	Sergui Ciobanu	Clonliffe Harriers	34:31:00
			60	Brian MacMahon	Clonliffe Harriers	35:29:00
			66	Cian McLoughlin	Clonliffe Harriers	35:54:00
			75	Lorcan Cronin	Clonliffe Harriers	36:47:00
			86	Gary O'Hanlon	Clonliffe Harriers	38:55:00
06.02.2011	San Vittore Olona, ITA	Yes	10	Clonliffe Harriers	IRL	185
			36	Cian McLoughlin	Clonliffe Harriers	31:11:00
			52	Gary O'Hanlon	Clonliffe Harriers	32:03:00
			57	John Heneghan	Clonliffe Harriers	32:14:00
			40	Sergui Ciobanu	Clonliffe Harriers	31:26:00
			69	Paolo Doglio	Clonliffe Harriers	32:55:00
			75	Lorcan Cronin	Clonliffe Harriers	33:13:00
05.02.2012						
03.02.2013	Castellon, ESP	Yes	14	Clonliffe Harriers	IRL	233
			36	Sergui Ciobanu	Clonl;iffe Harriers	
			48	Gary O'Hanlon	Clonliffe Harriers	
			71	Michael Mac Diarmada	Clonliffe Harriers	
			78	John Heneghan	Clonliffe Harriers	
			81	Declan Power	Clonliffe Harriers	